MW00774055

Questioning Belief

Torah and Tradition in an Age of Doubt

Raphael Zarum

QUESTIONING BELIEF

Torah and Tradition in an Age of Doubt

London School of Jewish Studies
Maggid Books

Questioning Belief
Torah and Tradition in an Age of Doubt

First Edition, 2023

Maggid Books
An imprint of Koren Publishers Jerusalem Ltd.

POB 8531, New Milford, CT 06776-8531, USA
& POB 4044, Jerusalem 9104001, Israel
www.korenpub.com

Cover art: Jacqueline Nicholls, www.jacquelinenicholls.com

The publication of this book was made possible
through the generous support of *The Jewish Book Trust*.

ISBN 978-1-59264-619-7, *hardcover*

Printed and bound in the United States

In memory of

Brian Roden – Benjamin Ben Joel Hacohen z"l

A man of few words and many good deeds.
A man of truth and compassion.
He was a wonderful role model and source of support and love to his children, grandchildren, and wider family.

The publication of this book is dedicated

in loving memory of

Averil Grose

יונה חוה בת שמואל יוסף

Contents

Foreword

"We Ask Not Because We Doubt But Because We Believe"

Gila Sacks

The first time I heard Rabbi Dr. Raphael Zarum teach I was seventeen. He was teaching a first pilot of what would go on to become his *Torah L'Am* course. Over four short classes, he opened up the windows of Torah and flooded our classroom with light. He walked us through the structure of the Torah, grounding us in its facts, its history, maps, and characters. And then he taught us to ask questions of any text, to have confidence in our ability to find answers to those questions, and to give a *dvar Torah*.

The effect that this had on the participants in our class was profound. By the end of these sessions, our group – of multiple generations, diverse religious backgrounds, and varying degrees of familiarity or comfort with Torah and Jewish learning – stood a little taller. The Torah had become a little less mysterious. It didn't need to be translated or refracted through generations of rabbis, but was there for them to hold in their hands, and read, and have a view on. And for me, a sheltered Orthodox teenager, watching this all happen was transformative.

At the time, I thought that the magic of what Rabbi Zarum was doing in that classroom was giving legitimacy to our questions. But that is not unique – indeed, to be told that our questions are valid has rightly become a more mainstream expectation for today's students of Torah. Instead, over time, as I saw him teach more, I realized he was doing something else – he was teaching us to take seriously the pursuit of answers. Questions might take confidence, but answers take work. We needed to take seriously the work involved in finding answers to our questions, because while all questions may be valid, all answers are not. In his teaching, rooted as it always was in facts, in history, in scholarship, Rabbi Zarum modeled the pursuit of answers.

And so, at least for me, his student, it is very fitting that Rabbi Zarum has written this book of serious answers to serious questions. The content matters – but so too does the process he is showing us. Readers here will be fortunate to have a glimpse of what it is like to sit in Rabbi Zarum's classrooms – the excitement, the clarity, the challenge, and the humanity of his explorations and arguments. But perhaps more than that, they will come away knowing they cannot just let their questions hang in the air – they have a responsibility, and an ability, to work hard on their answers.

Of course, it should not really be me writing this foreword. My father, Rabbi Jonathan Sacks, *zt"l*, would without a doubt have filled these pages with his pride and affection for Raphael and his work, because he was a close *talmid* of Rabbi Sacks, and they learned much from each other over many years.

Rabbi Sacks had great faith in Raphael and what he was trying to do. He supported and celebrated Raphael's work to revive Jews' College, the institution he himself had led, and transform it for a new generation into the London School of Jewish Studies. He admired Raphael's work to raise the bar of adult education for the entire UK community, to lift people's expectations of what Jewish learning could and should look like. And while his approach is fully his own, Raphael shares many of the traits which shaped Rabbi Sacks's work: the hunger for knowledge and to integrate and synthesize wisdom from all sources; the drive to set a long-term vision and challenge us to do likewise – a vision not just for his own work or institution, but for the whole community.

There are those who ask for the sake of the question. For them, to question is perhaps an attempt to shrug off the yoke of responsibility, or free themselves from the ties that bind us to each other. And there are some who ask for the sake of the answer. For them, to question is to commit to the search for meaning, for truth, to commit to being part of the story, not a dispassionate observer. In this book – I hope the first of many – Rabbi Zarum shares some of his answers and helps us to be part of the story. As Rabbi Sacks wrote:

> Judaism is not the suspension of critical intelligence. To the contrary: asking a question is itself a profound expression of faith in the intelligibility of the universe and the meaningfulness of human life. To ask is to believe that somewhere there is an answer.… Far from faith excluding questions, questions testify to faith – that history is not random, that the universe is not impervious to our understanding, that what happens to us is not blind chance. We ask not because we doubt, but because we believe. ("The Art of Asking Questions," in *The Jonathan Sacks Haggada*)

Acknowledgments

In Edgware, the London suburb where I grew up, Dayan Michoel Fisher was one of the great community teachers. Every Shabbat afternoon my father, Arieh Zarum, would take me to hear him give a class in his home. By then he had retired from his role as head of the Federation of Synagogues Beis Din. Although their backgrounds were very different, Dayan Fisher and my father liked each other enormously. One grew up in Grodno, then in Imperial Russia, and was a brilliant Litvishe Talmudist; the other was a Yemenite Jew, born in Tel Aviv in pre-state Israel, who knew the Bible by heart and adored Maimonides. They shared a deep love of Torah and would talk for hours. Both have continually influenced my thinking and learning.

One lasting memory about their relationship was Dayan Fisher's interpretation of the phrase in *Pirkei Avot* "Make for yourself a teacher" (1:6). He said that that my father had *made* him into a teacher because when he knew Arieh Zarum was to attend his class, he would spend all day before preparing, often late into the evening – "burning the midnight oil" were his exact words – so that he would be thoroughly ready for anything my father might ask or say.

Something similar has happened to me. Stuart Roden and I have met regularly for several years to study together. His questions always home in on the heart of the issue. Stuart rightly expects the Torah to be intelligible and ethically grounded. His gentle probing of the text and its meaning constantly challenge me. His curiosity has spurred my returning to key questions again and again, looking for more considered responses that make sense to both of us and point to a deeper understanding. I cannot thank him enough for his encouragement and support in the years it has taken to write this book. He has made me a teacher, and I am honored to have him as a friend.

Four more people have aided me immensely on this journey. Joanne Greenaway, the CEO of London School of Jewish Studies (LSJS), always kept me on track, helping me to keep going despite any other commitments. Her input and belief in this project have been very precious. Rabbi Dr. Harvey Belovski and Dayan Ivan Binstock both took the time to read the book thoroughly and provided many helpful comments on content, referencing, and style, and I am appreciative for all their time and effort. The insights and encouragement of Rabbi Joseph Dweck, the Senior Rabbi of the S&P Sephardi community in the UK, have also been invaluable.

Many other friends and colleagues have taken the time to read parts or all of the manuscript, discussed it with me, and given their remarks and criticisms. They have all made this a much better book. I would like to thank Uri Berkowitz, Harris Bor, Benjamin Ellis, Yehoshua Engelman, Gila Fine, Samuel Lebens, Jason Marantz, Hannah Mays, Neil Moss, Jacqueline Nicholls, Michael Rainsbury, Barnea Selavan, Zahavit Shalev, Abe Sterne, Lindsey Taylor-Guthartz, Dan Sacker, Gila Sacks, Archie Sinclair, Jonathan Sive, Evelyn Stern, Adam Taub, Oriel Weinberg, Adrian Weller, Ramon Widmonte, Peter and Alonet Zandan, and Gitta Zarum.

You will find that I have quoted Rabbi Moshe ben Maimon, the great twelfth-century rabbinic scholar and philosopher, known as Maimonides or Rambam, more than anyone else in this book. His influence on Judaism is immeasurable. Though he lived over eight centuries ago, his writings are still so exciting and challenging to read. The Yemenite community held him in such high esteem that they included his name in their version of the *Kaddish* prayer. As a Jew of Yemenite descent, I am very proud of this association.

For over a decade I had the privilege to meet regularly with Rabbi Jonathan Sacks, *zt"l*. His approach to learning Torah, living meaningfully, and leading responsibly has had a profound effect on my life. I treasure those years of friendship and continue to be guided by his writings. I am honored to hold the Rabbi Sacks Chair in Modern Jewish Thought at LSJS, established by the Zandan family. He always encouraged me to write, and I have tried to live up to his advice: always be crystal clear, justify your arguments, check all the sources, and never be boring.

In 2018, LSJS published a booklet I co-wrote entitled "Big Questions, Brief Answers." It gave short, easy-to-read responses to thirty-three questions about Judaism. The positive feedback received, and the requests for a longer work, encouraged me to write this book. My co-author for the booklet, Maureen Kendler, *a"h,* was an expert at writing sensitively and personally. Maureen was a wonderful teacher who lectured at LSJS for over a decade and was loved by her many students. She was a mentor to the teaching staff, and her kindness, warmth, and great humor helped us all. Maureen too is a part of this book.

I am especially grateful to Irving Grose and his family for dedicating the book in memory of his wife Averil Grose. Irving has been a thoughtful and loyal student for many years, and I am honored by his care and support.

Thanks also go to all the staff at LSJS for their constant support, and to publisher Matthew Miller, editorial director Reuven Ziegler, and the rest of the Maggid staff, in particular Ita Olesker, Caryn Meltz, Aryeh Grossman, Tani Bayer, Taly Hahn, and Debbie Ismailoff. I am grateful to editor Rookie Billet and to Rabbi Yitzchak Blau for his helpful comments.

Finally, I'm indebted to my family: to Jacqueline and our daughters, Levona and Sapira, for their constant love and support. And thank you all especially for smiling knowingly every time I said I was *almost* finished.

Of course, there are mistakes in this book. But as the Beatles sang, "With every mistake we must surely be learning." No idea is ever fully formulated, no vision entirely realized, and no book complete. We are all on a journey in which we occasionally take a break to gather our thoughts, and these are mine. If I have misread any reference or misunderstood any idea, I apologize. My only aim has been to open curtains and shed new light on our wonderful tradition.

"Abba, who made God?" "Abba, if Joshua and the Israelites marched round Jericho sounding trumpets for seven days until the walls came down, does that mean they blew on Shabbat?" These questions and so many more, said my father, were what I would nag him about in my childhood. He always said he loved my questions and those of my sisters, Alonet and Deganit. His patient responses, quoting verses the length and breadth of the Bible, ingrained in us a love of our tradition and a belief in its eternal relevance and ever-expanding possibilities. And so, my personal dedication for this book is to my Abba, *avi mori,* Arieh ben Moshe veOra. May his memory and his deep love of God and the Torah be a blessing for us all.

Introduction

Do you firmly believe in God? Do you think all the stories in the Torah are true? And are its laws still ethical for today? If you are not certain, then you are not alone.

The modern world has dramatically changed us all. Scientific innovation and instant online access have increased our knowledge exponentially. Radical changes in social norms have profoundly affected our attitudes and values. New discoveries about human history, culture, and psychology force us to constantly reassess our sense of humanity and its purpose.

Jews, of course, are not exempt. These changes have led many of us to ask deep and difficult questions about our faith. Some find the Torah to be antiquated and unscientific, with little to say on contemporary issues. Some query the morality of Jewish law when it clashes with modern sensibilities. Some search for an authentic relationship with God and wonder why they have never experienced it. Most worrying of all, some feel that Judaism lacks relevance and personal meaning in their lives.

In my experience as both a lecturer and a rabbi, the questions being asked are rarely intended to provoke or belittle Judaism. On the contrary, they come from an honest desire to better appreciate our religious tradition. At times, when questions are expressed forcefully, they may come from feelings of frustration or even anger, but they tend to arise from a genuine desire to live a fulfilling Jewish life.

Judaism was always meant to be a religion that encourages questioning: "Ask your father, who will tell you, your elders who will speak to you" (Deut. 32:7). From the inquisitive child at the Passover Seder to the confused yeshiva student who questions their teacher's lecture, Jewish tradition is suffused with a culture of curiosity. Abaya, the fourth-century Babylonian rabbinic sage, would often say, "I am open and ready to answer anyone asking questions about the Torah."[1]

And yet, I have spoken with many people who feel that their questions have been left unanswered. This might be because they found the responses unsatisfying, or simply because they never found anyone whom they felt comfortable enough to ask. This can open the door to disillusionment and a gradual disengagement from Jewish life.

A weak reply to a real question, or ignoring it completely, confirms the feeling in the questioner that Judaism is ill-equipped to respond to contemporary issues. Besides being insensitive, teachers who give flippant or dismissive answers fail to understand the religious angst of the sincere individual who stands before them. Receiving a pat answer can cause further problems. It shuts down the asker rather than opening them up to further exploration. Answering a question with a quick and clever retort comes across well at the time, but often crumbles when scrutinized. Rabbi Yehoshua Engelman, a teacher of mine and a good friend, is fond of saying, "Never ruin a first-rate question with a second-rate answer."

Many intelligent adults no longer even bother to ask questions about Judaism because they fear that their doubts will never be convincingly addressed. To stay committed, they feel that they must sacrifice some of their intellectual integrity and, as Micah Goodman notes, "put their critical thinking aside whenever they enter a synagogue or *beit*

---

1. Rashi on Kiddushin 20a, s.v. *amar Abaye*. See also Rashi on Sota 45a, s.v. *hareini kven Azzai*. Rava, Abaya's contemporary, also made this statement; see Rashi on Eiruvin 29a, s.v. *hareini kven Azzai*. These sources show that both rabbis were inspired by the second-century scholar known as Ben Azzai.

midrash (religious study hall)."[2] Meanwhile, when teenagers and college students do not receive meaningful responses to their questions, they tend to disengage and drift away from Jewish life. In their wake are hurt and distraught parents who lack the knowledge and experience to cope.

So, what do I know? Well, to be honest, I have been asking many of these questions myself for a very long time. I too was frustrated with many of the stock responses and formulations with which I was routinely presented. And so I went looking for something better. I sought out ideas, books, and people that might help me. Years of learning with some wonderful rabbis, pursuing academic studies, exploring my Yemenite-Ashkenazi heritage, reading widely, teaching reflectively, and having endless late-night conversations have enabled me to forge a path.

I believe serious questions should be treasured. They reveal a genuine interest; they show that the asker is trying to make sense of what they are learning and attempting to see how it fits into their view of the world. Inquiry is the springboard to further knowledge and new perspectives.

There is a risk in mistaking the Jewish tradition for a vast supercomputer. Press a button and a specific, timeless answer to any question just pops out. An exact solution for every problem and possibility! But this misses the point that our tradition spans thousands of years and encompasses multiple different approaches which are often subtle and complex. That is why I prefer the term "responses." Responses are not universal; they are situated in place and time. They engage with the questioner. They encourage comebacks and further discussion.

Our understanding of Jewish tradition changes and adapts, depending on when and where we live. And so, the responses given in this book are not meant for *all* times; rather, they are how I think about the many challenges of modernity *right now*. They are based on my experience of engaging with people and their opinions, just as much as on my reading and research. I know that responses can never be conclusive, but I have done my best to make them as reasonable and helpful as possible.

This book is a collection of my approaches to some of the most challenging questions on the Torah, the text at the heart of Judaism. The

---

2. Micah Goodman, *The Wondering Jew*, trans. Eylon Levy (Yale University Press, 2020), 3.

range of issues addressed reflects the many fascinating people, passionate seekers, and casual inquirers who have contacted me over the years. Of the thousands of questions I've been asked, the ones in this book are those that arise most often, in some form or another. They deserve decent responses.

Responses and Interpretations

I begin each chapter by expanding on the question posed and exploring its various elements. Often, I include a critique of the standard answers given. This reduces the natural tendency for confirmation bias, the temptation to present information in a way that just reaffirms my values and assumptions. All of us are inclined to such bias when it comes to emotionally charged topics or deeply held beliefs. Then I share my own responses to each question. These involve presenting and analyzing a range of traditional Jewish sources and modern texts, often in novel ways. Says the Talmud, "One person's way of thinking differs from the next, just as one person's face differs from the next."[3] And so, of course, these responses express my personal way of thinking about these questions.

Rabbi Yehuda Henkin (1945–2020) once asked his grandfather, the prominent halakhist Rabbi Yosef Eliyahu Henkin, whether it was permissible to interpret non-legal parts of the Torah in ways different from those of the rabbinic sages. "Yes," he answered, "provided the intention is to strengthen *yirat shamayim* (reverence for God)."[4] This is my intention here: to suggest new ways of seeing and understanding the Torah that make sense to the modern mind and facilitate a deeper connection with our traditions and our Creator.

You may be thinking: Is all this just apologetics then? In its everyday usage, being an apologist has a negative connotation, referring to the process of conjuring up a host of justifications that avoid or excuse the issue at hand and fail to address deeper concerns. However, the technical definition of apologetics is the defense of some value, cause, or religious belief through systematic argumentation and discourse. This is exactly

---

3. Berakhot 58a; see also Rosh HaShana 18a.
4. Yehudah Henkin, *Equality Lost: Essays in Torah Commentary, Halacha, and Jewish Thought* (Urim, 1999), 6.

what I want to do here. The book responds to modern challenges to the Torah by making a case based on well-researched and reasonable arguments. Over the next twelve chapters, I try to be a passionate and even-handed advocate for Judaism who takes questions very seriously.

Of course, my arguments have strengths and weaknesses. I am deeply committed to Judaism, but that does not mean I am unaware of substantial challenges to its principles. Indeed, it is my commitment that makes me open to hearing these challenges. I am intrigued to understand how our Jewish sources might be formed into responses. It has always seemed to me that we are meant to grapple intelligently with God about living and finding meaning in a religious life, as it says in Isaiah, "Come now, let us reason together, says God" (Is. 1:18).

My approach to researching and responding to each question is inspired by a comment of Maimonides concerning the proper way of studying rabbinic texts:

> When you encounter a word of the sages which seems to conflict with reason, you should pause, consider it, and realize that this utterance must be a riddle or a parable. You should sleep on it, trying anxiously to grasp its logic and context, so that you may find its true intellectual intention.[5]

This takes time, but I have found that it is well worth the effort. My faith that our tradition has resources designed to respond to changing times makes me confident to address each question, mull it over, and present some reasonable responses. I have tried to be clear and compelling, and never to sacrifice my critical faculties in the process.

I am not expecting to provide definitive proofs to you, the reader. There are no incontrovertible answers to these kinds of questions. But what I can do is present rational responses that make belief possible and that ground commitment on meaningful foundations. The process of researching and responding to each question has forced me again and again to rethink simplified answers. My approach is to present

5. Maimonides, *Introduction to Perek Ḥelek, Commentary on the Mishna.*

innovative applications and interpretations of traditional texts that show their relevance for today.

I have ordered my responses to twelve questions into three parts. The first part concerns the Torah's origin narratives; the second, some of its ethical positions; and the third, its presentation of God and belief. Taken together, these interpretations offer a way of being a committed Jew today and being able to embrace, rather than avoid, the huge impact of modernity.

Each is a considered response requiring a methodical analysis of the issues. It takes time to build the argument. A range of sources, both classical and modern, are marshaled and interwoven. Each response is a journey with many stages along the way. I hope you take the time to read through them and think about them. Nothing worthwhile should be rushed, but this advice is often under-appreciated. Maimonides makes this point with an incisive parable:

> Suppose you awaken any person, even the most simple, as if from sleep, and say to them, "Do you desire to know what the heavens are? What is their number and form?... How did the creation of the whole world happen? What is its purpose? How are its various parts related to each other? What is the nature of the soul?..." And so on. They would undoubtedly say "Yes," and show a natural desire for the true knowledge of these things. But they would want to satisfy that desire and to attain to that knowledge by listening to just a few words from you. And if you ask them to interrupt their usual pursuits for a whole week, until they learn all this, they would not do it. They would be contented to remain with misleading notions. They would refuse to believe that there is anything which requires so much preparatory study and persevering research.[6]

We all want answers, but who is willing to give up a week of their lives to get them? Maimonides reminds us to invest the time needed to gain a decent understanding of a topic.

6. Maimonides, *Guide for the Perplexed* 1:34.

The Age of Doubt

The European Enlightenment caused a radical shift in human thought. Cherished beliefs of the devout, Jews and Christians alike, came into question. Long-held assumptions firmly rooted in biblical teaching were challenged by new sources of knowledge. For the deferential and religiously minded European society of the nineteenth century, the rapid succession of discoveries and realizations in numerous fields of study was devastating.

Geological research by Charles Lyell extended the age of the world far beyond what the Bible implied.[7] The discovery of ancient hand tools by John Evans and Joseph Prestwich proved that humanity was much older than Adam.[8] Charles Darwin's theory of evolution challenged the account of species formation in Genesis.[9] Ancient inscriptions translated by the Assyriologist George Smith and others questioned the uniqueness of the Creation and Flood narratives.[10]

The growing influence of philosophers such as Spinoza (1632–1677) and Voltaire (1694–1778) on leading nineteenth-century scholars led to a dismissal of the Torah's description of a personal God who communicated with humankind.[11] Victorian novels, like those of George Eliot, focused on character-driven narratives that championed human agency and the capacity to love over religious belief.[12] The German

---

7. Charles Lyell, *Principles of Geology* (Penguin Classics, 2005). Originally published 1830–1833.
8. Clive Gamble, *Making Deep History: Zeal, Perseverance, and the Time Revolution of 1859* (Oxford, 2021).
9. Charles Darwin, *The Origin of Species* (Penguin Classics, 2009). First published in 1859.
10. George Smith announced his discovery in 1872. T. C. Mitchell, *The Bible in the British Museum: Interpreting the Evidence* (The British Museum, 2004), 26–27, 80.
11. See, for example, Rebecca Newberger Goldstein's *Betraying Spinoza: The Renegade Jew Who Gave Us Modernity* (Schocken Books, 2009).
12. See, for example, George Eliot's *Middlemarch*, which was first published in 1872. On Eliot's turbulent life and attitude to religion, see David Brooks, *The Road to Character* (Allen Lane, 2015), ch. 7. On the rise of the modern novel, see Joshua Berman, *Created Equal: How the Bible Broke with Ancient Political Thought* (Oxford, 2008), 135–37.

biblical scholar Julius Wellhausen confronted the unity of the Torah, portraying it as a synthesis of four independent narratives.[13]

The emerging field of anthropology revealed the remarkable similarities between biblical rituals and those of other ancient cultures, thereby also throwing doubt on the divinity of the Book of Books.[14] Founders of social science, such as Emil Durkheim and Max Weber, recast religion as nothing more than a human construct.[15] And Sigmund Freud's research into psychoanalysis, especially the unconscious, undermined the biblical emphasis on human choice and personal responsibility.[16]

All this intellectual richness caused a growing crisis of faith:

> Never has an age in history produced such a detailed literature of lost faith, or so many great men and women of religious temperament standing outside organized religion.[17]

So many of the challenging issues we have concerning the Torah today can be traced back to this age of doubt:

> The debates about religion and science that flared in nineteenth-century Britain predate by almost two centuries the "new" atheism that has evolved today, undermining many of its claims for originality.[18]

13. Julius Wellhausen, *Prolegomena to the History of Israel* (Cambridge University Press, 2013). First published in English in 1883.
14. See, for example, James George Frazer's *The Golden Bough: A Study in Magic and Religion* (Oxford, 2009). First published in 1890.
15. See, for example, Ian McIntosh, *Classical Sociological Theory: A Reader* (Edinburgh University Press, 1997).
16. Sigmund Freud, *The Interpretation of Dreams* (Penguin, 1991). First published in 1900.
17. Quoted in Christopher Lane, *The Age of Doubt: Tracing the Roots of Our Religious Uncertainty* (Yale University Press, 2011), 3.
18. Ibid., 4.

Initially, the religious establishment dismissed, downplayed, or simply ignored the results of all this new research. However, as the new ideas and discoveries gained wider recognition, such reactions could not be sustained. Priests and rabbis needed to respond to mounting questions from their congregants. Some doggedly continued to deny or deride what they portrayed as newfangled theories or dangerous ideas. They retreated from modernity, preferring to intensify their religious practice. Others were unwilling to reject the mounting evidence and research and, over time, have learned ways in which to accommodate many aspects of this knowledge into their religious outlooks. Rather than weakening belief, they find that understanding these new discoveries and ideas uncovers creative avenues to reinterpret ancient texts and renew religious commitment.[19]

Of course, this does not mean uncritically embracing all the fruits of ongoing research. Modern religious leaders, scholars, and academics continue to engage thoughtfully with new findings, in evolving fields such as neuroscience, thermodynamics, and artificial intelligence, seeing their potential for explaining and energizing the meaning of faith and the purpose of tradition.[20] For me, the process of investigating challenging questions has uncovered fresh readings and insights that have had a transformative effect on my understanding of Judaism. They have led to a reassessment of many topics and allowed me to see them in a new light. In the end, my thinking moved me from a defense of Judaism to a reevaluation of it for the modern age.

---

19. See, for example, Geoffrey Cantor, "Anglo-Jewish Responses to Evolution," in *Jewish Tradition and the Challenge of Darwinism*, ed. Geoffrey Cantor and Marc Swetlitz (University of Chicago Press, 2006), 23–46; Jeremy Brown, *New Heavens and a New Earth: The Jewish Reception of Copernican Thought* (Oxford, 2013), 274–86; and Tova Ganzel, Yehudah Brandes, and Chayuta Deutsch, eds., *The Believer and the Modern Study of the Bible* (Academic Press: Boston, 2019).
20. See, for example, Mario Beauregard and Denyse O'Leary, *The Spiritual Brain: A Neuroscientist's Case for the Existence of the Soul* (HarperOne, 2007); Jeremy England, *Every Life Is on Fire: How Thermodynamics Explains the Origins of Living Things* (Basic Books, 2020); and Harris Bor, *Staying Human: A Jewish Theology for the Age of Artificial Intelligence* (Cascade, 2021).

Keeping My Faith

As the dean, my day job is teaching at the London School of Jewish Studies. The school dates back to 1855, when it was established as Jews' College by Chief Rabbi Dr. Nathan Marcus Adler and Sir Moses Montefiore. Ever since, it has been Anglo-Jewry's premier center of teacher training, Jewish scholarship, and adult learning. It is an Orthodox establishment that appreciates the value of studying Jewish texts in their historical context. When I read the books and articles of the scholars who have worked and taught here, I am amazed at their breadth of knowledge and capacity for providing fascinating insights and clear explanations. I only hope to be able to continue this tradition.

Many people are afraid to ask probing questions. They are worried about being judged or condemned for raising them. There is an apocryphal story about Galileo, the seventeenth-century Italian astronomer, who was convicted of heresy by the Catholic Church for publishing a book asserting that the earth revolves around the sun, rather than the reverse. Galileo questioned the accepted view of his day: that the earth was the unmoving center of the universe created by God. He was publicly forced to recant his views. After he confirmed his allegiance to the church, he is said to have defiantly muttered under his breath, *Eppur si muove*, "And yet it moves!"

On a visit to the Museum of Enlightenment and Modernity in Valencia, my family and I watched a dramatic retelling of this moment, but in truth Galileo never spoke those words.[21] Nonetheless, the many times the story has been retold certainly highlights the historic tension and fear of recriminations and reprisals that occurred between dogmatic traditionalists and those promoting new discoveries. In the West today, we are not forced to hide or retract our questions and doubts about religion. Yet many Jews are still nervous to rock the religious boat by challenging accepted beliefs in any serious way. And when their rabbi says something which they find unconvincing or questionable, they just ignore it or mutter under their breath. "Better to keep *shtum* about such questions" is the attitude I come across.

---

21. Jeremy Brown, *New Heavens and a New Earth: The Jewish Reception of Copernican Thought* (Oxford, 2013), 239.

Over time, though, unanswered questions eat into faith, eroding it from the inside. This is another reason why I wrote this book: to shine a light on challenging questions and make it more acceptable to talk about them. Religious belief and practice can only really flourish in an atmosphere of openness that values questions, rather than being anxious and embarrassed of them. Hillel, the first-century BCE sage, used to say: "A person who gets embarrassed cannot learn."[22] Rabbi Obadiah Bartenura (1445–1515, Italy) explained: "He refers to one who is embarrassed to ask questions for fear of being made fun of, for they will always remain with their questions."[23] Our sages had no desire to shut down questions. Through their teaching they hoped to create an atmosphere in which the questioner was gently encouraged rather than promptly dismissed.

Should there be any limits to questioning belief? In 1787, Thomas Jefferson wrote to his nephew concerning religion:

> Your reason is now mature enough to examine this.... Question with boldness even the existence of a God; because, if there be one, He must more approve of the homage of reason, than that of blind-folded fear. Your own reason is the only oracle given you by heaven, and you are answerable not for the rightness but uprightness of the decision.[24]

Five years later, in *A Vindication of the Rights of Woman,* Mary Wollstonecraft addressed the same issue with an even more positive conclusion:

> It is not impious thus to scan the attributes of the Almighty: in fact, who can avoid it that exercises his faculties? For to love God as the fountain of wisdom, goodness, and power, appears to be the only worship useful to a being who wishes to acquire either virtue or knowledge.[25]

---

22. Mishna Avot 2:5.
23. Commentary of the Bartenura on this mishna.
24. https://tjrs.monticello.org/letter/1297.
25. Penguin, 2004, ch. 3.

The words of Jefferson and Wollstonecraft remind me of the experience of Moses on Mount Sinai, when he displayed his inquisitiveness to God: "Let me know Your ways, please, so that I may know You.... Show me, please, Your glory" (Ex. 33:13, 18).

God was not at all perturbed by these questions and proceeded to respond to Moses in a way he could understand.[26] It seems that since we have been created with the power of thought, God expects us to use it.

In researching and writing this book, I have no doubt made some errors along the way, and I apologize for them. There is always the danger of misunderstanding. Some biblical verses and rabbinic texts can be notoriously difficult to comprehend fully. I take comfort from the criticism that the sages of the Talmud leveled at one another:

> If you read this text once, then you certainly did not read it a second time in greater depth; and if you read it a second time, then you certainly did not read it a third time; and if you read it a third time then it was not adequately explained to you, as it is clear that you do not understand it properly.[27]

There are wonderful writers who have addressed modern challenges to the Torah, and I have quoted some of them in my responses. This book, however, reflects my own thought process. It represents my personal outlook and the fruits of a long journey. It contains many of the reasons why I keep my faith. If you have comments or questions, please contact me. I welcome and value your thoughts. It would be good to talk. My sincere hope is for this book to be helpful to you and to anyone, religious or not, Jewish or not, who is questioning belief.

---

26. Berakhot 7a examines the contents of this conversation.
27. R. Yehuda HaNasi said this to R. Ḥiyya in Moed Katan 16b, and R. Ḥiyya said it to R. Yonatan in Berakhot 18a.

Part I
ORIGINS

Chapter 1

Is Creation at Odds with Modern Science?

EXPLORING THE QUESTION

On December 21, 2020, there was a chance to observe a once-in-a-lifetime phenomenon. Just after sunset, the two largest planets in our solar system were visible above the horizon side by side. Jupiter overtakes Saturn in its orbit around the sun every twenty years, but what made this "great conjunction" special was the unobscured view from Earth and the fact that these planets had not been observed this close to each other for almost eight hundred years. As I watched the serene specks in the London sky, I thought about just how much the modern science of astronomy has learned about the vastness and makeup of space, and the implications for us on Earth. According to the popular British physicist, Professor Brian Cox:

> The exploration of the Solar System has brought out the best in us.... We are compelled to understand that we are one species among millions, living on one planet around one star amongst billions, inside one galaxy amongst trillions. The beauty of our planet is made manifest, enhanced immeasurably by the juxtaposition with other worlds.[1]

1. Brian Cox and Andrew Cohen, *Wonders of the Solar System* (Collins, 2010), 15.

This is an inspiring view of the universe, but does it sit comfortably with traditional Judaism?

The afterglow of the Big Bang that birthed our universe fills all of space and continues to reach our earth from every direction with almost uniform intensity. Astronomers have measured this cosmic background radiation to determine that the universe is about fourteen billion years old.[2] Our sun was formed some nine and a half billion years later and was followed by the planets in our solar system, including Earth. Investigations into the ancient fossil record have concluded that it took another billion years for the earliest forms of life on Earth to appear.[3]

Even considering the margins of error, these calculations appear to entirely contradict the Torah, which describes the Creation of the universe, from nothingness to humankind, in just seven days: "For in six days God made the heavens and the earth… and rested on the seventh" (Ex. 20:11). Why does the Torah talk about Creation over a few days when we now know from modern science that the process spanned billions of years?

To answer this contradiction, some suggest that each "day" described in the first chapter of Genesis might have been much longer than twenty-four hours. A description of God from the book of Psalms lends support to this approach: "For a thousand years in Your eyes are like yesterday, like a watch in the night" (Ps. 90:4). Likewise, fourteen billion years might have been only a week from God's perspective. Kabbalistic texts and relativistic physics have both been employed to justify this approach.[4]

Though intriguing, there are several problems here. First, the Hebrew word for "day," *yom*, occurs over eighty times in the book of Genesis alone and its meaning is straightforward. So how could *yom* refer to a few billion years only in the first chapter?

---

2. Steven Weinberg, *The First Three Minutes: A Modern View of the Origin of the Universe* (Basic Books, 1993).
3. Stephen Jay Gould, *Wonderful Life: The Burgess Shale and the Nature of History* (Vintage, 2000), 58.
4. Respectively, see Aryeh Kaplan, *Immortality, Resurrection, and the Age of the Universe: A Kabbalistic View* (Ktav, 1993), and Gerald Schroeder, *Genesis and the Big Bang: The Discovery of Harmony Between Modern Science and the Bible* (Bantam Doubleday, 1991).

Second, why is the word *yom* used at all for the Creation narrative? A day is defined as a period of twenty-four hours because that is how long it takes the earth to rotate on its axis, but the earth was only formed on the third day of Creation, so what meaning could *yom* have before that?

Third, all six days of creation end with the phrase "And there was evening and there was morning" (Gen. 1:5, 8, 13, 19, 23, 31). This refers to the cycle of the setting and rising of the sun each day, but such terminology only makes sense when there is an actual sun to set and to rise, and according to Genesis 1 the sun was not formed until the fourth day of Creation. What meaning could sunrise and sunset have before then?

Fourth, why would the Torah present a description of Creation that could only be understood by later generations who would require mysticism or science to explain it? The language needed to be intelligible to the Israelites who stood at Sinai.

There is, however, an overarching problem with the view that the days of Creation lasted much more than twenty-four hours. It relies on the underlying assumption that the *order* of the various acts of creation in Genesis 1 is broadly in accordance with that described by science. But apparently it isn't. Through the dating of meteorites that have fallen from space, science has confirmed that the formation of our sun preceded the earth by millions of years.[5] This directly contradicts Genesis, which describes the formation of the earth on the third day of Creation, and the sun only on the fourth day (Gen. 1:10).

Additionally, the biological process of plant growth requires water and sunlight, but according to Genesis the first plants also sprouted on the third day, before there was any sun to shine (Gen. 1:12). It has also been shown that *Archaeopteryx*, the oldest bird-like creature ever discovered, evolved from land dinosaurs,[6] and yet in Genesis the creation of fish and birds occurred on the fifth day, which preceded the creation of land animals on day six (Gen. 1:20–21, 25).

5. G. Brent Dalrymple, *Ancient Earth, Ancient Skies: The Age of Earth and Its Cosmic Surroundings* (Stanford University Press, 2004), 205–14.
6. Richard Fortey, *Dry Store Room No. 1: The Secret Life of the Natural History Museum* (Harper Perennial, 2008), 81–84.

These inconsistencies imply that any attempt to parallel the Creation narrative with the development of our solar system and life on Earth is doomed to fail because the basic order is incorrect. To counter these problems, some quote the words of Rashi (1040–1105, France), our foremost biblical commentator:

> The Torah does not intend to teach the order of Creation (*seder haberiya*).... Its presentation confirms nothing about what came earlier or later in the Creation sequence.[7]

Does this imply that Rashi thought there was no significance to the ordering of Genesis 1 at all? This is difficult to accept because Rashi makes this comment only in order to solve an apparent contradiction in the opening two verses; it is not a general statement. Indeed, he comments later, "In fact all the productions of heaven and earth were created on the first day, but each of them was put in its place on that day when it was so commanded."[8] Also, if Genesis 1 is not meant to be read as a well-ordered historical account, then why does it read like one? The arrangement of the text must have *some* significance.

More generally we could ask: If the Torah is essentially a guide to life, then why have an origin story at all? Relating to the clash with science, we might also question why God would give us a text which begins with creation in just seven days, knowing full well that just a few centuries later human progress would lead to the discovery of overwhelming evidence that Earth was in fact billions of years old and that life developed in an entirely different way than what is written there? Finally, there is the question of why the Torah presents Creation as an incremental process lasting *seven* days:

> One day... a second day... a third day... a fourth day... a fifth day... the sixth day... the seventh day. (Gen. 1:5, 8, 13, 19, 23, 31; 2:3)

---

7. Rashi on Genesis 1:1.
8. Ibid., 1:14.

Unlike other measures of time, the seven-day week has no basis in astronomy. The time of day can be determined from the position of the sun in the sky. The day of the month can be calculated from the waxing and waning of the moon. And the month of the year can be deduced from taking note of the relative positioning of the planets at night. But the day of the week is different; it cannot be determined by just looking at the sky. The Talmud confirms this with a discussion as to when Shabbat should be celebrated if you were to be washed up on a desert island with no calendar, as there would be no practical way to determine the seventh day of the week.[9]

Moreover, a seven-day week is neither universal nor original. The native calendar of the Javanese employs a five-day week, while the Romans originally followed an eight-day market week which they inherited from the Etruscan civilization of seventh century BCE. It is generally understood that the seven-day week originated in ancient Mesopotamia, well before the Torah was given at Mount Sinai, which might suggest that the account in Genesis is just an imitation.[10]

On reflection, would it not be reasonable to adopt the commonly held view that the Torah is just a product of its time? In the ancient world people thought up origin stories to suit the needs of their societies. They imagined super-powered beings that magically made the earth and all it contains. Thus, the Torah too comes up with a Creation story that puts its deity front and center as the Creator of every part of this world and who, because of His immense power, could pull the whole thing off in just one week. Would that not make more sense?

RESPONDING TO THE QUESTION

Chief Rabbi of the United Kingdom Dr. Joseph H. Hertz (1872–1946), in his classic commentary on the Torah, had an elegant response to the clash between modern science and the first chapter of Genesis:

9. Shabbat 69b.
10. Anthony R. Michaelis, "The Enigmatic Seven," *Interdisciplinary Science Reviews* 7, no. 1 (1982): 1–3.

> Now, while the *fact* of Creation has to this day remained the first of the articles of the Jewish Creed, there is no uniform and binding belief as to the *manner* of creation.[11]

In other words, core to Jewish belief is that God created the universe, but exactly *how* this happened is not. Hertz continues:

> The manner of divine creativity is presented in various forms and under differing metaphors by Prophet, Psalmist and Sage; by the Rabbis in Talmudic times, as well as by our medieval Jewish thinkers.

There are at least five distinct biblical accounts of the Creation. Though Genesis begins with the best-known account spread over seven days, in the second chapter it seems to start all over again: "These are the generations of the heaven and the earth when they were created, in the day that the Lord God made earth and heaven" (Gen. 2:4). The story is then retold with a focus on humanity:

> No shrub of the field was yet on the earth, and no plant of the field had yet sprouted, for the Lord God had not caused rain to fall on the earth and there was no human to till the soil.... Then the Lord fashioned the human. (Gen. 2:5, 7)[12]

A third account can be found in Psalm 104, known as *Barkhi nafshi*, "Bless the Lord, my soul." It is dedicated to a poetic celebration of God as the Creator:

> Cloaked in a robe of light, You have spread out the heavens like a tent. He roofs His upper chambers with water.... He has fixed

---

11. J. H. Hertz, *The Pentateuch and Haftorahs* (Soncino, 1937), 193.
12. Rashi's verse-by-verse commentary seeks to integrate these two versions of Creation, whereas, for example, Rabbi Soloveitchik beautifully described the philosophical significance in contrasting them; see Joseph B. Soloveitchik, *The Lonely Man of Faith* (Maggid, 2012).

> the earth on its foundations so that it will never be shaken." (Ps. 104:2–3, 5)

We read a fourth account in Proverbs, in which "Lady Wisdom" tells of how she was created by God and became His assistant:

> The Lord created me at the outset of His way, the very first of His works of old.... When He founded the heavens, I was there, when He traced a circle on the face of the deep... when He set to the sea its limit... when He strengthened the earth's foundations. (Prov. 8:22, 27, 29)

And a fifth account appears in the climax of the book of Job when God proclaims His power over the anguished prophet:

> Where were you when I founded earth?... Who fixed its measures, do you know, or who stretched a line upon it? In what were its sockets sunk, or who laid its cornerstone? (Job 38:4–6)[13]

Each of these biblical accounts is analyzed and interpreted across hundreds of pages of Talmud and midrash. The rabbinic sages derived countless philosophical and practical lessons from these varied descriptions of Creation. However, they analyzed very few literal aspects of the text, preferring to focus on metaphorical interpretations. Chief Rabbi Hertz was arguing that it is a mistake to have a blind attachment to a literal understanding of the first chapter of Genesis. It should be understood as one of several biblical accounts that are elucidated through the lens of rabbinic exegesis.

In line with this approach, Maimonides warned of the danger in attempting to read the beginning of Genesis at face value:

> The account given in the Torah of the Creation is not, as is generally believed, intended to be completely literal.... The literal meaning of the words might lead us to conceive corrupt ideas and

13. God's speech on this subject continues until the end of chapter 39.

> to form false opinions about God, or even to entirely abandon and reject the principles of our faith.... It is, however, right that we should examine these biblical texts using the intellect, after having acquired a knowledge of demonstrative science, and of the hidden meaning of the prophets.[14]

Unsophisticated readings could result in a misunderstanding of Torah, God, and Judaism, and lead people dangerously astray. That is why, adds Maimonides, the sages warned against lecturing publicly about Creation to an uneducated audience.[15] Note that he mentions three requirements for studying this topic. It should be analyzed with intelligence and thoughtfulness, with an appreciation of the relevant scientific knowledge, and with an understanding of how the sages reached their metaphorical interpretations of the biblical prophets. These will ensure that conclusions are not drawn that ignore or clash with accepted science or traditional talmudic analysis.

As well as Maimonides, many medieval rabbinic commentators gave non-literal explanations to various words and phrases in the opening chapters of the Torah. These include Saadia Gaon (882–942, Iraq), Abraham ibn Ezra (1089–1164, Spain), Moses ben Nahman, known as Nahmanides (1194–1270, Spain), Ovadia ben Jacob Sforno (1475–1550, Italy), and Isaac Abarbanel (1437–1508, Portugal). Responding to the advances of science in the nineteenth century, this approach was further developed by rabbinic scholars such as Samson Raphael Hirsch (1808–1888, Germany), Meir Leibush ben Yechiel Michel Wisser, known as the Malbim (1809–1879, Russia), and David Zvi Hoffmann (1843–1921, Germany).

One practical example of this non-literalist mindset appears in the dating of legal documents such as a *ketuba*, the Jewish marriage contract. In translation, mine begins as follows:

14. Maimonides, *Guide for the Perplexed* 2:29.
15. See Ḥagiga 11b.

> On the first day of the week, on the fourth day of the month of Shevat, in the year 5754 since the creation of the world, *according to the counting which we count…*

Following the simple biblical chronology, the world is less than six thousand years old. If this is to be taken literally, why does every *ketuba* use the subjective phrasing "according to the counting which we count"? It is because the Jewish year is recognized as the conventional way we count time, rather than a definite statement about the absolute astronomical age of the world.[16]

Though the perspective of Chief Rabbi Hertz is very helpful, we are still left with the thorny problem of why the first chapter of Genesis *reads* like a highly ordered historical account, with days, seas, stars, species, and all the rest of it. We need to understand why it is such a strictly ordered text. What can be gained from this form of presentation? And, of course, any response should be mindful of Maimonides's requirements for studying the Creation.

Using traditional and modern sources, we will examine three complementary ways of understanding this text, each of which may deepen our appreciation of its meaning and purpose and will serve to resolve the queries raised above. These three ways can be labeled: *three-stage Creation, anti-idolatry Creation,* and *word-concept Creation.* After explaining each one, we will also look at possible reasons for why there are specifically seven days in the Creation story.

1. Three-Stage Creation

The seven days of Creation contain a literary structure which has been called the "frameworks interpretation." For over a century, biblical scholars have noticed that there are similar parallels between days 1 and 4, days 2 and 5, and days 3 and 6.[17] Below is a table with phrases that illustrate these parallels:

---

16. This same phrasing is also used in writing a *gett,* the Jewish bill of divorce. See Maimonides, *Mishneh Torah, Hilkhot Geirushin* 4:13.
17. Meredith G. Kline, "Because It Had Not Rained," *Westminster Theological Journal* 20, no. 2 (May 1958): 146–57; Umberto Cassuto, *Commentary on Genesis: Part One – From Adam to Noah,* trans. Israel Abrahams (Magnes Press, 1998), 17.

Framework	Content
Day 1: Light and Dark	*Day 4*: Sun, Moon, and Stars
Day 2: Waters and Sky	*Day 5*: Fish and Birds
Day 3: Land and Vegetation	*Day 6*: Land Animals and Humans
Completion – *Day 7*: Shabbat	

Each of the first three days serves as a setting, a "framework," which is then populated by the formations of each of the next three days. Thus sun, moon, and stars (day 4) are embodiments of light and dark (day 1), fish and birds (day 5) occupy seas and sky (day 2), and animals and humans (day 6) live on land and consume vegetation (day 3). This process is completed on the Shabbat with God's rest (day 7). The text signals this structure using the Hebrew word *vayikra*, "And God called," on each of the first three days of Creation (Gen. 1:5, 8, 10). The verb "to call" is how God establishes the three frameworks in which content will be formed.

What is the purpose of this framework? It implies that rather than being a straightforward chronological account, the text has an alternative, more essential ordering. The three sets of parallel days lead to a *three-stage structure of Creation*. This can be explained in two different ways, one which focuses on human proximity and the other on divine creativity.

The first explanation of the three-stage structure places humanity in relation to its surroundings. It teaches us our place in the cosmos. Most distant from us are the planets that reside beyond the earth's atmosphere and light up the night sky. They appear as permanent and unchanging and are located at the outermost limits of human sight. Until very recently, humankind was unable to have any contact with these at all. This first stage is represented by day 1 and day 4.

Next are two locations that we can survive in temporarily but not for any extended period – the skies and the seas. They are inhabited by creatures whose physical mobility – flying or swimming – is essentially different from our own. Although we have developed ingenious methods to catch, store, and devour these creatures, they inhabit environments that are alien to us. This second stage is represented by day 2 and day 5.

Finally, we reach a place that is our own, where we are physically comfortable. We share the land with the other animals. This third stage is represented by day 3 and day 6.[18]

We see that the order of Genesis 1 is the relationship of humankind to its surroundings, progressing from distant to close.[19] The three stages gradually home in on humanity, which is the culmination of Creation and the focus of the Torah. Hence, we are later commanded to rest on the seventh day in order to be at peace in the world, just as God was when Creation was completed (Ex. 20:8–11). This may be illustrated by the diagram below.

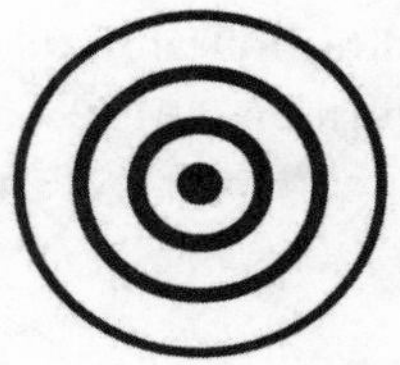

- Outer band: far away, the planets
- Middle band: brief excursions, sky and seas
- Inner band: our home, land
- Center dot: humankind

A second explanation of the three-stage ordering centers on the use of a particular verb in Genesis 1. In creating the universe, several verbs recur: God speaks, sees, separates, calls, and makes. Though all of these are part of God's creative process, the verb "to create" is only actually employed in three instances: once in each of

18. Similar points are mentioned in Malbim's commentary on Genesis 1:25: "The beast still shares with Man the same surface of the Earth, whereas Man's greater biological distance from the birds is matched by the fact that they inhabit the air which is inaccessible to Man. As for the fish, they are even further removed biologically, as evidenced by the fact that they live in the forbidding oceans to which Man would have to descend in order to reach them."
19. This whole formulation also explains why the Torah gives the impression of being geocentric, i.e., that the Earth is at the center of the universe, and everything revolves around it, when in fact the Earth is just one of the eight planets in our solar system, all revolving around the sun. From a physical point of view, our solar system is heliocentric, but from the Torah's point of view it is geocentric because the Earth is the home to humankind, which is the focus of the Torah.

the three stages of Creation described above. It occurs in stage one, when referring to the overall project of Creation: "In the beginning God *created* the heavens and the earth" (Gen. 1:1); in stage two, when referring to the appearance of the first living creatures: "And God *created* the great sea creatures and all the other teeming life that comes from the waters" (Gen. 1:21); and in stage three, when referring to the uniqueness of humanity: "And God *created* the human species in God's image" (Gen. 1:27).[20]

According to the traditional commentaries, the triple use of the verb "to create" relates to three milestones in the development of God's Creation. The first is the creation of *matter* itself, *ex nihilo,* something from nothing.[21] The second is the creation of *life,* which began in the seas.[22] The third is the creation of a refined *consciousness* which makes humankind uniquely in God's own image.[23]

What is the significance of these three milestones? Aptly, they match what continue to be three of the great mysteries of modern science. The American science journalist John Horgan describes them as follows:

> Where did the universe come from?
> How did life begin?
> How, exactly, does a chunk of meat make a mind?[24]

---

20. Translating *adam* as "human species" can be inferred from the commentary of Nahmanides on Genesis 5:2.
21. *Guide for the Perplexed* 2:30; commentaries of both Nahmanides and Sforno on Genesis 1:1.
22. Commentary of Ohr HaḤayim on Genesis 1:21. Though plant life is referred to earlier, the Torah reserves the word *nefesh* for moving creatures; see Genesis 1:20, 21, 24, 30.
23. "God's own image" is variously interpreted as: intellect (Maimonides, *Guide* 1:2); soul (Radak on Gen. 1:27), angel-like (Ḥizkuni, ibid.); mirroring God in potential (Sforno, ibid.); perception (Ohr HaḤayim, ibid.); conscience (Hirsch, ibid.); and free will (Meshekh Ḥokhma, ibid.).
24. John Horgan, *The End of Science: Facing the Limits of Knowledge in the Twilight of the Scientific Age* (Basic Books, 2015), preface.

Horgan thinks these three mysteries – the origin of matter, the beginning of life, and the nature of consciousness – might be unsolvable. This may or may not be true, but James Le Fanu, the British doctor and author, discusses how scientific research into these three questions has resulted in an appreciation of the underlying *non-material* nature of reality. First, investigations into the essence of *matter* have led to the discovery of non-observable subatomic particles. Second, investigations into the essence of *life* through the various genome projects have revealed that

> the genes "code for" the nuts and bolts of the cells from which all living things are made – the hormones, enzymes and proteins of the "chemistry of life" – but the diverse subtlety of form, shape and colour that distinguishes snowdrops from tulips, flies from frogs and humans, is *nowhere to be found.*[25]

And third, investigations into the essence of the human *mind* have led to advanced brain-scanning techniques, but they have had limited success in explaining how our neuronal circuits relate to emergent properties such as memory, free will, and our sense of self.[26]

Thus, matter, life, and consciousness all elude an explicit material-based comprehension in science. Humanity has reflected on these mysteries from the earliest times, and they continue to vex us. Therefore, it is fitting that for just these three mysteries, Genesis 1 assigns God's unique ability "to create."

This is not to imply that a comprehensive understanding of these is forever beyond our reach; rather, the implication is that they are fundamental to the formation of the universe. Matter, life, and consciousness are the very building blocks of reality. The more we understand them, the closer we will come to comprehending all existence and, ultimately, God. Thus, after the first six days, in which the word "create" appears three times, we have the Shabbat, on which we are commanded to rest

---

25. James Le Fanu, *Why Us? How Science Rediscovered the Mystery of Ourselves* (HarperPress, 2010), 16.
26. Le Fanu, *Why Us?* 176–229.

in imitation of God (Ex. 20:8–11). This may be illustrated by the diagram below. The triangle shape symbolizes an increase in complexity and sophistication from base matter, to animate life, to human consciousness and ultimately God.

- God
- Consciousness
- Life
- Matter

2. *Anti-Idolatry Creation*

Numerous cultures of the ancient world have creation myths. These tell of rivaling deities whose fierce battles lead to the formation of the world:

> The internecine strife of the gods, the personified forces of nature, is an outstanding characteristic feature of polytheistic cosmogonies. That is why polytheistic accounts of creation always begin with the predominance of the powers of nature, and invariably describe in detail a titanic struggle between two opposing forces.[27]

Among the ancient myths of Mesopotamia, names of gods appear that relate to Hebrew terms found in the book of Genesis. The *Epic of Creation* recounts the vicious battle between Tiamat, the goddess of the sea, and several other gods.[28] Tiamat is philologically related to the Hebrew word *tehom,* the primordial deep mentioned as Creation begins (Gen. 1:2).[29] In the *Epic of Gilgamesh,* the sun god Shamash intervenes in a contest between two other deities.[30] Shamash is related to *shemesh,* the

27. Nahum M. Sarna, *Understanding Genesis* (Schocken Books, 1978), 21.
28. Henrietta McCall, *Mesopotamian Myths* (British Museum, 2004), 52–59.
29. Sarna, *Understanding Genesis,* 22.
30. McCall, *Mesopotamian Myths,* 23.

Hebrew word the Bible employs for the sun, one of the "two great lights" God fashioned on the fourth day of Creation (Gen. 1:16).[31]

Investigations into Egyptian mythology have also revealed associated terminology. When God began creating, all was "void and desolate (*tohu vavohu*) and there was darkness (*ḥoshekh*) on the face of the deep (*tehom*)" (Gen. 1:2). The Hebrew terms roughly correspond to Hehu, Keku, and Nun, three of the eight Egyptian gods of primordial chaos.[32]

What makes the Genesis account revolutionary is how it undermines these Mesopotamian and Egyptian myths of ancient gods. This is achieved by treating what were perceived to be deities as mere *physical* components of the universe, which were all created in an orderly fashion by the one and only God. Thus, Torah demythologizes the beliefs of ancient cultures by reducing their deities to concrete objects. Similarly, the following biblical verse is recited daily in the morning prayer service:

> For all the gods of the peoples are mere idols;
> it was the Lord who made the heavens. (I Chr. 16:26)[33]

The role of the Bible was "to resist these polytheistic traditions and to purify the religion of Israel and its Scripture from any and all mythological-pagan elements."[34] Genesis replaces the chaos and one-upmanship of competing gods with the calm and organized description of a single divine designer.

The difference between one God and many gods is more than just a number; these different worldviews reveal alternate perceptions of reality. The existence of multiple deities implies the incessant competition of disparate parts, born of fractious and tumultuous origin

---

31. The first mention of *shemesh* appears in Genesis 15:12.
32. James K. Hoffmeier, "Some Thoughts on Genesis 1 and 2 and Egyptian Cosmology," *Journal of Ancient Near Eastern Society (JANES)* 15, no. 1 (1983): 39–49.
33. See *The Koren Shalem Siddur*, with commentary by Rabbi Lord Jonathan Sacks (Koren Jerusalem, 2019), 66. The verse is part of a collection recited after *Barukh She'amar.*
34. Avigdor Shinan and Yair Zakovitch, *From Gods to God: How the Bible Debunked, Suppressed, or Changed Ancient Myths and Legends,* trans. Valerie Zakovitch (Jewish Publication Society, 2012), 5.

stories, whereas one God implies cohesion and harmony, an integrated and holistic universe, emanating from a unified "mind." Note also that the formation of the gods *themselves* is included in ancient Egypt and Mesopotamia creation narratives. Genesis differs entirely. God stands *outside* of Creation, alone and ever-present, with no struggle for supremacy.

This explains the highly organized structure of Creation. Each of the first six days begins with the divine pronouncement "And God said" (Gen. 1:3, 6, 9, 14, 20, 24). Similarly, each ends with the words "And there was evening and there was morning" (1:5, 8, 13, 19, 23, 31). Another refrain, "And God saw that it was good," is repeated on each of the six days and acts as a chorus of approval (Gen. 1:4, 10, 12, 18, 21, 25, 31).[35] Indeed, after the opening verse, *every* one of the thirty verses in the first chapter of Genesis 1 begins with the word "and," a further sign of this cohesive literary arrangement.

The Torah's preoccupation with order stands in grand defiance of the ancient myths of the Middle East, and later it served as an antidote to the seductive power of Greek mythology. Rabbi Professor Umberto Cassuto (1883–1951) writes:

> All kinds of wondrous stories about the creation of the world were widespread throughout the lands of the East, and many of them assumed a literary form in epic poems or other compositions....
>
> They began, as a rule, with a theogony, that is, with the origin of the gods, the genealogy of the deities who preceded the birth of the world and mankind; and they told of the antagonism between this god and that god, of frictions that arose from these clashes of will, and of mighty wars that were waged by the gods. They connected the genesis of the world with the genesis of the gods and with the hostilities and wars between them; and they identified the different parts of the universe with given deities or with certain parts of their bodies....
>
> Then came the Torah and soared aloft, as on eagles' wings, above all these notions. Not many gods but One God... not wars

35. The refrain appears twice on the third day.

> nor strife nor the clash of wills, but only One Will, which rules over everything... not a deity associated with nature and identified with it wholly or in part, but a God who stands absolutely above nature, and outside of it, and nature and all its constituent elements, even the sun and all the other entities, be they never so exalted, are only His creatures, made according to His will.[36]

Idolatry is the cult veneration of physical representations of forces *within* nature, rather than understanding that there is a sole Creator *outside* of nature. Genesis 1 is thus a sustained rejection of idolatry; it plays an integral part in the Bible's purpose "to educate a nation, purify its beliefs, cleanse it of the dust of idolatry and myth, and wash it of vulgar expressions and faulty morality."[37] Ultimately, the orderliness of the Torah's presentation of Creation is a mark of the oneness of God:

> Over against the polytheistic naturalism of Babylonia and the confused consubstantial ideas of the Egyptian pantheon, Israel affirmed, "The Lord our God, the Lord is one" (Deut. 6:4).[38]

Modern science too craves unity and consistency. The holy grail of particle physics is the Grand Unified Field Theory, which seeks to demonstrate how all the forces of nature are interconnected and emerge from one integrated conception. The belief that this underlying structure exists and can be found is an outgrowth of the idea of order and coherence that Genesis 1 conveys.

3. *Word-Concept Creation*

Another distinctive aspect of Genesis 1 is that God creates through *speech*. While human speech is used for expression and communication, God's speech in this chapter causes the construction of reality itself:

---

36. Umberto Cassuto, *Commentary on Genesis: Part One*, 7–8.
37. Avigdor Shinan and Yair Zakovitch, *From Gods to God*, 268.
38. William A. Irwin, "The Hebrews," in Henri Frankfort et al., *The Intellectual Adventure of Ancient Man: An Essay on Speculative Thought in the Ancient Near East* (University of Chicago, 1977), 224.

> God *said*, "Let there be light," *and there was* light. (Gen. 1:3)
>
> God *said*, "Let the waters under the heavens be gathered in one place so that the dry land will appear," *and so it was.* (Gen. 1:9)
>
> God *said*, "Let there be lights in the vault of the heavens…" *and so it was.* (Gen. 1:14–15)
>
> God *said*, "Let the earth bring forth living creatures…" *and so it was.* (Gen. 1:24)

Likewise, we find God's ability to create with words mentioned in Psalms:

> By the word of the Lord the heavens were made, and by the breath of His mouth all their array…
> For He spoke and it was;
> He commanded, and it was established. (Ps. 33:6, 9)[39]

And we also refer to this daily in the morning prayer *Barukh She'amar*:

> Blessed is He who spoke, and the world came into being…
> blessed is He who speaks and [thereby] acts.[40]

The sages took note of this too and counted up the number of times "God said" in Creation: "With ten sayings the world was created."[41] The strength of God's words is further emphasized on the first three days of Creation. God gives *names* to five basic components of reality: two chronological – "day" and "night" (Gen. 1:5) – and three spatial – the "heavens" above (Gen. 1:8) and the "earth" and "seas" below (Gen. 1:10). All this implies a more intimate relationship between language and the physical world than might first be appreciated.

---

39. The second verse is part of the collection of verses reciting each morning in *Yehi Kavod*, before *Ashrei*, see *The Koren Shalem Siddur*, 70.
40. Ibid., 62.
41. Mishna Avot 5:1. These are listed in Genesis Rabba 17:1.

Building on this perspective, certain Hebrew words that appear in the first chapter of Genesis could be understood in a more expansive way than they normally are. They can be called "word-concepts" because they introduce ideas that are fundamental to the fabric of reality. Rather than merely being the linguistic expression of a physical object, they define the concept underpinning that object. This perspective can help to make sense of the Torah's use of the Hebrew words *yom* (day), *or* (light), *erev* (evening), and *boker* (morning), even before God made the sun on the fourth day of Creation.

The word *yom* normally means "day," referring to the time period that we mark by sunrise and sunset. But in the opening verses of the Creation narrative it states, "And God called the light, day" (Gen. 1:3). Light is a substance that enables us to see or make things visible in *space*, whereas a day is a measurement of *time*, so what does this deceptively simple phrase mean? If we understand *yom* as a word-concept, then it becomes more intelligible. *Yom* refers to a fundamental *unit of reality*. Such a unit can refer to a measure of space, time, or some other fundamental structure of reality. This is a further reason why the ordering of the acts of Creation is at odds with what science teaches us. The seven days are in fact seven conceptual units that underpin the physical world. It is not a chronological narrative.

Some rabbinic sages did not think the *or* (light), which God called *yom*, was sunlight. They understood it to be metaphysical light which enables humanity to perceive reality as a whole, but which was subsequently hidden.[42] Meanwhile, modern physics teaches that reality exists in at least four dimensions, called the space-time continuum, and that light is a form of electromagnetic radiation, one of the fundamental forces of nature. Both perspectives give credence to the understanding of *or* and *yom* as word-concepts that underpin reality.

To be clear, this is not meant to imply that certain words in the Torah were lying in wait for millennia so that one day modern science could miraculously explain them. Rather the point is that the Torah is written in a style somewhat akin to poetry, which enables deep insights to be expressed in simple ways that resonate with scientific formulations.

---

42. Ḥagiga 12a.

Erev and *boker* in the Creation narrative are also word-concepts. A number of commentators, including Rashi, Nahmanides, Abraham ibn Ezra, and Rabbi Samson Raphael Hirsch, have pointed out that the Hebrew word *erev* essentially refers to a blurred or confused mixture,[43] while the word *boker* essentially refers to an investigation, from the Hebrew root *levaker,* "to clarify."[44] So at the end of each *yom* (unit of reality), instead of: "And there was evening and there was morning," the Torah is actually saying something like, "And there was confusion and then there was clarity." In other words, further definition and refinement was being given each time to what was disordered and chaotic.

Before any act of Creation there was just *tohu vavohu,* "nothingness and emptiness" (Gen. 1:2). God then used words to create conceptual structures which firmed up reality, step by step. Thus, with the completion of each *yom* the Torah gives the recurring refrain of *erev* and *boker* to summarize what had been achieved.

Seven Days

As has already been explained, although the day of the week cannot be determined just by looking up, the origin of the seven-day weekly cycle might still be related to the contents of the sky. Well before telescopes, the earliest astronomers had to rely on the naked eye to make their observations. There is evidence that several ancient civilizations followed a lunar calendar whose monthly cycle divides into four phases of seven days each.

For instance, four thousand years ago the Babylonians considered the 7th, 14th, 21st, and 28th of the month to be holy days.[45] Additionally, while the stars appear fixed in their positions when viewed from Earth, there are seven bodies that we see gradually moving through the sky in regular patterns. These are the sun, moon, Mercury, Venus, Mars, Jupiter, and Saturn. The Babylonians associated each of these planets with a different god or goddess, and they named the days of the week

43. See their commentaries on Exodus 8:20 and 12:38.

44. See their commentaries on Leviticus 19:20 and Ezekiel 34:11–12.

45. Referenced in Anthony R. Michaelis "The Enigmatic Seven," *Interdisciplinary Science Reviews* 7, no. 1 (1982): 1–3.

after them. This custom was later adopted by the Romans. In English today, Sunday, Monday, and Saturday retain their origins in Roman gods while the names of the other days are derived from Anglo-Saxon gods.

Thus, the origins of the seven-day week seem to lie in a combination of the astronomical observations of the four lunar phases and the seven moving luminaries. Historians assume that the Babylonians inherited the seven-day week from the Akkadians before them, although no one is sure why they adopted it.[46] In any case, the seven-day week gradually spread throughout the region, including what was to become the Land of Israel. This, though, was centuries before Abraham, so it is generally thought that the Torah just adopted the seven-day week from the cultural surroundings.

There are, however, substantive problems with tracing the seven-day biblical Creation to the lunar phases or moving luminaries. First, a lunar month is not exactly four weeks; it is just over twenty-nine and a half days. Without adjustments, seven-day weeks are soon out of sync with the monthly cycle, as they are in our calendars today. This is why a new month might start on any day of the week. A second issue is the fact that the Torah itself does *not* identify the planets as a way of counting the seven-day week:

> And God said, "Let there be luminaries in the firmament of the heaven to separate between the day and the night; and they shall serve as signs, and for festivals and for days and years." (Gen. 1:14)

If "days and years" are mentioned, why not weeks? The verse clearly states that the planets are meant to mark the passage of time for us. Specifically, the motion of the sun would determine the time of the day, the cycle of the moon would determine the date of the festivals in the month, and the pattern of the stars would determine the time of the year. So why is *shavua,* the word in biblical Hebrew for "weeks," missing here? It should certainly have appeared if the Torah's seven-day week was based on the moving planets, because these are the very "luminaries" referred to in the verse! The word *shavua* does appear

46. Ibid.

later in Genesis, and in every book of the Torah, but not here. This implies that the choice of seven days for Creation was not adopted from the outside but was particular to the Torah. In which case, we can still ask, why *seven*?

If we adopt word-concept Creation and understand the word *yom* as a unit rather than a day, then there is no reason to assume that the seven days of Creation are a time measurement at all. Instead, they could be some other sevenfold structural aspect of the world. In which case, the correct place to search for an explanation of "why seven?" might be in nature, not space. And, of course, in order to be meaningful, this seven-part structure would need to be easily observable in the ancient world. What might it be? At this point we enter the arena of speculation, as there is little to substantiate the two options which I will now present. Nevertheless, they are offered as intriguing possibilities.

Many geometric shapes can be observed in the natural world, but the hexagon is surprisingly common. For instance, hexagons appear in honeycombs, basalt columns, insects' compound eyes, green sea turtle shells, great star coral, soap bubbles, and snowflakes. This is due to their economical use of space and energy. The hexagon shape neatly fills a plane with equal size units. Hexagonal packing of spherical objects (eggs, balls, atoms) is over 90 percent efficient. If we add that its symmetry is simple, it easily tessellates, and it stablizes surface tension, then it is clear why nature favors this structure.

An individual hexagon is associated with the number six, obviously, because it is six-sided. However, this is not how they appear in nature. They always occur in the form of hexagonal packing, which associates them with the number seven, because each one is surrounded by six others. This repeated pattern of seven may have been recognized as a building block of the natural world, hence its use in Genesis.

The second possibility is even simpler. There are seven openings in your head that allow you to interact with the world around you: two ears, two eyes, two nostrils, and a mouth. If, as mentioned before, humankind is the pinnacle of Creation, then the human head, the seat of our awareness, is surely its quintessential component. These seven openings allow us to hear, see, smell, and taste the world. It is not unreasonable to suggest that a seven-part structure of Creation would remind humanity of how it physically interacts with its environment and dwells with it.[47]

Interestingly, the two (ears), two (eyes), two (nostrils), and one (mouth) structure is reminiscent of the frameworks interpretation discussed earlier. Spatially speaking, it is similar to the shape of the *Menorah*, the golden candelabrum with three branches on each side of a central column, an essential object in the Tabernacle, which itself becomes a central focus of much of the Torah (Ex. 25:31–40).

Subtle Is the Lord

Attempting to uncover why Creation occurs in seven parts, coupled with three ways of understanding the purpose of the presentation of Creation in the Torah, shows it to be a highly nuanced and methodical text. From three-stage Creation we learn about humankind's position in the universe and the mysteries of matter, life, and consciousness; anti-idolatry Creation reveals to us the oneness of God and the essential unity of all existence; and word-concept Creation demonstrates how words are used in Genesis 1 to frame primary concepts. Additionally, the seven "days" might be symbolic of the seven openings in the human head through which we come to *know* Creation.

In sum, the account of the origin of the universe in Genesis was never meant to be a historical description or a scientific treatise. Rather, it belongs in the realm of theology and philosophy, presenting us with profound ways to perceive and conceive the world and our existence. Is Creation at odds with modern science? Yes, if we adhere to a strictly literal reading of the Torah text, but Judaism has never been limited by that approach, as testified by centuries of metaphorical interpretation.

From a religious point of view, scientific knowledge should be welcomed because it can deepen our understanding of both our world and

47. This point, of seven openings in the head, can be traced back to the seventeenth-century Italian astronomer Francesco Sizzi. See Francis Bacon, *A Selection of His Works*, ed. Sidney Warhaft (Macmillan, 1965), 17; J. J. Fahie, *Galileo, His Life and Work* (1903), 103. Of course, "touch," the fifth sense, is missing from the analysis. This might be because touch is not limited to the head as there are sensory receptors embedded in all parts of the skin, which is the largest organ in the human body.

of the Torah. There is no need to be fearful of apparent inconsistencies and contradictions between modern physics and the Jewish tradition. It is unnecessary to oversimplify one or ignore the other just so you can sleep soundly at night with no questions to keep you awake. The immense complexities of the Creation make it difficult to fully comprehend; nevertheless, our Creator gave us the ability to make sense of it through the in-depth study of Torah and a deep appreciation of scientific development.

This is neatly summarized by a sentence that was inscribed in 1930 above the fireplace in the faculty lounge of the mathematics building at Princeton University. It reads, *Raffiniert ist der Herrgott aber boshaft ist Er nicht.* This is a German quotation by Albert Einstein and translates as, "Subtle is the Lord, but malicious He is not."[48] For Einstein, God represents the complicated laws of nature, which though subtle and nuanced are, ultimately, intelligible and deducible. Scientific discovery can often be infuriatingly slow and difficult, but there was never any mischievous intent on the part of the Creator.

In truth, science and religion have always had a complementary relationship. Since ancient times, religion has been humankind's way of seeking the purpose and meaning of life. Along with that search, scientific methods were developed to analyze observable phenomena systematically in order to deduce how they are fundamentally related. Religious wondering was thus the main driver and shaper of scientific inquiry.[49]

When they work together, the discoveries of science coupled with the interpretative skills developed by religious thought guide us as we constantly reevaluate ourselves and the universe in which we live. Only when they become detached is there a danger of religious fundamentalism on the one hand and fanatical atheism on the other.[50] As Einstein concluded:

---

48. Abraham Pais, *Subtle is the Lord: The Science and the Life of Albert Einstein* (Oxford, 2008), vii.
49. The history of this relationship between religion and science is described in a fascinating book co-authored by an artist and a scientist, Roger Wagner and Andrew Briggs, *The Penultimate Curiosity: How Science Swims in the Slipstream of Ultimate Questions* (Oxford, 2016).
50. "The fanatical atheists," wrote Einstein in a letter, "are like slaves who are still feeling

> Science can only be created by those who are thoroughly imbued with the aspiration towards truth and understanding. This source of feeling, however, springs from religion. To this there also belongs the faith in the possibility that the regulations valid for the world of existence are rational, that is, comprehensible to reason. I cannot imagine a scientist without that profound faith. The situation may be expressed by an image: science without religion is lame, religion without science is blind.[51]

Rabbi Jonathan Sacks viewed science and religion as the two great partners in human development. "Science takes things apart to see how they work," he wrote, while "religion puts things together to see what they mean."[52]

This perspective has been held by many great scientists, such as James Clerk Maxwell (1831–1879), who first developed the theory of electromagnetic radiation. He was so inspired by the biblical verse "Great are the works of the Lord, discovered by all who desire them" (Ps. 111:2) that he had it carved in Latin over the door of the Cavendish Laboratory in Cambridge University, the site of so many world-changing scientific discoveries.[53] The more we achieve scientifically, the more profoundly we will come to appreciate the God of Creation. Maimonides wrote:

> What is the path that leads to love of God? When a person contemplates God's great works and wonderful creations, and from them obtains a glimpse of God's wisdom which is incomparable and

---

the weight of their chains which they have thrown off after their struggle. They are creatures who – in their grudge against traditional religion as the 'opium of the masses' – cannot hear the music of the spheres." Quoted in Walter Isaacson, *Einstein: His Life and Universe* (Simon and Schuster, 2007), 390.

51. Albert Einstein, "Science and Religion," in *Ideas and Opinions* (Crown, 1982), 46.
52. Jonathan Sacks, *The Great Partnership: God, Science and the Search for Meaning* (Hodder and Stoughton, 2011), 77.
53. Wagner and Briggs, *The Penultimate Curiosity*, 400–405.

> infinite, they will certainly come to love, praise, and glorify God, yearning with a tremendous desire to know God's great Name.[54]

The wonders of this world can never clash with our religious outlook; they only serve to enhance it. Again, Einstein expressed this eloquently:

> The most beautiful emotion we can experience is the mysterious. It is the fundamental emotion that stands at the cradle of all true art and science. He to whom this emotion is a stranger, who can no longer wonder and stand rapt in awe, is as good as dead, a snuffed-out candle. To sense that behind anything that can be experienced there is something that our minds cannot grasp, whose beauty and sublimity reaches us only indirectly: this is religiousness. In this sense, and in this sense only, I am a devoutly religious man.[55]

---

54. Maimonides, *Mishneh Torah, Hilkhot Yesodei HaTorah* 2:2.
55. Quoted in Isaacson, *Einstein: His Life and Universe*, 387.

Chapter 2

Has Evolution Made Genesis Redundant?

EXPLORING THE QUESTION

"The hinges in the wings of an earwig, and joints of its antennae, are as highly wrought, as if the Creator had nothing else to finish."[1] So wrote the Christian scholar William Paley in *Natural Theology,* one of the most influential books of the early nineteenth century. Paley introduced the analogy of a watchmaker to demonstrate the existence and wisdom of God. Just as a watch has an intricate design that could not have occurred by accident, so too the universe must have an intelligent designer. The book initially inspired the young Charles Darwin, but after decades of research, the father of evolution came to reject it:

> The old argument of design in nature given by Paley, which formerly seemed to me so conclusive, fails, now that the law of natural selection has been discovered. We can no longer argue that, for instance, the beautiful hinge of a bivalve shell must have

---

1. William Paley, *Natural Theology, or Evidence of the Existence and Attributes of the Deity, Collected from the Appearance of Nature,* edited with an introduction and notes by Matthew D. Eddy and David Knight (Oxford, 2008), 280. The book was first published in 1802.

> been made by an intelligent being, like the hinge of a door by man. There seems to be no more design in the variability of organic beings and in the action of natural selection, than in the course which the wind blows.[2]

At first glance, Paley's perspective seems to reflect that of the Torah. Every plant and animal species is described as being designed individually, for God made each one "according to its kind." In its various constructions, this phrase is repeated ten times in the first chapter of Genesis.[3] Meanwhile, at the heart of Darwin's theory of evolution is the extremely slow mechanism of natural selection that enabled the multitude of species we see today to evolve from just a few original forms. Why does the Creation narrative repeatedly use the phrase "according to its kind" when there is overwhelming evidence for the underlying biological interconnectedness and common ancestry of all life, which does not require a divine being?

Today there are those who still say that evolution is unproven and is "just a theory." They try to argue that certain complex organic processes cannot be accounted for by evolution and hence reveal God's hand in creation. However, their approach has been debunked time and again.[4] Evolution is harnessed in laboratories around the world for biological research every day, especially in the design of molecules, enzymes, and drugs for life-enhancing and life-saving medical purposes.[5] Evolution is now accepted as the central unifying concept in the field of biology.

---

2. Charles Darwin, *Autobiographies* (Penguin, 2008), 50.
3. Once in Genesis 1:11, twice in verses 12, 21 and 24, and three times in verse 25. The first three refer to plant life, and the other seven refer to animal life of the air (once), sea (once), and land (five times).
4. See, for instance, Kenneth Miller's book, *Only a Theory: Evolution and the Battle for America's Soul* (Viking, 2008). The teaching of evolution or creationism is still an ongoing debate in many American public schools. This is examined in Michael Berkman and Eric Plutzer, *Evolution, Creationism, and the Battle to Control America's Classrooms* (Cambridge, 2010).
5. Kenneth R. Miller, *Finding Darwin's God: A Scientist's Search for Common Ground between God and Evolution* (Harper Perennial, 2007), 51–53. In 2006, evidence compiled from evolutionary data was decisive in the release of six medical workers who had been held and tortured in a Libyan jail for eight years, accused of deliberately

How then can you believe in the Torah *and* accept evolution when the two seem to contradict each other so fundamentally? This disturbed me when I first investigated the topic. I had spent years studying theoretical physics in university but knew little about the science of evolution. Surely a committed Jew could not also subscribe to evolutionary biology?

The argument that humankind evolved is particularly contentious. According to Genesis 1, humans were created "in God's image" (Gen. 1:27). No other life-form has this distinction. Genesis 2 further establishes human uniqueness: "God formed the human species from dust of the ground and breathed into its nostrils the soul-breath of life; and the human became a living being" (Gen. 2:7). In contrast to all other species, God created humankind with both external ("dust from the ground") and internal ("soul-breath") actions. This primal human was given dominion over all other life-forms, which it then named, one by one (Gen. 1:28, 2:20). All this cements the exclusivity and superiority of humankind and accentuates its separateness from the rest of creation.

Of course, evolution theory seems to negate all this and radically recasts the role of humankind. We humans are just another branch of the ancient and evolving tree of life. We might be sophisticated and advanced creatures, but we are not essentially dissimilar to all others. Darwin wrote:

> There is no fundamental difference between man and the higher mammals in their mental faculties.... The difference in mind between man and the higher animals, great as it is, certainly is one of *degree* and not of *kind*.[6]

Evolution pushed humankind off its pedestal. We are merely intelligent apes, with a biological makeup common to many other species.

Does this imply that God's role in the creation of life on Earth is completely nullified? Well, no. Darwin was careful to title his famous

---

infecting hundreds of children with the HIV virus – see Jonathan Silvertown, ed., *99% Ape: How Evolution Adds Up* (Natural History Museum and the Open University, 2008), 7–10.

6. Charles Darwin, *The Descent of Man* (Penguin, 2004), 86, 151.

book on this subject "*On the Origin of Species*,"[7] not "*On the Origin of Life*." Once some basic forms existed, he argued, his theory could account for how we ultimately arrived at the almost infinite variety of life-forms we see today. The prior existence of these basic forms was essential for Darwin, but speculation about how they came into being, he felt, was futile:

> It will be some time before we see slime and protoplasm generating a new animal.... It is mere rubbish thinking at present of the origin of life; one might as well think of the origin of matter.[8]

Modern biology continues to investigate the complexity and interrelationship of life, rather than its origin. The Open Tree of Life project is a collaborative online database for species classification with free public access, which already includes more than two million species.[9] Meanwhile, the Darwin Tree of Life project forms the UK's contribution to this global effort which aims to sequence all one and a half million known eukaryotic species on Earth.[10]

Reading *The God Delusion* by Richard Dawkins – which is a passionate but vitriolic polemic against religion and belief – I was intrigued to see how he would handle this point. What was his explanation for the origin of life? After all, Darwin had said that it was "mere rubbish" to try to comprehend this "at present"; but that was well over a century ago, so maybe now science was finally ready to address it. Surprisingly, Dawkins dealt with this in just one paragraph:

> The origin of life is a flourishing, if speculative, subject for research. The expertise required for it is chemistry, and it is not mine. I

---

7. Published in 1859, the full title of the first edition was *On the Origin of Species by Means of Natural Selection, or the Preservation of Favoured Races in the Struggle for Life*. It was already onto its sixth edition in 1872. Darwin made some changes to each new edition, which will be discussed.
8. Letter to J. D. Hooker, March 29, 1863, in *The Life and Letters of Charles Darwin*, Francis Darwin, ed., 1887.
9. https://opentreeoflife.github.io/.
10. See https://www.sanger.ac.uk/science/collaboration/darwin-tree-life-project. Eukaryotes are organisms whose cells have a nucleus enclosed within membranes.

> watch from the side-lines with engaged curiosity, and I shall not be surprised if, within the next few years, chemists report that they have successfully midwifed a new origin of life in the laboratory. Nevertheless, it hasn't happened yet and it is still possible to maintain that the probability of its happening is, and always was, exceedingly low – although it did happen once![11]

This is far from convincing. To date, a new origin of life has not been "midwifed," and his quip "although it did happen once!" made me smile, because it plainly answers nothing. Reproducibility is an essential tool for scientific investigation.[12]

The role of randomness in evolutionary theory is another assault on God as Creator. The birth mutations that Darwin describes in his theory of natural selection are unpredictable and arbitrary. The environment plays a central role in determining which and how many young will reach maturity and reproduce. No impetus or guidance from God is needed. Randomness is a real problem for religion because it appears to be the very opposite of divine providence, a staple of almost every theological approach. Where is God when we know evolution relies on blind chance?

Darwin was aware that his theory had the potential to undermine religious belief. This is why in *On the Origin of Species* he discussed natural selection only in terms of plants and animals but avoided any overt discussion of humans. Although the book's implications for the origins of humankind were not hard to fathom, Darwin made them explicit only in a subsequent book, *The Descent of Man,* which he published more than a decade later.[13] Fellow researchers such as Sir Richard Owen, the eminent biologist who coined the term "dinosaur" and was responsible for the building of the Natural History Museum in London, had trouble accepting that humans could be part of Darwin's evolutionary theory.

---

11. Richard Dawkins, *The God Delusion* (Black Swan, 2006), 165.
12. There is some recent progress in understanding the origins of life based on Jeremy England's theory of "dissipative adaptation." See Jeremy England, *Every Life Is on Fire: How Thermodynamics Explains the Origins of Living Things* (Basic Books, 2020).
13. *The Descent of Man, and Selection in Relation to Sex* was first published in 1871.

The debate was not confined to the scientific community but seeped into public consciousness. Benjamin Disraeli, then British prime minister, voiced his unreserved rejection:

> Is man an ape or an angel? I, my lord, I am on the side of the angels. I repudiate with indignation and abhorrence those newfangled theories.[14]

Nonetheless, Darwin's approach has won out over time. As science has progressed, the principles of evolution are repeatedly confirmed and developed in fields such as embryology, genetics, and paleontology.

A symbolic validation of the centrality of Darwin's work to all branches of modern biology was staged by London's Natural History Museum in 2009. For ninety years a bronze statue of Sir Richard Owen held pride of place on the landing of the museum's Central Hall. As part of the celebrations for Darwin's two hundredth birthday, Owen's statue was relocated to make way for the marble one of Darwin. This was followed by the completion of a huge new "Darwin Center." Opened by Prince William and the world-renowned broadcaster and natural historian Sir David Attenborough, it enables the public to learn about the diversity of life and how the museum cares for its twenty million specimens and uses them for ongoing research.[15]

In sum, I am unwilling to reject evolution. It has too much well-researched and fruitful science behind it, endorsed by the overwhelming majority of the global scientific community. So is Genesis largely redundant and God's role in Creation diminished? More explicitly: Are the randomness of natural selection, the interconnectedness of all species, and the non-uniqueness of humankind in any way compatible with a religious view of the world?

---

14. Speech given on November 25, 1864, at a meeting of the Oxford Diocesan Society; printed in *The Times*, November 26, 1864.
15. See www.nhm.ac.uk/visit/galleries-and-museum-map/darwin-centre.html.

RESPONDING TO THE QUESTION

The study of evolution can actually enhance Jewish faith.[16] We will see how the life and thought of Charles Darwin himself demonstrates this. His notes and publications, as well as most of his letters to fellow researchers and faith leaders, have been digitized, and these serve as an invaluable resource.[17] Darwin's views about the religious implications of evolution, as well as the rocky journey his own life and faith took, are also helpful in addressing these thorny issues.

In the first edition of *On the Origin of Species,* Darwin seems to have had no desire to upset the religious establishment. He opens with a quote from the philosopher and statesman Sir Francis Bacon:

> Let no man upon a weak conceit of sobriety or an ill-applied moderation think or maintain that a man can search too far, or be too well studied in the book of God's word, or the book of God's works; divinity or philosophy; but rather let men endeavor an endless progression or proficience in both.[18]

With this insertion, Darwin was clearly advocating respect for both religion and science. In the second edition, which appeared a few months later, Darwin also added a reference to God in the book's iconic concluding sentence:

> There is grandeur in this view of life, with its several powers, having been originally breathed by the Creator into a few forms or into one; and that, whilst this planet has gone cycling on

16. Some strands of Orthodoxy still reject evolution, for example, Rabbi Avigdor Miller, *The Universe Testifies* (Simchas Hachaim, 1995), and this letter from the Lubavitcher Rebbe: https://www.chabad.org/library/article_cdo/aid/112083/jewish/Theories-of-Evolution.htm. However, the Rabbinical Council of America, North America's leading organization of Orthodox rabbis, publicly endorses evolution; https://ncse.ngo/rabbinical-council-america (published October 1, 2008).
17. John van Wyhe, ed., The Complete Work of Charles Darwin Online (2002), http://darwin-online.org.uk/.
18. Francis Bacon's *Of the Proficience and Advancement of Learning, Divine and Human* was first published in 1605.

> according to the fixed law of gravity, from so simple a beginning endless forms most beautiful and most wonderful have been, and are being, evolved.[19]

By adding the phrase "by the Creator," he hoped to soften the book's impact and head off criticism by declaring to the Christian establishment that he fully recognized God's role in the *origin* of life, even if not in the *evolution* of species.[20] Years later, he wrote to his local vicar, J. B. Innes:

> I hardly see how religion and science can be kept…distinct… [but] there is no reason why the disciplines of either school should attack each other with bitterness.[21]

Darwin always wanted a respectful engagement between the two. His aim was to further science, not attack religion.

God of Chance

Is the unpredictability of mutations in Darwin's theory of natural selection problematic for Judaism? If natural selection depends on chance then God would appear to have no role. However, it transpires that the Bible has little issue with a God that deals in randomness. For instance:

> The lot is cast in the lap,
> but the decision is all from God. (Prov. 16:33)

In his commentary, the Malbim explains the verse as follows:

> There are things that appear given to chance but are actually determined by God's providence.… "The lot is cast in the lap" means that it is hidden from the eye of Man and given over to chance.

---

19. It is interesting to note that the word "evolution" does not actually occur anywhere in *On the Origin of Species*. The popular use of the term came from the last word of the book.
20. Darwin kept this emendation in all subsequent editions of *On the Origin of Species*.
21. Letter of November 27, 1878.

> Nevertheless, the eye of God's providence shows up in it, and "the decision" that the lot causes is not chance but "from God."

This explanation turns out to be surprisingly similar to the truth behind the so-called randomness of mutations in Darwin's theory. Pure chance does not occur in the natural world. Randomness is a mathematical construction rather than a physical reality. We use the word "random" to refer to an event whose cause is contingent on such a multitude of complex factors that we are unable to determine in advance how it will turn out. For example, theoretically the roll of a die results in an exactly equal chance of landing on any of the six numbers. However, in the real world, the result of the roll of an actual, physical die *could* be determined using the laws of motion *if* we had enough information about it: the exact weight distribution of the cube, the velocity, direction, and spin of the thrower, and the air dynamics in the vicinity of the die. We only call the roll of a real die "random" because we lack complete knowledge about every aspect of the event.

Likewise, when Darwin wrote about random mutations, he did not mean that they were indeterminable by physical laws. He was explaining how the absence of the myriad of details concerning the organism and its environment meant that these laws could not be successfully applied; hence a biological mutation *is* random from our point of view. We now know that these mutations function on a genetic level – a feature beyond the science of Darwin's era – but they are still effectively indeterminate.[22] Malbim's explanation fits very well here. The unlimited knowledge of God implies that the results of a lottery are knowable from the perspective of divine providence, but still incalculable, and thus random, to us.

---

22. Recent developments in genome biology have uncovered some factors that influence mutations; see J. G. Monroe et al., "Mutation Bias Reflects Natural Selection in *Arabidopsis thaliana*," *Nature* 602 (2022): 101–5, https://doi.org/10.1038/s41586-021-04269-6.

Brutal Nature

Brought up as a devout Christian, Darwin was in the process of training to become an Anglican minister when, in 1831, he gained the opportunity that changed his life: a five-year voyage aboard HMS *Beagle,* in which his many up-close encounters with the natural world eventually led to his innovative theory of evolution. What began to challenge Darwin's religious faith was not only the randomness of natural selection, but also its brutality.

This issue is worthy of serious consideration: Why would a benevolent God allow for the vicious competitiveness of the animal kingdom? The Christian evolutionist Asa Gray questioned Darwin about the problematic implications for religion that come from an evolutionary theory reliant on such violent and incessant competition between species. Darwin's response was intriguing:

> I cannot see as plainly as others do, and as I wish to do, evidence of design and beneficence on all sides of us. There seems to me too much misery in the world. I cannot persuade myself that a beneficent and omnipotent God would have designedly created the Ichneumonidae (wasps) with the express intention of their (larva) feeding within the living bodies of caterpillars, or that a cat should play with mice.... On the other, I cannot anyhow be contented to view this wonderful universe and, especially, the nature of man, and to conclude that everything is the result of brute force. I am inclined to look at everything as resulting from designed laws, with the details, whether good or bad, left to the working out of what we may call chance. Not that this notion at all satisfied me. I feel most deeply that the whole subject is too profound for the human intellect. A dog might as well speculate on the mind of Newton. Let each man hope and believe what he can.[23]

In these words, you can hear Darwin's internal struggle. He could not accept that the brutality of nature was designed by God. Equally, he could not believe that there was no design to nature at all. How can

23. Letter to Asa Gray, May 22, 1860.

nature be, as the poet Tennyson wrote, "red in tooth and claw"[24] and at the same time divinely created? Darwin thought this paradox was beyond our comprehension and compared the attempt to fathom God's intent to a mere animal trying to understand human thought: "A dog might as well speculate on the mind of Newton." I am sure he was aware of the irony of this comparison – given that it was he who had argued that humans and animals are not that different in evolutionary terms. However, it is his final point that has enabled me to feel an affinity with his thinking: "Let each man hope and believe what he can." Here Darwin admits the complexity and inscrutability of these issues, yet still he wants each of us to retain our faith as much as possible.

A further brutality of biology is the natural spread of disease. Experiencing a prolonged sickness or having to watch others suffer immense pain can challenge the faith of the most devout. Worst of all are incurable congenital defects that cause the victims to deteriorate and die well before their time. But this is part and parcel of natural selection. The philosopher and biologist Herbert Spencer originated the term "survival of the fittest" (which Darwin later adopted) to describe the mechanism of this selection process. Less well-adapted organisms are much more likely to die out before reproducing, thus allowing the fittest to survive. Though this can be dispassionately understood on the grand scale that spans generations, when considering an individual case, it becomes a cruel reality. As a result of random mutations, any child might be born with a degenerative disease or with a physiology that makes them more likely to contract illness later in life.

Darwin faced these experiences within his own family. His second child, Mary Eleanor, was born in September 1842. She was a small, weak baby who lived for only three weeks. In June of 1850 his bright and beloved eldest daughter, Annie, also fell sick and, after a painful illness, died in April of 1851, aged ten. Faced with these tragedies, Darwin's faith in Christianity had been dwindling for some time. He had stopped attending church. On Sundays, though, he would often accompany his

24. Alfred Lord Tennyson, *In Memoriam A. H. H.*, section 56 (1850).

wife Emma as far as the church gate and then go for a walk.[25] Both grieved the loss of Annie, but Charles was overwhelmed.

> For Charles, lacking Emma's faith, alert to the seeming inevitability of suffering according to his theory and having witnessed every moment of his daughter's agonizing and degrading death, Annie's loss was simply unbearable…the last remnants of his belief in the good, personal, just, loving God of Christianity died, at Easter 1851, with his dearly beloved daughter.[26]

In the end, Darwin's loss of faith was more a result of his personal life, rather than his professional one. He could not reconcile human pain and anguish with his religious beliefs.

Why God created a world that has so much or even any suffering, is a question that many ask. Though it pained him personally, Darwin's theory gave a reasonable biological explanation. The only way for life to constantly grow and evolve was to have a mechanism that propagated hugely diverse variations in the reproductive process. Unfortunately, these variations inevitably lead to some unsustainable or failing life-forms.

Judaism recognizes the value of variation in living species, and there is even a blessing for it. On seeing unusual people or animals – an experience that testifies to the sheer diversity of life – the Talmud instructs that the following blessing be recited: "Blessed are You, Lord our God, King of the Universe, *meshaneh habriyot*, who makes [all] creatures different."[27]

Meanwhile, the question of why people suffer unfairly is such an important one that it appears just a few pages into the first tractate of the Talmud.[28] Although the rabbis proposed possible explanations, ultimately, they believed that pain and suffering were beyond human

25. John van Wyhe, *Darwin: The Story of the Man and His Theories of Evolution* (London: André Deutsch Ltd., 2008), 41.
26. Nick Spencer, *Darwin and God* (SPCK, 2009), 71. He did, though, retain some form of belief in God, as we shall see later.
27. *The Koren Shalem Siddur*, 1002. This blessing is based on Berakhot 58b.
28. Berakhot 7a.

comprehension and laid the question at God's door. Said Yannai, a third-century sage:

> It is not in our hands to explain either the comfortable life of the wicked or even the suffering of the righteous.[29]

Natural or *Super*natural Selection?

Darwin argued that the numerous species of nature have a common ancestry and that the diversification of these species came about over millions of years, through the process of *natural* selection. He rejected the notion that God painstakingly designed and created each species individually. However, he did not think that this had to be seen as a denigration of God. In fact, he suggested the exact opposite:

> I see no good reason why the views given in this volume should shock the religious feelings of any one.... A celebrated author... has written to me that "he has gradually learned to see that it is just as noble a conception of the Deity to believe that He created a few original forms capable of self-development into other and needful forms, as to believe that He required a fresh act of creation to supply the voids caused by the action of His laws."[30]

Surely, thought Darwin, a God who created creatures that could evolve into other creatures is just as great as a God who created each species individually!

Even if we agree with Darwin that God's role would not be diminished by the common ancestry of all species, this still seems to clash with the Torah's account of the formation of each one "according to its kind," spread over different days of Creation. A response to this problem can found in the Malbim's analysis:

---

29. Mishna Avot 4:15. We will return to the issue of human suffering in the last two chapters of this book.
30. *On the Origin of Species,* 2nd ed., chap. 14. The "celebrated author" is Charles Kingsley in a letter (November 18, 1859).

> More advanced creations incorporate in a perfected form those things that have appeared earlier. Thus, the plant includes both the specific features that identify vegetative life as well as the inorganic elements. The animal comprises the processes of the plant – nourishment, growth – in addition to possessing the animate soul. Humankind does not lack the capacities of the animal, even as it is imbued with the intellectual soul.[31]

Malbim based himself on a midrash:

> Compare this to a country that received its supplies from ass-drivers who would ask each other: "What was the market price today?" Those who supplied on the sixth day would ask this of those who supplied on the fifth day; the fifth of the fourth, the fourth of the third, the third of the second, the second of the first.... So it was with Creation, the action inquired of its predecessor, "What creations did God create on your day?" The sixth asked of the fifth, the fifth of the fourth, the fourth of the third, the third of the second, and the second of the first.[32]

Each "action" responds and builds upon the previous day's "action." Thus, each time the Torah mentions "according to its kind," it is understood as identifying a further stage in the development of what already came before. The process of biological evolution is compatible with this idea. Though Malbim never mentions Darwin, it is clear from his Torah commentary, written from 1867 to 1876, that he was well aware of recent scientific advances in a range of fields, "and was trying to educate his readership who may have otherwise remained ignorant or received their scientific education from less pious sources."[33]

Maimonides explained that the literary style of the biblical prophets was to name God as the *direct cause* of an occurrence which, in reality, was a multi-staged process only *initiated* by God:

---

31. Commentary on Genesis 1:25.
32. Genesis Rabba 8:2.
33. Shai Cherry, *Coherent Judaism* (Academic Studies Press, 2020), 289.

> It is clear that everything produced must have an immediate cause which produced it, and that cause again a cause, and so on, until the First Cause, i.e., the will and decree of God, is reached. The prophets therefore sometimes omit the intermediate causes and ascribe the production of an individual thing directly to God, saying that God has made it.... I will give you examples and they will guide you in the interpretation of passages.... As regards phenomena produced regularly by natural causes, such as the melting of the snow when the atmosphere becomes warm, the roaring of the sea when a storm rages, "God sends His word and melts them" (Ps. 147:18); "And God spoke and a storm-wind rose up and lifted up its waves" (Ps. 107:25).[34]

According to this, God does not directly melt snow or raise up waves, even though the text says unequivocally that God does indeed do those things. In truth, God established the meteorological system that ultimately *results* in these phenomena. Applied to Genesis 1, this implies that God does not need to be involved meticulously in the creation of each and every species, because God established the entire system for this in the first place. What Darwin taught us, then, is the *mechanism* of this system, and that is natural selection.[35]

Three of my predecessors at Jews' College addressed evolution in their writings, and all viewed the theory as broadly consistent with traditional Jewish thought. In 1900, Rabbi Michael Friedlander wrote:

> We may be able to discover numerous facts in evidence of this theory, we may well conceive the idea of a protoplasm developing into a whole system of worlds, and yet our belief in the truth of the Biblical account of the Creation is not shaken in the least. The

34. Maimonides, *Guide for the Perplexed* 2:48.
35. For an in-depth treatment, see Natan Slifkin, *The Challenge of Creation: Judaism's Encounter with Science, Cosmology, and Evolution* (Zoo Torah, 2018), ch. 21, "Common Ancestry," and ch. 22, "Evolutionary Mechanisms and Intelligent Design."

> laws of evolution are the *result* of the creative act of the Almighty, and not its *causes*.[36]

In 1954, Rabbi Isadore Epstein wrote:

> There is nothing in the evolutionary theory which is inimical to the fundamentals of Jewish religious teaching and which must necessarily be rejected by him who is convinced of the truth thereof.[37]

And in 2012, Rabbi Jonathan Sacks wrote:

> The constantly evolving, ever-changing nature of life revealed by biology after Darwin fits the theological vision far more than did the controlled, predictable, mechanical universe of eighteenth-century science.[38]

Humans Too?

"Is it on your grandfather's or grandmother's side that you claim descent from the apes?" This was the biting put-down Bishop Samuel Wilberforce threw at biologist Henry Huxley during a famous debate between them at Oxford in 1860. For many religious people, the fact that the human species also evolved by natural selection is possibly the largest hurdle to accepting Darwin's theory.

Wilberforce's quip oversimplifies the argument since, according to Darwin, humans and apes are relatively recent branches of the tree of life, which goes back hundreds of millions of years until we reach some

---

36. Michael Friedlander, *The Jewish Religion* (Vallentine and Son, 1900), 180. Rabbi Friedlander was Principal of Jews' College from 1865 to 1907 and produced the first major English translation of Maimonides's *Guide for the Perplexed,* in 1881.
37. Isadore Epstein, *The Faith of Judaism* (Soncino, 1954), 200. Rabbi Epstein was principal of Jews' College from 1945 to 1961 and was the managing editor of the first major English translation of the Talmud (Soncino Press, 1935–1952).
38. Sacks, *The Great Partnership,* 216. Rabbi Sacks was principal of Jews' College from 1984 to 1990 and authored many books on Jewish thought and modernity, as well as producing new translations and commentaries for the *siddur* and various *maḥzorim*.

far simpler life-forms. Given its physical characteristics, it has been suggested that the humble Pikaia, the world's first-known chordate, might have been our earliest ancestor, some five hundred million years ago.[39] For many, it seems impossible to imagine that over the eons humans evolved from simple, worm-like organisms, or to reconcile this with the biblical account of the unique creation of humankind in God's image.

Remarkably though, when you look at the actual six-day structure in the opening chapters of Genesis, the distinctiveness of humankind begins to crumble. First, why were animals and humans created on the same day of Creation (Gen. 1:24–31)? If humans were created separately, why were they not given their very own creation day? When teaching this topic, I often ask people to list exactly what God made on each day of Creation from memory. They instinctively give humankind its very own day and then get confused about how to fit everything into the previous days. When I point out that animals and humans were *both* formed on the sixth day, they are often surprised. Both being introduced on the same day implies an essential connection between them.

Second, the Torah employs similar wording in describing the formation of animal and human. When the Creation story is retold in the second chapter of Genesis, the identical phrase is used for both: *Vayitzer Adonai Elohim*, "And the Lord God formed" (Gen. 2:7 and 2:19); also, in both cases, they are produced *min haadama*, "from the soil." This suggests a similarity between animals and humans. Now consider the whole of the earlier verse:

> And the Lord God formed the human species from dust of the earth and breathed into its nostrils the soul of life; and the human became a living being. (Gen. 2:7)

This clearly describes two parts to the formation of the human: "dust of the earth" and "soul of life." Did these two parts happen simultaneously? The verse could easily be understood as occurring in two stages, reading "and" as "and then." Also, the verse need not be taken completely

39. Stephen Jay Gould, *Wonderful Life: The Burgess Shale and the Nature of History* (Vintage, 2000), 321–23.

literally;[40] "breathed into" can be understood as some kind of divine process of refinement. First there was the formation of the animal body from the earth, and then there was the breathing into this body to give it a soul. The sages associated this soul with "the image of God," described in the formation of humanity in Genesis 1, which they understood as the development of human consciousness.[41]

It can be inferred from the commentary of Nahmanides that the creation of humankind followed this two-stage process: first a physical body with a life force like the other animals, and then a higher consciousness given by God.[42] It is also implied by Sforno in his Torah commentary:

> At first the human species was just a living being (*ḥaya*), unable to speak [like the animals], until it was creatively endowed with God's image.[43]

Since the time taken for this "breathing into" process is not specified and, as explained in the previous chapter, the days in the Creation narrative are not necessarily twenty-four-hour periods, this process could have taken an extremely long time, even millions of years. Hence, this verse could easily be understood as not contradicting the gradual evolutionary process at all, for it implies a slow and continuous creative process from animal to human.

Rabbi Gedaliah Nadel (1923–2004), who was an influential rabbi in Israeli's *ḥaredi* community, came to a similar conclusion. He wrote:

> The creation of man in the image of God was the conclusion of a lengthy process, which began in a non-rational being under the category of animals, that processed to develop until it acquired human intellect and also the physiological appearance of man with which we are familiar.... The evidence of Darwin and of

40. Maimonides's non-literal reading of the Creation narrative was discussed in chapter 1.
41. See the commentaries explaining "the image of God," also in chapter 1.
42. See Nahmanides's commentary on Genesis 1:26 and 2:7.
43. Comment of Sforno on Genesis 2:7.

> palaeontologists, regarding the existence of earlier stages, appears convincing. As long as there is recognition of the Divine Will that functions in nature via spiritual forces, there is no need whatsoever to negate the description of events that scientific investigation presents today. There are discoveries of skeletons of bipeds with a small skull, whose brain could not have been like the brain of the human being that we know. The man about whom it is said, "Let us make man in Our image," was the final stage of a gradual process.[44]

The Torah's purpose in describing how humankind began as animal-like creatures who evolved into something much more is given a full treatment by the great talmudic scholar and philosopher Rabbi Joseph Soloveitchik (1903–1993), in his book *The Emergence of Ethical Man*:

> While the background of Man's existence is his involvement in the natural biological occurrence, his vistas are almost endless. His origin is the earth, the mother of the wildflower and the insect; his destiny, destination and goal are placed in the sublime heights of a transcendental world. Man is a simple creature ontically [essentially], but a very complicated one ethically.[45]

He explains that by placing humankind's origins firmly within the six days of Creation, the Torah teaches our intimate connection and responsibility to nature. But this is just the beginning. By appreciating the evolutionary processes involved in human development, he describes how we progressed beyond our biology:

> Man as a natural being suddenly begins to discover in himself not only identity but also incommensurability with nature. Thus,

44. Gedaliah Nadel, *BeTorato Shel Reb Gedaliah* (Sheilat, 2004), 100. For translation and other relevant material, see Natan Slifkin, *The Challenge of Creation: Judaism's Encounter with Science, Cosmology, and Evolution* (Zoo Torah, 2018), ch. 24, "The Ascent of Man."
45. Joseph B. Soloveitchik, *The Emergence of Ethical Man* (Ktav, 2005), 13.

> he enters into a new phase of viewing nature from a distance and meeting other beings who act in a similar manner. Man can simultaneously be both unique and universal.... At this phase, the personality begins to assume shape and the ethical norm attains its full meaning.[46]

Self-awareness bred moral responsibility. This enabled humankind to connect to God and deepen its own self-understanding. Rabbi Soloveitchik reveals the nuanced way the Torah tells the story of the birth and growth of humanity's ethical dimension. It begins with the framing of Adam in nature and the birth of human personality in the first chapters of Genesis, and moves on to the development of a sophisticated moral, theological, historical, and covenantal consciousness as expressed in the lives of the patriarchs in Genesis and of Moses in Exodus, culminating at Mount Sinai. Thus, he acknowledges the Darwinian view of humankind's origins and how that impacts the spiritual and ethical way we might live today, as much as does the fact we were created in God's image:

> Perhaps more than man-as-a-divine-person, man-as-an-animal needs religious faith and commitment to a higher authority. God takes man-animal into His confidence, addresses him, and reveals to him His moral will.[47]

Thank God for Evolution

Charles Darwin was buried in Westminster Abbey in 1882. In admiration of his mutual appreciation of science and religion, the pallbearers included both clergymen and scientists. During the service there was a choral rendition of some apt words taken from the book of Proverbs:

> Happy is the person who finds wisdom, and the person that attains understanding... She is a tree of life to those who grasp her, and whoever holds on to her is happy. God founded the

46. Ibid., 80.
47. Ibid., 5.

> earth by wisdom; He established the heavens by understanding. (Prov. 3:13, 18–19)

Darwin's body was laid to rest near the grave of Sir Isaac Newton. They had achieved similar feats. Darwin did for biology what Newton had done for astronomy. Both deduced some of the fundamental rules by which the universe is governed – Newton's laws of planetary motion and Darwin's laws of evolution by natural selection. These scientific laws were established by the Almighty so that the universe could exist and function, but after that, as Maimonides often asserted, "the world goes its customary way (*olam keminhago noheg*)."[48]

Thus, divine guidance is not necessary for every step of natural selection, variation by variation, just as it is not required to direct the orbits of planets around a star, moment by moment. Darwin himself realized this, but knew that this thinking challenged the religious attitude of his contemporaries:

> Why should you or I speak of variation as having been ordained and guided more than does an astronomer in discussing the fall of a meteoric stone? He would simply say that it was drawn to our earth by the attraction of gravity.... Would you have him say that its fall at some particular place and time was "ordained and guided without doubt by an intelligent cause on a preconceived and definite plan"?[49]

Both Darwin and Newton allowed us to peek behind the curtain, as it were, to see how God structured our universe. At the beginning of the daily evening service we say:

> Blessed are You, Lord our God, King of the Universe,
> who by His word brings on evenings,

48. Maimonides expanded the meaning of this talmudic phrase from Avoda Zara 54b and discussed this important principle a number of times in his writings. See *Mishneh Torah, Hilkhot Melakhim uMilḥemoteihem* 12:1; *Guide for the Perplexed* 2:19, 25, 29.
49. Letter to Charles Lyell, August 21, 1961.

> by His wisdom opens the gates of heaven,
> with understanding makes time change and the seasons rotate,
> and by His will
> orders the stars in their constellations in the sky.
> He creates day and night,
> rolling away the light before the darkness,
> and darkness before the light.
> He makes the day pass and brings on night,
> distinguishing day from night.[50]

We understand this to mean that the sun, moon, and stars follow laws that were initiated by God and not that God puts each of them individually in their place on a daily basis. Similarly, we can now understand that the multitude and diversity of species on earth evolved and continues to evolve according to laws initiated by God, rather than God having to form each species separately, including humankind. Rabbi Jonathan Sacks put it succinctly, "The Creator made creation creative."[51]

All in all, not only is evolution compatible with Genesis but the study of evolutionary biology serves to enhance our appreciation of the biblical narrative as well as deepen our understanding of humankind's place in the universe. As the Malbim says:

> The more each succeeding generation ponders the works of God and the secrets of nature, the more it recognizes in them wisdom and wonders that were hidden from earlier generations, and this next generation improves God's works by increasing its goodness and wisdom over what had been until now, so that every new generation will realize that the generation before it did not properly understand God's works.[52]

---

50. *The Koren Shalem Siddur*, 244.
51. Sacks, *The Great Partnership*, 216.
52. This is Malbim's comment to the phrase "One generation to another will praise Your works" (Ps. 145:4). Rabbi Dr. Norman Lamm suggested that the Malbim derived this interpretation from the verse's use of the word *yeshabaḥ*, "will praise," being similar

For instance, we are told: "And the human gave names to all the cattle and to the fowl of the heavens and to all the beasts of the field" (Gen. 2:20). This human ability to classify nature ultimately led to the work of Carolus Linnaeus, the eighteenth-century Swedish botanist and zoologist who ushered in modern taxonomy with his standardization of a system for naming all organisms. Darwin himself was involved in biological classification as a young man, in his hunt for new species of beetle:

> No pursuit at Cambridge was followed with nearly so much eagerness or gave me so much pleasure as collecting beetles. It was the mere passion for collecting, for I did not dissect them and rarely compared their external characters with published descriptions, but got them named anyhow. I will give a proof of my zeal: one day, on tearing off some old bark, I saw two rare beetles and seized one in each hand; then I saw a third and new kind, which I could not bear to lose, so that I popped the one which I held in my right hand into my mouth. Alas it ejected some intensely acrid fluid, which burnt my tongue so that I was forced to spit the beetle out, which was lost, as well as the third one.[53]

In his youthful exuberance, Darwin displayed a passion for understanding nature and how it was organized. Such an attitude can only deepen our affection for the often-prayed phrase "How many are your works, O God; You made them all with such wisdom, the earth is full of Your creations" (Ps. 104:24). In 2014, a new species of beetle was named in Darwin's honor.[54] The search to comprehend and the desire to know more continues forever. Darwin was right; there is grandeur in this view of life.

---

to *yashbiaḥ*, "will improve." See Norman Lamm, *Torah Umadda: The Encounter of Religious Learning and Worldly Knowledge in the Jewish Tradition*, 20th anniversary edition (Maggid, 2010), 93, note 43.

53. Nora Barlow, ed., *The Autobiography of Charles Darwin 1809–1882* (London: Collins 1958), 62.
54. Christine Dell'Amore, *National Geographic*, published February 13, 2014. See: www.nationalgeographic.com/news/2014/2/140213-darwin-beetles-new-species-science-animals/.

Fragility and Humility

Darwin's account of natural selection reminds us of the fragility of life:

> A grain in the balance will determine which individual shall live and which shall die, which variety or species shall increase in number and which shall decrease, or finally become extinct.... The slightest advantage in one being, at any age or during any season, over those with which it comes into competition, or better adaptation in however slight a degree to the surrounding physical conditions, will turn the balance.[55]

The phrase "which individual shall live and which shall die" is reminiscent of the memorable *Unetaneh Tokef* prayer, the high point of the repetition of the Musaf *Amida* prayer on the High Holy Days:

> On Rosh HaShana it is written, and on the fast of Yom Kippur it is sealed: *how many will pass away and how many will be born, who shall live and who shall die.*

Our faith humbles us when we contemplate the flimsiness of our existence. The study of the precarious evolution of multiple species in the natural world, as well as the constant threat of extinction, only serve to reinforce this perspective. Thomas Halliday gives us an idea of just how much occurred before humans made their mark on this planet:

> If all 4.5 billion years of Earth's history were to be condensed into a single day and played out, more than three million years of footage would go by every minute. We would see ecosystems rapidly rise and fall as the species that constitute their living parts appear and become extinct.... The mass extinction event that extinguished pterosaurs, plesiosaurs and all non-bird dinosaurs would occur 21 minutes before the end. Written human history would begin in the last tenth of a second.[56]

---

55. Charles Darwin, *On the Origin of Species,* ch. 14.
56. Thomas Halliday, *Otherlands: A Work in the Making* (Penguin, 2022), xiv.

The Talmud learns a moral message from humankind's late arrival:

> Why was humankind created on the eve of Shabbat? ... So that if they become too proud of themselves, they can be reminded that the smallest species of gnat preceded them in Creation.[57]

Humankind is the culmination of Creation that began with very simple creatures indeed. This puts our humanity into perspective. And while the study of evolution enables us to comprehend how the almost infinite variety of species developed, it is religious belief that reminds us how this process was initiated, and religious practice that teaches us to respect and appreciate the wonder of life.

57. Sanhedrin 38a.

Chapter 3

Does the Flood Story Still Hold Water?

EXPLORING THE QUESTION

It is a story that captures the imagination of every child. The picture of an old man, caring for an ark-load of raucous creatures, while storms rage all around, has an epic, memorable quality to it. But does the Torah's description of Noah and his family on a floating zoo taking flight from a global deluge really stand up to critical examination? Can this fantastical account be sensibly justified? There are four major problems with this story: its recent dating, its inclusion of *all* life, its worldwide scope, and its supposed uniqueness.

First, the story of the great Flood is set just a few thousand years ago.[1] There should be *some* physical evidence for its occurrence, given its relative recency in geological terms. Interestingly, an important aim for early researchers in the field of geology was to substantiate the biblical text:

> Those investigating nature were confident that they would not only confirm the truth of a global flood but discover how cleverly

1. According to the traditional biblical chronology, the Flood occurred in the twenty-fourth century BCE.

> God pulled it off... [yet as they discovered more,] certainty in the reality of Noah's Flood led to imaginative ideas for reconciling geological evidence with biblical stories. But instead of resolving the issue, these efforts created new divisions, because the harder people looked for evidence of a global deluge, the less convincing the case for one became.[2]

For example, the seventeenth-century Dane Niels Stensen, better known as Steno, made deductions about rock formations and fossils that led to foundational principles of modern geology, which are still in use today. However, his attempt to explain the Flood by fitting it into geologic history has not stood the test of time.[3] Nothing in the Earth's sedimentary strata suggests worldwide flooding in such a recent period, and the fossil record belies the possibility that a small but diverse group of living species (the flood survivors) spread to repopulate the earth from one place. So, the question stands: How could this relatively recent episode not have left even a trace?

Second, there is the question of how two representatives of every land-based living species on the planet could have possibly lived together in the confines of Noah's ark, which was less than a third of the size of the *Titanic*: "Three hundred cubits was the ark's length, fifty cubits its width, and thirty cubits its height" (Gen. 6:15).[4] These dimensions might have accommodated a few thousand species, but not the millions that have now been classified. If you reduce this number by counting only each biological *family* of terrestrial species, then there might have been room.[5] However, the Torah explicitly states, "from *all* that lives, from *all* flesh" (Gen. 6:19).

Even if they could fit, how exactly would all these diverse species have shared the space in harmony? The carnivores would have had a

---

2. David R. Montgomery, *The Rocks Don't Lie: A Geologist Investigates Noah's Flood* (W. W. Norton and Co., 2012), 51.
3. Ibid., 56–63.
4. This adds up to about 43,500 cubic meters, while the *Titanic* was about 136,000 cubic meters.
5. This is suggested by a number of traditional commentaries. See Rabbi David Luria's commentary on *Pirkei DeRabbi Eliezer* 23, and *Haamek Davar* on Genesis 6:20.

feeding frenzy. The woodpeckers and woodworm would have compromised the ark's integrity. And with only "two of each ... male and female" (ibid.), even one fatality would have ended the future of an entire species. The midrash recognized these difficulties and explained that God forged a special covenant with Noah to protect and sustain the ark and all its precious cargo.[6] But if this kind of miraculous intervention is required to make the story work, then why does Genesis have such an elaborate description of building and waterproofing a ship according to very specific instructions that have the semblance of realism?

Third, the prospect of a catastrophic storm causing the *entire planet* to be submerged under water, including the highest mountaintops, flies in the face of conventional meteorology and climatology.[7] Global coverage of this magnitude would have required three times the total amount of water in the world's atmosphere and seas. The sustained downpour would have raised the temperature of the Earth to a lethal level due to the latent heat of vaporization. No organic life could possibly have recovered from such an environmental devastation. After months afloat, the ark came to rest "upon the mountains of Ararat" (Gen. 8:4). The largest mountain range in the Middle East, named after the biblical Ararat in the Middle Ages, has an elevation of 5,137 meters at its highest point, but it is by no means one of the tallest in the world – Mount Everest is three times as high.

The nineteenth-century commentator Rabbi Naftali Zvi Yehuda Berlin was troubled by this and proposed that Ararat was the world's highest mountain range *at the time,* but that the Flood precipitated massive physical upheavals, causing other mountains to then rise and dwarf it.[8] Our systematic knowledge of geological strata, however, makes this extremely difficult to accept. All in all, an ecological disaster on this scale seems to defy all scientific sense.

Finally, the Torah is not the only ancient text with a flood story. There are Sumerian and Akkadian versions that contain many of the key

---

6. Genesis Rabba 31:12, based on Genesis 6:18.
7. Genesis 7:19–20 states the Flood's waters reached fifteen cubits above all the high mountains, that is, about seven meters.
8. Commentary of *Haamek Davar* on Genesis 7:20.

elements that occur in the Bible: a deluge, an ark, two of every species, a zookeeper, sending out birds to check if the waters had receded, and a sacrifice offered up in thanks for surviving.[9] Research into these Mesopotamian accounts shows them to have been recorded long before the giving of the Torah.[10] In fact, there are many ancient flood narratives from around the world.[11]

A pair of geophysicists from Columbia University have suggested that such catastrophic water-related stories evolved to give meaning to a purely physical phenomenon, namely, the end of the last Ice Age, about 10,000 years ago, which caused rapid climate change and devastating floods as the glaciers melted and receded. They demonstrate how one huge flood in the region of the Black Sea about 7,600 years ago might have inspired the Flood narrative we know.[12]

Meanwhile, some archaeologists argue that both the biblical and Mesopotamian versions were inspired by a local deluge that occurred some 5,000 years ago and point to the identification of a flood deposit layer in excavations at Ur, Kish, and other sites in Iraq.[13] As archaeology uncovers more ancient cuneiform tablets, the uniqueness of the Torah narrative is ever more challenged. There are too many similarities to argue that all these versions are unrelated, and our reliable dating of ancient tablets means that it's tough to argue convincingly that the Torah's account is the most authentic.

With these four overwhelming challenges, how can the story of Noah and the Flood be taken seriously? Why not just admit it is an enchanting magical tale for children? It fails to stand up to scientific

---

9. For a good overview of all these versions, see Irving Finkel, *The Ark Before Noah: Decoding the Story of the Flood* (Hodder and Stoughton, 2014), 87–98.
10. Henrietta McCall, *Mesopotamian Myths* (The British Museum, 1990), 38–51.
11. Finkel, *The Ark Before Noah,* 84–85.
12. William Ryan and Walter Pitman, *Noah's Flood: The New Scientific Discoveries About the Event That Changed History* (Touchstone, 2000). In 2019 I visited the Rhine Falls, the most powerful waterfall in Europe, with up to a quarter of a million gallons of water rushing over every second. It too was created from the gradual recession of the last Ice Age and is still shifting. Standing almost beneath it, I had a profound and urgent sense of its awesome primal force.
13. Samuel Noah Kramer, "Reflections on the Mesopotamian Flood," *Expedition Magazine* 9, no. 4 (1967): 12–18.

scrutiny and cannot be read as real history. What purpose does the book of Genesis have for expending three and a half chapters, eighty-six verses in all, on this unbelievable episode?

One simple answer to all four challenges is to say that the entire event was a divine miracle in every way. God introduced vast quantities of additional water to the whole planet, from beneath the ground and beyond the skies, as the verse says: "All the wellsprings of the great deep burst, and the casements of heaven were opened" (Gen. 7:11). This massive upheaval confounded the geological strata and moved mountains. Simultaneously, God must have carefully regulated the deluge to ensure it did not spiral into an irrevocable global and geological calamity.

Also, despite its considerable size, the ark must have been miraculously bigger on the inside (like Doctor Who's TARDIS) in order to have enough room to house all the millions of earth's life-forms. Finally, we would have to say that all the other civilizations with a flood story just imagined or falsified their versions, or based them on other events, or somehow copied Genesis.

Of course, all the above is *possible*. After all, belief in God means recognizing that divine power is unlimited, so this approach is tenable, as far as it goes. But for many, including me, it is not satisfactory. To begin with, as Nahmanides points out, reliance on miracles is far from ideal:

> God made the ark large in order to reduce the miracle, for such is the way with all the miracles in the Bible: whatever is humanly possible is done, with the balance left to heaven.[14]

But my main query is this: If it was all a miracle, then we must also admit that the planet was *restored in just such a way as to look as if the Flood never happened in the first place*. This is an outlandish proposition. Why would God do that? Why allow future generations to question the veracity of the Flood by making it appear that it never actually occurred? It would certainly have been useful to have left at least a few irrefutable physical traces to dispel the inevitable naysayers.

---

14. Comment of Nahmanides on Genesis 6:19.

This is the very reason explorers hunt for remains of Noah's ark. The discovery of physical evidence, they believe, would surely silence the skeptics. Their meager findings over the years, such as hazy aerial photos, weathered wood remains, and quantities of animal bones are dubious in the extreme. The Talmud does record an opinion that three regional hot springs were a remnant of the Flood, but these sites of geothermal activity are perfectly explainable natural phenomena.[15]

In the end, treating the Flood as a great global miracle compels us to ignore the extensive scientific evidence – coming from a whole host of disciplines – which challenges this event. But it is more than that. *It means casting doubt on the whole endeavor of science.* For if God not only suspends the laws of physics but also *makes it appear as if they were never really suspended,* then everything we have deduced and measured in this world might, in truth, be mistaken. Thus, it might *appear* as though dinosaurs once roamed the Earth, but in fact they did not. It might *appear* as though the world is billions of years old, but in fact it is only a few thousand. It might all just be an elaborate hoax, miraculously staged in accordance with some ineffable divine plan. And if we take this approach to the extreme, then we cannot rely on anything at all. Maybe the universe is only seconds old and its entire backstory – the planets, life on Earth, and human history – has just been put there to make it appear that the universe has a past. Such an approach makes a mockery of any attempt at objective scientific study. Everything we think we know might just be a mirage, and there are no consistent or measurable features in the physical universe.

This is a lot to swallow. Why would God deceive us so? Every day, before the morning *Amida,* we say, "True is the eternal God, our King."[16] In the book of Psalms it says, "The essence of Your word is truth" (Ps. 119:160). God does not deceive. Aren't we meant to use our God-given faculties to make sense of our God-given world? In the end, the "it's-all-a-miracle" tactic throws up more questions than it answers. In which case, our primary question remains: How do we possibly explain the fantastical flood story?

---

15. Sanhedrin 108a.
16. *The Koren Shalem Siddur,* 102.

RESPONDING TO THE QUESTION

The Flood narrative has moments of high drama and hyperbole that are not meant to be understood completely literally. To begin with, the story employs some unusual language. As mentioned above, the rain arrived through the release of the "wellsprings of the deep" and the "casements of the heavens." These two Hebrew phrases, *maayanot tehom* and *arubot hashamayim,* mark the beginning and end of the rain (Gen. 7:11 and 8:2). They appear together nowhere else in the Bible. Rain is mentioned dozens of times, but never again coming from these sources. Anyway, how could this "rain" (*geshem* in Hebrew) come from above *and* below? It normally just *falls*. Furthermore, *mabul* – the Hebrew word for "flood" – only ever appears in reference to this unique event.[17]

Perhaps, the unique use of such words and phrases is an indication that we are meant to read the story in a more sophisticated way. The narrative could be understood to contain both literal elements and figurative ones. It is rooted in recognizable human experience but introduces vivid images in order to convey its message. By blending realism and hyperbole, the reader is carried along by the drama of the story while also appreciating that there are deeper layers of meaning to be uncovered. The Talmud readily acknowledges the use of hyperbolic language in the Bible:

> R. Ami said: the Torah spoke with exaggerated (*havai*) language and books of the prophets spoke with exaggerated language.... The Torah spoke with exaggerated language, as it is written, "Great cities and fortified to the heavens" (Deut. 1:28);[18] the books of the prophets spoke with exaggerated language, as it is written, "And all the people marched up after him [King Solomon], with the people piping away on pipes and rejoicing with such great joy that the very earth split from the sound" (I Kings 1:40).[19]

---

17. The Hebrew word *mabul* is mentioned thirteen times in the Bible, and every instance refers to this Flood (twelve times in Genesis, chapters 6–11, and once in Psalms 29:10).
18. See also Deuteronomy 9:1 for the same phrase.
19. Ḥullin 90b. See also Tamid 29a. Maimonides discusses the Bible's use of exaggerated language in *Guide for the Perplexed* 2:47.

In other words, the Canaanite cities that the Israelites would have to conquer were not really "fortified up to the heavens," *they were just very high*. Similarly, when King Solomon was coronated, the music and rejoicing did not really cause a crack in the earth, *it was just very loud*. In both cases, the text employs hyperbole to dramatize the events.

With this blended approach in mind, we can begin to address three of the four major problems discussed above. Put simply, the Flood could be read as a *regional event,* one that happened in a limited area in Mesopotamia. The overflowing of the Tigris and the Euphrates Rivers there are regular occurrences that occasionally have devastating consequences for the local populations.[20]

Once the Flood story is not treated as a global occurrence, many of the problematic scientific issues it raises fall away. No extra water is needed; the global ecosystem remains intact; there is ample room for the many regional species within the dimensions of the ark as described; and Ararat is a reasonable resting place as the highest mountain range in the area. A regional flood also overcomes the need to save every land-based life-form. Those rescued may have been picked from just those that people were familiar with – domesticated animals such as pets, livestock, and load-bearing animals, as well as some wilder ones.

All Life over All the Earth?

Rabbi David Zvi Hoffmann in the nineteenth century and Rabbi Gedaliah Nadel in the twentieth century, both highly respected traditional scholars, proposed that the Flood affected only the human settlements of a specific geographic area, what was the known world at the time.[21] For instance, we are told that the Flood would destroy every living thing "from under the heavens" (Gen. 6:17). Why this particular phrasing? Rabbi Nadal suggested it refers to *the heavens above the region in which Noah's civilization lived* rather than the entire world.

---

20. The British archaeologist Sir Charles Leonard Woolley (1880–1960) was one of the first archaeologists to propose a regional flood after identifying a flood-stratum at Ur some 400 miles long and 100 miles wide. See L. Woolley, *Ur of the Chaldees* (Ernest Benn Limited, 1929), 31.
21. See David Zvi Hoffmann, *Sefer Bereishit* (Netzach, 1969), 140–41; and Gedaliah Nadel, *BeTorato Shel Reb Gedaliah* (Sheilat, 2004), 116–18.

But, you may still be asking, doesn't treating the Flood as a regional event fly in the face of most of the Genesis text? In the verse just quoted, Noah is told that the Flood is coming "to destroy *all* flesh that has within it the breath of life" (ibid.). Surely this must mean every living species on the planet? Later, the dove sent out by Noah can find no resting place, "for the waters were over *all* the earth" (Gen. 8:9). Does this not imply the entire globe? Not one pre-modern rabbinic commentator proposed that the Flood was anything less than a global occurrence. We have already seen in chapter 1 that some of them treated the Creation story as allegorical. None, however, extended this to the Flood. So how could Rabbis Hoffmann and Nadel even entertain the possibility of a regional flood?

An important passage in the writings of Saadia Gaon, the tenth-century rabbi and philosopher, will help us here. His book *Sefer HaNivḥar BaEmunot uVaDeot* is an early example of the foundational principles of Judaism being described in a rational and systematic way. In it he confirms the traditional approach that biblical texts should, in the main, be read literally, but presents four types of exceptions. Only the first one concerns us here. This states that reading a biblical text literally is unacceptable when it can be "rejected by the observation of the senses." He gives a compelling example:

> Such as the statement, "And the man called his wife's name Eve (*Chava*) because she was the mother of *all* living (*chai*)" (Gen. 3:20), whereas we see that the ox and the lion are not offspring of womankind. Hence we must conclude that the implication of the statement embraces human descendants only.[22]

Humans only beget humans, so Eve could only have been the mother of all *human* life. Saadia Gaon thus limits the word "all" (*kol*) in the verse just to humans because that is what he has observed in nature.

Note that this was not his only interpretative option. He could have suggested that things were different in the Garden of Eden, and that

22. Saadia Gaon, *The Book of Beliefs and Opinions*, trans. Samuel Rosenblatt (Yale, 1989), 265.

Eve did indeed miraculously give birth to multiple species. Or he could have suggested that the biological makeup of biblical characters was different from ours, and that Eve somehow had the potential to mother *all* life. The fact that he does not take either of these two paths means that he is confident in applying his rational faculties and observational abilities, rather than simply relying on some kind of miraculous explanation.[23]

This approach could be applied to the Flood. When God says that "all flesh" will be destroyed, and that the Flood will cover "all the earth," these phrases should not be taken literally, as they would certainly contradict our current understanding of science. Just as Saadia Gaon limited the meaning of "all" with Eve, perhaps the word "all" in the Flood story was limited to the animals of a particular region, extending only to places familiar to the Mesopotamian peoples of the time. It is surprising to see just how often the word "all" appears in the Flood narrative. The extent of its recurrence is staggering:

- The phrase "all flesh" occurs thirteen times (Gen. 6:12, 13, 17, 19; 7:15, 16, 21; 8:17; 9:11, 15 [twice], 16, 17)
- Referring to life as a whole, "all" is used nine times (Gen. 6:19 [twice], 20; 7:4, 22 [twice], 23; 8:19, 21)
- Referring to animals and beasts, eight times (Gen. 7:2, 14 [twice]; 8:1 [twice], 17, 19, 20)
- To crawling things, five times (Gen. 7:8, 14, 21; 8:17, 19)
- To birds, five times (Gen. 7:14 [three times]; 8:19, 20)
- The phrase "all the earth" occurs twice (Gen. 7:3; 8:9)
- And "all humankind," once (Gen. 7:21)

The sustained use of the word is clearly a central motif of the story. Rather than being literal, "all" acts as a literary device signaling to the reader an expression of hyperbole. Similar hyperbole is used later in Genesis when describing the seven years of famine predicted by Joseph:

23. Somewhat similarly, both Rashi and Ibn Ezra readily interpret the phrase "And you shall circumcise the foreskin of your heart" (Deut. 10:16) in a non-literal way. Though very similar language is used to refer to actual physical circumcision (see Gen. 17:11), this is never entertained here.

> And the famine was over *all* the face of the earth. And Joseph laid open whatever had grain within and sold provisions to the Egyptians. And the famine grew harsh in the land of Egypt. And *all* the earth came to Egypt, to Joseph, to get provisions, for the famine had grown harsh in *all* the earth. (Gen. 41:56–57)

Are we seriously meant to entertain that this was a worldwide famine for which only Egypt had prepared, and that every nation on earth came there to buy grain? More probably, the recurrent "all" is hyperbole here too, aiming to show the superiority of Egypt, and how Joseph had established this dominance on a grand scale. This famine, just like the Flood years before, was a limited regional phenomenon.[24] However, from the perspective of those who experienced it, as mentioned earlier, it encompassed all the face of the earth.

This can also explain why no pre-moderns questioned the global spread of the Flood. It is because the extent of their knowledge of the earth sciences and ancient civilizations at the time would not have necessitated such a reading. The globe was not circumnavigated until the sixteenth century; the ancient civilizations of South America and the Far East were largely unknown, only a relatively small number of animal species had been identified, and an appreciation of global meteorology was well beyond their reach. At the time, the idea of a planet-wide flood and an huge floating ark housing all life were not unreasonable possibilities, so they had no need to question them.

Today however, with the exponential growth in science and technology, the Flood story now qualifies for Saadia Gaon's first type of text – i.e., one that cannot be taken literally when it clashes with our observations and knowledge. Hence, we find commentators that suggest a regional Flood, such as Hoffmann and Nadal, only much more recently.

The "all" motif even extends to the central character of the Flood story. After God gave Noah the instructions on how to build the ark and whom to house within it, the Torah says, "And this Noah did – *all* that

24. Even in a legal context the word "all" can be understood as a limiting factor: "One approach holds that the use of the word 'all' is to add, while another approach holds that it is to reduce" (Bekhorot 3a).

God commanded him, so he did" (Gen. 6:22). Many commentaries commend Noah for carrying out God's directions to the letter.[25] However, in line with the use of "all" throughout the story, it has a limiting sense. Yes, Noah did "all" God said, *but nothing more*. He failed to challenge God and advocate for arresting the coming Flood. "Noah was silent, saying nothing, not pleading for mercy."[26] Thus the "all" motif also exposes Noah's limited abilities.[27]

Challenges to a Regional Flood

There are some traditional sources that appear to clash with viewing the Flood as a regional event. For instance, the third-century sage R. Ḥama b. Ḥanina taught that Pharaoh's advisors told him not to fear any retribution from the God of Moses if he ordered the drowning of the Israelite baby boys, because it was well-known that God had promised never to destroy the earth again with a flood. They were wrong, however, says R. Ḥama, "because his advisors did not realize that while God will not bring a flood upon all the world, He may bring destruction by water upon one particular nation (i.e., Egypt)."[28] This seems to imply the Flood in Noah's time was global. Again, it can be countered that the phrase "all the world" (*kol ha'olam kulo*), refers to all the inhabited places and established nations at that time, i.e., the known world, not the entire globe.

A second challenge comes eight centuries later from Abraham ibn Ezra. On the verse "And God wiped out *all* existing things from the face of the earth" (Gen. 7:23), he commented:

> This is an overwhelming response to those of our fellow Jews who lack understanding, saying that the Flood was not across the whole earth.[29]

25. For example, the commentaries of Rashi, Nahmanides, and Ḥizkini on this verse.
26. Zohar 1:106a. Noah is critiqued for not challenging God as Abraham and Moses later did. See Deuteronomy Rabba 11:3; Zohar 1:67b–68a, 3:14b–15a.
27. Thanks to Dr. Aviva Gottlieb-Zornberg for pointing this out to me.
28. Sota 11a.
29. Ibn Ezra's comment on Genesis 7:23.

His opinion is particularly interesting because it reveals that there were people already questioning the literal truth of the Flood story way back in the twelfth century when Ibn Ezra lived. They did not have modern scientific data to back up their skepticism, but even then, new routes were starting to open up for intercontinental trade, and the rapid expansion of the known world may have fueled challenges to long-established beliefs. Ibn Ezra himself traveled widely and may well have been aware of these challenges, which he hoped to counter. His insistence on a global Flood is somewhat compromised, however, because even in his own commentary he identifies a whole clan of people who were unaffected, implying that it was not a universal phenomenon.[30]

It may be that Ibn Ezra's concern about reducing the Flood's reach was the possibility that it might undermine God's power. Divine supremacy is diminished if this was not a seminal worldwide event, but just a regional incident with limited influence. This, though, is a practical concern and is less about the facts of the narrative than its educational impact. In Ibn Ezra's time, an awesome story with a global scope would still inspire the masses. Today, however, rejecting a regional interpretation could put off those of a more questioning nature, especially if they are familiar with modern science.

While not directly stating it, several rabbinic sources may be marshaled in support of the Flood encompassing neither all life nor all the earth. For instance, one talmudic opinion states that the Flood did not reach the Land of Israel.[31] A second states that the remains of all those who died in the Flood were only to be found in the lower region of Mesopotamia.[32] And a third brings a verse to prove that aquatic life was left unharmed:

> R. Ḥisda said: During the generation of the Flood, no decree was decreed upon the fish in the sea, as it is stated, "all that was on dry land died" (Gen. 7:22), but not the fish in the sea.[33]

30. Ibn Ezra's comment on Genesis 6:4.
31. Zevaḥim 113a.
32. Shabbat 113b.
33. Zevaḥim 113b. See, though, Sanhedrin 108b, which implies the waters of the Flood

As well as limiting "all life" to terrestrial life, Rabbi Ḥisda's statement also contradicts the possibility of a deluge on a global scale, because that would have necessitated the mixing of fresh water and seawater, which is deadly to most species of sea creature.

Furthermore, a midrash suggests the sea creatures were also meant to board the ark somehow, but survived instead because "they fled to the *Okeanos*."[34] *Okeanos* is a Greek word meaning the "Great Sea," or the "Outer Ocean." Ancient civilizations believed this was a vast belt of water which surrounded all the earth's land masses. Thus, aquatic creatures saved themselves by retreating beyond the known earth of the time. As we now know, this is topologically inaccurate, but again the implication is that the Flood did not affect all forms of life.

Lessons from Hyperbole

If we accept the Flood as a regional occurrence, then what is the purpose of the sustained use of hyperbole in the story? Why keep repeating "all" life over "all" the earth? Perhaps it was written in this way to sensitize us to the fragility of humankind and the "all"-encompassing moral failures and utter corruption of ancient Mesopotamian civilization. Indeed, this is God's opening declaration to Noah:

> The end of all flesh is come before Me, for the earth is filled with their violence, and I am now about to destroy them, with the earth. (Gen. 6:13)

God's moral outrage drives the biblical narrative. This stands in stark contrast to comparable versions found in ancient Mesopotamia. We come then to the fourth problem – mentioned at the beginning of this chapter – the Torah's similarity to other ancient flood narratives. Rabbi Professor Umberto Cassuto's introduction to his commentary on the Flood is an invaluable resource here.[35]

---

were boiling hot, which certainly would have killed all life in the seas.

34. Genesis Rabba 32:11.

35. Umberto Cassuto, *Commentary on Genesis: Part Two – From Noah to Abraham*, translated by Israel Abrahams (Magnes Press, 1998), 3–47. Cassuto was the chief

Cassuto presents a thorough comparison of the biblical Flood and the ancient Mesopotamian versions. He details nineteen similarities between the two, including the ark specifications, narrative timetable, sealing the entrance, where the ark comes to rest, and the age and role of the hero – Utnapishtim in the Sumerian *Epic of Gilgamesh*, Atrahasis in the Akkadian version, and Noah in Genesis. The extent of the similarities makes it evident that these three versions have a common origin. However, Cassuto then lists sixteen specific and essential differences between the Mesopotamian and biblical texts. These differences reveal an entirely different purpose to the narratives. Let us focus on four of them:

1. In one Mesopotamian version, the storm god Enlil wanted to destroy humanity because they were making too much noise and he could not sleep; in another version no reason is given at all – it was an arbitrary decision of the gods. Meanwhile, the Torah opens its account with a crystal-clear cause: "All flesh had corrupted its ways on the earth" (Gen. 6:12). The Flood is decreed as retribution for widespread unethical behavior. This is completely absent from the Mesopotamian versions.
2. In the Mesopotamian versions, the gods quarrel before the Flood and continue to do so, with more recriminations, after it. The Torah has none of this. God displays absolute justice and has complete authority.
3. The *Epic of Gilgamesh* portrays the gods as frightened by the deluge and in search of refuge. They are overcome by the forces of nature they have unleashed. In the Torah, God is in complete control of the Flood. God commands and nature responds. There is no limit to God's power. The Flood has no effect on God, who is clearly outside, or beyond, the destruction that occurs.

---

rabbi of Florence for eleven years before being appointed professor of Hebrew and Literature at the University of Florence, and then of Rome. In 1938, antisemitism led to his emigration to Israel, where he was appointed professor of Bible at the Hebrew University of Jerusalem. Sadly, he died in 1951 before he could complete his multifaceted Torah commentary.

4. The climax of the Akkadian version is the exaltation of the zoo-boat captain hero to divine status. In fact, the reason this story appears at all in the *Epic of Gilgamesh* is because the Sumerian king Gilgamesh was in pursuit of the secret of eternal life. Meanwhile, in the Torah, Noah remains mortal. The division between humanity and deity is not blurred. In fact, God establishes a covenant with Noah and all living flesh to preserve life. Rather than ending in personal reward, the story is concluded with an eternal commitment.

Taken together, these differences are overwhelming. In the Mesopotamian versions, competing gods with limited power and lacking a just cause release an almost uncontrollable flood, rewarding the human survivor with a seat at their table. Conversely, God in the Torah is prompted by an ethical purpose that is carried out in a controlled and systematic way, ending with a lasting covenant between God and all life on earth. This startling contrast underlines the completely different orientations of the narratives. Cassuto writes:

> Not only does the Torah exclude any reference to the will of the various gods or natural forces apart from the will of the Lord of the universe; not only does its concept of God transcend completely the world of nature; and not only is it free from any blurring of the boundaries between the human and the Divine… [but the attributes of gods] who act arbitrarily, cunningly and give deceitful counsel are changed to [a God with] qualities of uprightness, of love for creatures that are deserving of it, and of paternal care for them. Thus, the story that to begin with was amoral becomes a source of ethical instruction.[36]

The lasting impact of God's intervention is the purpose of the dramatic narrative. The frequently repeated "all"-motif is a literary device to support this. And so, in the rabbinic tradition, the Flood becomes a seminal moment. Seven universal ethical laws were affirmed in the period of Noah. Human

---

36. Cassuto, *Commentary on Genesis: Part Two*, 28.

societies must establish justice systems, refrain from idolatry, blasphemy, murder, theft, sexual immorality, and consuming living flesh.[37] This was at a time when legal systems were being established in order to enable early civilizations to flourish and not descend into violence and destruction.

Building on Cassuto, other Jewish scholars have described the Flood as an ethical reframing of older narratives.[38] According to these approaches, the Torah took an ancient regional catastrophe and invested it with ethical meaning and moral lessons. In light of this, the issue of whether the Flood affected all life over the entire world is relatively unimportant:

> If the Torah has a specific educational purpose in retelling the story of the Flood from its ethical-religious perspective, we have little reason to think that its statement that every species was included in the ark was meant to give divine confirmation of that specific detail of the pagan story and to exclude the possibility that some esoteric species from far-away New Zealand (unknown to Noah) had survived the Flood.[39]

Co-opting the Rainbow

Finally, we need to consider the rainbow at the end of the story. A simple reading of the Torah here would lead us to think that the appearance of the rainbow in the clouds was not originally part of the world's weather, and that, miraculously, God created a new phenomenon as a sign to assure humanity that there would never be another flood:

> And God said, "This is the sign of the covenant that I set between Me and you and every living creature.... My bow I have set in the cloud." (Gen. 9:13)

37. Sanhedrin 56a–b.
38. See Joel Wolowelsky, "A Note on the Flood Story in the Language of Man," *Tradition* 42, no. 3 (2009): 41–48. Here it is also mentioned that this approach might be inappropriate to teach too early in a child's schooling. See also Joshua Berman, *Inconsistencies in the Torah: Ancient Literary Convention and the Limits of Source Criticism* (Oxford, 2017), 251–68.
39. Joel B. Wolowelsky, "Teaching the Flood Story: The Importance of Cultural Context," *Ten Da'at* 9, no. 1 (Winter, 1996): 91–92.

The problem is that a rainbow can be explained in purely meteorological terms and does not require divine intervention. Nahmanides recognized this in his Torah commentary:

> We should trust the words of the Greeks [i.e., their philosophers] that the rainbow is a natural result of the heat of the sun falling upon damp air, for even in a vessel containing water which stands in the sun, there is the appearance of a rainbow.[40]

He is describing the process of refraction, which is a basic part of the science of optics.

To resolve this problem, Nahmanides goes on to explain that the rainbow was indeed a preexisting phenomenon, and his proof is compelling. A close reading of the text reveals that God mentioned the rainbow in the past tense, "My bow I have set in the cloud," i.e., "I have *already* set," not "I *will* set." This makes it clear that it existed in nature from the very beginning. After the Flood, the rainbow was repurposed by God to act as a sign of assurance. Rainbows are the result of an increase of water in the atmosphere, and often occur on rainy days, especially in the summer months. This makes them a fitting reminder of the downfall that began the Flood. The occurrence of a rainbow in the wake of an unexpected downpour is an ideal signal to remind people that while a Flood *could* happen again, it *will not,* because of God's promise.

Nahmanides teaches that, in essence, God was saying, "The rainbow that I have set in the clouds ever since the Creation will be from this day forth a sign of the covenant between Me and you, and whenever I will see it, I will remember the covenant." Observed by God above and us below, the rainbow was co-opted as a visual representation of this covenantal commitment. This explanation employs a similar device to the one already used in this chapter. The Torah takes a preexisting natural phenomenon – occasional catastrophic flooding in the Mesopotamia region – and invests it with deep and lasting religious significance.

It is not so surprising that depictions of the Flood story in art and culture have tended to focus on the physical nature of the event. We are

40. Nahmanides's commentary on Genesis 9:12.

delighted by illustrations of a colossal boat with giraffe and elephant heads protruding from the sides on a stormy sea. Beautiful portrayals of Noah and the animals under a shining rainbow are also a common favorite. At the same time, when the Flood story is analyzed from a modern perspective, its believability as a historic event is usually the major concern.

Traditional Jewish commentaries work in a very different way. They concentrate on the ethical implications of the story rather than its physicality or historicity. The immorality of the Flood generation and the responsibilities of Noah are their focus. Some technical details are explored insofar as they enable the narrative to make sense to the reader. So, for instance, the rabbis thought that the broad base of the ark (300 by 50 cubits) as compared to its height (30 cubits) was reasonable enough to ensure that it would not capsize.[41] They also discussed how many hundreds of subcompartments would be necessary in order to house the multitude of animals, as well as what was contained on each of the three decks of the ark.[42] However, ethical lessons are the main focus when examining these details.

For instance, there is a discussion about the makeup of a particular design feature of the ark: "Make a *tzohar* in the ark; within a cubit of the top you shall finish it" (Gen. 6:16). The third-century sage R. Abba bar Kahana understood this to be the window referred to later in the story, from which Noah sent out the raven (Gen. 8:6–7). Meanwhile, his contemporary, R. Levi, thought that the *tzohar* was a shining jewel in that window which helped to illuminate the ark.[43] This discussion, which is essentially about the brightness of the ark's interior, is generally understood to be addressing a moral issue:

> Noah needed to be able to differentiate between day and night in order to know when to feed each animal, as some ate only during daylight while others were nocturnal.[44]

41. Sanhedrin 108b.
42. Genesis Rabba 31:11.
43. Ibid.
44. Comment of Rabbi Enoch Zundel ben Yosef, *Etz Yosef*, on the midrash, based on Yerushalmi Pesaḥim 1:1 and *Tanḥuma*.

The *tzohar* thus enabled Noah to be more caring to the animals.

The Ark Today

Young children are exhilarated by the tale of Noah and the ark, while modern critics are skeptical. The rabbinic sages took a different approach: they analyzed it for moral insight. We would do well to follow their lead and look for the relevance of the story to our contemporary situation.

The reality of climate change and the threats to our global ecology point to viewing life on this planet as a delicate "ark" that is under growing danger of destruction. The Earth's biodiversity is declining. How do we protect life today?

God brought the Flood as a reaction to humankind's moral failings. Similarly, today, life on earth is in danger because of humanity's choices. The number of species that have become extinct through human activity is growing exponentially:[45]

> According to estimates by a team of experts in 2004, climate change alone, if left unabated, could be the primary cause of extinction of a quarter of the species of plants and animals on the land by midcentury. The list of species erased is already long.... Gone are the golden coqui, a Puerto Rican tree frog; the lotis blue butterfly of California; Bachman's warbler, a migratory species of the eastern United States; and all three of the land birds found uniquely in Guam, including the brilliantly coloured cardinal honeyeater.[46]

The remains of these creatures, and so many more, fill the rows of collectors' shelves. They have been lost from the ark of life. How many more will we lose before we take responsibility for the unintended consequences of our industrial policies?[47]

---

45. Jeff Tollerson, "Humans Are Driving One Million Species to Extinction," *Nature* (May 6, 2019). See https://www.nature.com/articles/d41586-019-01448-4.
46. E. O. Wilson, *The Creation: An Appeal to Save Life on Earth* (W. W. Norton and Company, 2006), 74.
47. See, for example, Dave Goulson, *Silent Earth: Averting the Insect Apocalypse* (Jonathan Cape, 2021).

The Global Challenges Foundation looks at the potential catastrophes that could occur due to human activity.[48] Their 2021 report about global catastrophic risks identified weapons of mass destruction and pandemics as major threats; however, the interrelated risks due to climate change dominates the agenda.

> When it comes to climate change, the most recent report from the Intergovernmental Panel on Climate Change (IPCC) has delivered a grim warning which UN Secretary General António Guterres called a "code red for humanity." It found Earth is expected to hit the critical threshold of 1.5°C warming due to greenhouse gas emissions within the next 20 years. Even if we take drastic action to reduce emissions, a lot of the impact is likely already baked in, with drastic consequences for many people around the world. Glaciers will continue to shrink for decades or centuries and sea levels will rise. The probability of low-likelihood, high-impact outcomes increases – massive ice sheet loss, the collapse of forests, or even the breakdown of the circulatory system in the Atlantic Ocean that regulates much of the northern hemisphere's weather and climate. As the impacts of man-made climate change and humanity's destruction of the natural environment worsen, so do the threats from future pandemics, especially zoonotic viruses that jump from animals to humans. A changing climate is also exacerbating conflict, food insecurity, refugee crises and extreme poverty.[49]

The Torah's foresight in framing the Flood in global terms is remarkable. Even though, as previously argued, it may well have been a regional phenomenon, describing it as a global catastrophe gives it dramatic weight which has profound significance today. We are more aware than ever of

---

48. See https://globalchallenges.org.
49. *Global Catastrophic Risks 2021: Navigating the Complex Intersections*, Ulrika Westin, editor in chief, published by the Global Challenges Foundation, 4. See https://globalchallenges.org/wp-content/uploads/2021/09/Global-Catastrophic-Risks-2021-FINAL.pdf.

the threat to our planet that unbridled human productivity and consumption is causing. With the danger of rising sea levels, the Flood story still holds water and continues to bear an urgent message for humanity. At every COP (Conference of the Parties), the annual UN Climate Change Conference, more of the world's nations make promises to cut emissions and increase their responsibility for the planet. We will see in the coming decades if they hold true to their commitments and if they are even enough to stem the tide.

There is an apt midrash which imagines a conversation between Abraham and Noah's son, Shem:

> "What gave you the merit to survive the ark?" Abraham asks. "Because of all the *tzedaka* (righteous acts of charity and care) we did!" Shem replies. "But what *tzedaka* was there for you to do? Were there any poor people there? Surely, there were just eight of you – Noah and sons and their partners!" "Yes, but we were doing *tzedaka* for the beasts, animals, and birds. We did not sleep all night because if we weren't caring for one of them, then we were caring for another!"[50]

This moral responsibility was the spark that ignited Abraham; as God later remarked about him:

> He directs his children and his household after him to keep the way of the Lord by doing what is right (*tzedaka*) and just. (Gen. 18:19)

This is what made him the founding father of the Jewish people. He learned so much from Noah and the Flood, and so must we.

50. *Midrash Tehillim* (*Shoḥer Tov*), 37. See also Genesis Rabba 30:6.

Chapter 4

Did the Exodus Really Take Place?

EXPLORING THE QUESTION

If the Exodus did not happen, then we really are in trouble. So much of Jewish tradition rides on it. The foundational story of our faith is that God saved the Israelites from their Egyptian oppressors, brought them to Mount Sinai to receive the Torah, and then led them to the Promised Land. We mention the Exodus again and again in our daily and Shabbat prayers, and it forms the basis of the festival of Passover.[1] Nevertheless, from a historical point of view, it seems impossible to prove conclusively that the events recounted at the beginning of the book of Exodus ever occurred.[2] To be honest, such an admission is deeply uncomfortable because *yetzi'at Mitzrayim,* the Exodus from Egypt, is central to Jewish

---

1. *The Koren Shalem Siddur,* 18, 68, 80, 100, 104, 146, and 198 (Morning service: after donning *tefillin,* collection of verses after *Barukh She'amar,* Song of the Sea, third paragraph of *Shema,* before the *Amida,* in *Taḥanun* of Mondays and Thursdays, and in the first of the Six Remembrances); 248 and 250 (Evening service: third paragraph of *Shema* and subsequent paragraph); 382 (Friday night Kiddush), 978 (Grace after Meals, *Nodeh lekha* paragraph).
2. There is no mention of a mass Israelite exodus or the name "Moshe" in any hieroglyphic writings and no physical evidence to substantiate the Exodus narrative anywhere near conclusively.

belief and provides the moral foundation for much of Jewish practice. And yet this has become a question asked by many Jews today and needs to be addressed.

When researching a historical event, verifying the essential details such as the date, location, key players, scale, and political context is a good place to start. However, as we shall see, the Torah seems to be surprisingly hazy and inconsistent about all of these.

God told Abraham that his descendants would be enslaved for 400 years in a foreign land (Gen. 15:13), but later the Torah states that they lived in Egypt for 430 years before they left (Ex. 12:40). Which one is correct? The commentaries seek a way to align these time spans, but they generally agree that *neither* one refers to the period our ancestors actually resided in Egypt.[3]

Meanwhile, the book of Kings states that Solomon began to build the First Temple in Jerusalem "in the four hundred and eightieth year after the Israelites left the land of Egypt" (I Kings 6:1). Given that Solomon's reign is set in the tenth century BCE, this dates the Exodus to the fifteenth century BCE, and yet, based on the well-attested ancient Egyptian chronology, thirteenth century BCE is a much more likely era for the Exodus. The Torah is clear only about the actual *day* and *month* they left – after midnight on the fourteenth of Nisan.[4] Note, however, that this way of counting time had only been introduced to Moses two weeks earlier, when God said, "This month will be to you the first of the months" (Ex. 12:2). So there is no way to relate this date to the chronology of ancient Egypt.

---

3. Genesis Rabba 91:2 and Exodus Ṛabba 18:11 agree that the Israelites were in Egypt for only 210 years. In his commentary on Exodus 12:40, Rashi discusses the basis for the 400 years stated in Genesis and 430 in Exodus, but is clearly uncomfortable with the explanation, conceding: "You are compelled to say [this], even though unwillingly." He even points out in his conclusion that this inconsistency was one of the texts altered by the rabbis when translating the Bible into Greek for King Ptolemy II (285–247 BCE), for fear it would be misunderstood (see Megilla 9a).
4. See Exodus 12. Note that the months have no names in the Torah, only numbers (see, for example, Lev. 23). The Hebrew names are based on the Babylonian calendar that the Israelites adopted in exile (see Nahmanides on Ex. 12:2).

The Torah also tells us that the enslaved Israelites lived in a place called Goshen.[5] Where is this on a map of Egypt? A verse in Psalms (78:12) says it was in the fields of Zoan, but this location is never given any geographical context. When Jacob and family first settled in Goshen, as described at the end of the book of Genesis, the region was called "the best land, in the land of Ra'amses" (Gen. 47:11). None of this enables us to be definitive about the location of Goshen.

Years later, the two store cities that the Israelite slaves built for the pharaoh were called "Pitom and Ra'amses" (Ex. 1:11). Where are these located and for which pharaoh were they built? In the Torah the Egyptian ruler is called only *paro* (pharaoh), or *melekh Mitzrayim* (king of Egypt), but no personal name is ever given.[6] From ancient Egyptian king lists, we know that the first three pharaohs of the Nineteenth Dynasty (1295–1186 BCE) were called Ramesses, Seti, and Ramesses II (pronounced Ram-seez). The similarity between the biblical word Ra'amses and the pharaonic name Ramesses has led scholars to connect them, which is one reason why the Exodus is often dated to the thirteenth century BCE.[7] They identify Seti I as the pharaoh who persecuted the Israelite slaves (Ex. 1:8–16), and when he died (Ex. 2:23), his son Ramesses II became the stubborn pharaoh who rejected Moses's request to set the Israelites free.[8]

---

5. Goshen is mentioned in Genesis 45:10, 46:28, 34, 47:1, 4, 6, 27, 50:8; Exodus 8:18, 9:26; Joshua 10:41.
6. Later in the Bible some pharaohs are mentioned by their personal names, e.g., Shishak (I Kings 11:40) and Necho (II Kings 23:29).
7. See, for example, Mitchell, *The Bible in the British Museum*, 41. One problem with this approach is that if Ramesses was already the name of the pharaoh in Jacob's time, and Moses was born a few hundred years later, then the Exodus from Egypt would have to be set in the tenth century BCE, which no one accepts.
8. The Torah gives no information whatsoever about this pharaonic transition of power. Most readers do not even notice that the persecutor of the Israelites in Exodus 1 is not the same person refusing Moses in Exodus 5. The reaction to the death of the pharaoh in Ex. 2:23 is followed, in the very next verse, with the Israelites sighing due to their enslavement. Rashi wonders why they did not rejoice at the death of the cruel pharaoh. He explains, based on a midrash from Exodus Rabba (1:34), that the pharaoh did not actually die. Rather, he contracted leprosy, which was "like" death, and bathed in the blood of slaughtered Israelite children to cure himself. Thus, from

The choice of Ramesses II as the best candidate for the pharaoh of the Exodus story is built on several factors, including his name, lasting success, preoccupation as a builder, and the seat of his kingdom. Until the Nineteenth Dynasty, most major royal cities and palaces were to be found along the Nile in southern Egypt, in places such as Thebes and Abydos, three hundred miles south of where Cairo is today. Due to increased trade and interactions with the coastal provinces of Canaan, Ramesses II was the first pharaoh to relocate his center of operations to the northern Delta region.[9] He built his capital city, Pi-Ramesses, just fifty miles from the Mediterranean coast.[10] He was also lauded as a great builder, constructing temples and other buildings all across Egypt. He ruled for sixty-six years (1279–1213 BCE), one of the longest reigns of any pharaoh.

We know about Ramesses II from numerous hieroglyphic inscriptions, including the fact that he had conquered much of Canaan, bringing it under his control. This only adds more confusion to the Exodus story, however, because after successfully leaving Egypt behind them, the Israelites would have met fresh Egyptian forces when they finally reached Canaan. Thus, even though there are many good reasons to identify Ramesses II as the main pharaoh of the Exodus story, not everything correlates.[11] Indeed, there are a number of accounts that endeavor to connect all the dots, but these are obliged to ignore or downplay one aspect or another, either from the archaeological record or from the Torah's account.[12]

---

a rabbinic point of view – just like the dispute about the number of years in Egypt – even supposedly straightforward information provided by the Torah about the details of the Exodus cannot be taken at face value.

9. Nahum M. Sarna, *Exploring Exodus* (Schocken Books, 1996), 19.
10. This is identified with the village of Qantir today (ibid., 20).
11. The actual dating for this approach is off by a few decades, too, as the traditional Jewish date for the Exodus is 1312 BCE (based on *Seder Olam Rabba*). Also, we know from hieroglyphic inscriptions that Ramesses II lived a long life and had many sons, and there is no mention of Israelite slaves or any kind of rebellion, all of which blatantly contradict the account in Exodus.
12. See, for example, K. A. Kitchen, *On the Reliability of the Old Testament* (Eerdmans, 2006), and David Arnovitz, ed., *The Koren Tanakh of the Land of Israel: Exodus* (Koren, 2019).

The story in the Torah is not a straightforward account. Much of the narrative is focused on the direct clash between Pharaoh and Moses. We are not told the titles or names of any of Pharaoh's advisors or of any of the elders of the children of Israel. Both are occasionally mentioned when challenging their respective leaders, but the Torah does not elaborate on their positions or on the part they play in this epic story. Rather, it is presented as a dramatic battle between hero and antihero.

We are not even sure of how many Israelites left Egypt. The Torah says that they numbered "about six hundred thousand on foot, adult men, aside from children" (Ex. 12:37). So, doubling up for women and including children, we reach a figure of two to three million people all in all. This is a staggeringly large total – the housing, food supply, sanitation, and general infrastructure requirements for such a mass of people in one location in that period are just plain unrealistic. In the late second millennium BCE, the large capital, Pi-Ramesses, is estimated to have had a population of 300,000, leading to a total Egyptian population of just a few million.[13] To make matters worse, one rabbinic thread suggests that many Israelites died in the ninth plague and that only one-fifth of them actually made it out of Egypt.[14] This would imply an Israelite slave population in Egypt of well over seven million!

In sum, from a historical point of view, we cannot be sure about the *who, what, when, where,* or even the *how many* of the Exodus story.

And then there are the miracles. The account in Exodus is teeming with them. To back up his message to Pharaoh, God shows Moses how to transform his staff into a snake and turn his hand leprous (Ex. 4:1–8). Next, on a much larger scale, come the unforgettable ten plagues, each of which adds to the devastation of Egypt (Ex. 7:14–12:30). These miracles culminate in the splitting of the sea, which puts an end to the Egyptian army's pursuit (Ex. 14:19–28).

What are we to make of these unbelievable contraventions of nature? One approach is to find a naturalistic explanation for every

13. Alan Bowman, "ancient Egypt" *Encyclopedia Britannica* (updated 7 March 2022), www.britannica.com/place/ancient-Egypt.
14. This is based on the word *ḥamushim* (Ex. 13:19), translated as either "armed for battle" or "a fifth of them" – see Rashi there and the *Mekhilta*.

miracle of the Exodus.[15] This, so the argument goes, makes them more believable. The miracle then lies in the *timing* – it happened just when it was needed. However, miraculous timing could be considered just as unnatural as the miracle itself! How then is a modern rational person meant to relate to miracles? Indeed, the Exodus is the most miracle-laden story in the Torah. Why is this the case?

I have been studying the Exodus for a long time. No matter how much I would like to, I know of no way to prove the veracity of the story as literally recounted in the Torah. An honest assessment of the information and facts precludes any scientific attempt to confirm its occurrence. Despite all this, the Exodus remains central to Jewish faith, of utmost importance to religious life, and essentially true, as will be explained.

RESPONDING TO THE QUESTION

David Ben-Gurion, the first prime minister of Israel, was not a religious man. Yet he believed in the Exodus story:

> An event which has been etched so deeply into the consciousness of the nation and whose reverberations are heard in almost all the books of the Prophets, in several books of the Writings, is without doubt an historical event; indeed, a central event in our history.[16]

Inspiring as it is, this is still no proof. What then is the academic view? A significant advance in assessing the historicity of the Exodus took place in San Diego in 2013. At the University of California, a transdisciplinary conference was held entitled, "Out of Egypt: Israel's Exodus Between Text and Memory, History and Imagination." It was possibly the largest academic gathering in modern times focused on the Exodus.

More than forty presentations were given by leading scholars from around the world in a range of disciplines, including Egyptology, archaeology, biblical scholarship, philosophy, history, ancient languages, geography,

---

15. For instance, Colin J. Humphreys, *The Miracles of Exodus: A Scientist's Discovery of the Extraordinary Natural Causes of the Biblical Stories* (2003, Continuum).
16. David Ben-Gurion, *Ben-Gurion Looks at the Bible,* trans. Jonathan Kolatch (W. H. Allen, 1972), 113.

and geoscience. A large volume of the proceedings was published in 2015 and has accompanied our family Seders ever since. The overwhelming conclusion is this: *In the second half of the second millennium BCE, some form of Israelite Exodus definitely happened.* After analyzing the biblical text in its Near Eastern context, unpacking its ancient literary portrayal, and evaluating it as a formidable cultural memory, the book makes it very reasonable to acknowledge a reality to the Exodus narrative.[17]

One paper at the conference even focused on the changing attitudes of Egyptologists to the Israelite Exodus history over the last century and ends with a survey of their latest attitudes. Most of the nineteen eminent respondents admitted they had not published directly on the topic, but when asked, "Do you think the early Israelites lived in Egypt and there was some sort of Exodus?" surprisingly, almost all of them answered in the affirmative. The paper concluded that

> Egyptologists, on the one hand, seem to accept the historicity of the biblical sojourn and Exodus narratives, but on the other hand either have no interest in investigating it using their discipline, or feel that ... the Exodus is a religious matter.[18]

This is a vital point because it shows that even Egyptologists, who could legitimately claim that studying the Exodus falls within their expertise, admit that it has many aspects that are beyond their field.[19]

---

17. The Bible scholar Richard Elliott Friedman argued this point in his book *The Exodus* (HarperOne, 2017). As a prominent proponent of biblical criticism, his voice is particularly significant. A similar approach is also taken in an excellent Bible encyclopedia which presents historical, archaeological, and literary explanations by numerous Israeli academics. See volume 2 on the book of Exodus: Shemaryahu Talmon, ed., *Sefer Shemot, Olam HaTanakh* [Hebrew] (Divrei Hayamim, 2002).
18. Thomas E. Levy, Thomas Schneider, and William H. C. Propp, eds., *Israel's Exodus in Transdisciplinary Perspective: Text, Archaeology, Culture, and Geoscience* (Springer, 2015), 206.
19. Even calling it the Exodus sets it apart from other ancient migrations. As Dr. Indiana Jones said to his students as he walks out the door in his fourth outing on the big screen, "When I come back, we'll discuss the difference between migration and Exodus." A response might be: one is the academic historical analysis of demographic change, while the other is the religious portrayal of a national foundation story.

However, we are still left with a major problem. While many Egyptologists have confidence in the historical grounding of the Exodus story, this is a far cry from affirming the truth of every single element of the biblical text. Did it all happen exactly the way it is written?

To respond to this question, we need to understand the various ways in which the Torah *presents* the Exodus narrative. To this end, three complementary aspects of the text will be discussed. These can be termed educational imperative, literary forms, and Egyptological resonance. Together, they return the Exodus to its appropriate position and rescue it from the unending, sterile, and ultimately unsatisfying debates about its literal historicity.

Educational Imperative

What is the *purpose* of telling the Exodus story in the Torah? It might seem an obvious question, the answer being "because that is what happened." But this is not convincing. As seen earlier, much important data is conspicuously absent if we read the narrative as a straightforward historical account. There is a lot more going on here. One vital aspect is the educational imperative. *The need to recall this event in the future is so essential that it is introduced into the event itself, while it is still happening.* As the drama of the story unfolds, it is interrupted on four separate occasions in order to teach how to remember and relive these events in future times.

We take up the narrative as God instructs Moses and Aaron on how the Israelites should prepare for their departure, which will take place in a fortnight, on the night of the final plague. Twelve verses provide detailed instructions on how to take and slaughter a lamb or kid, prepare its meat for eating, and daub its blood on the doorposts (Ex. 12:2–13). But then, God tacks on another seven verses about the future remembrance of this night:

> And this day shall be a remembrance for you; and you shall celebrate it as a festival to the Lord through your generations.... Seven days shall you eat unleavened bread.... And you shall observe the Feast of Unleavened Bread; for on this very day I brought out your battalions from the land of Egypt; and you

> shall observe this day through your generations, an everlasting statute... in all your dwelling places shall you eat unleavened bread. (Ex. 12:14–20)

This is extraordinary: the Exodus is still a fortnight away and God is giving directives about how it is to be remembered in some undisclosed time to come.

Moses now conveys this message to the Israelites in his own words. Following God's lead, he gives instructions both to prepare for the Exodus and how to recall it in the future. But while he spends three verses on the former (Ex. 12:21–23), he dedicates four to the latter:

> And you shall keep this thing as a statute for you and your sons, everlasting. And so when you come to the land that the Lord will give you... and when your child asks you, "What is this service to you?" you shall say, "A Passover sacrifice to the Lord, who passed over the houses of the Israelites in Egypt, when He scourged Egypt and our households He rescued." (Ex. 12:24–27)

Again, this is extraordinary: the night of the Exodus has not even arrived and yet Moses is instructing the people as to how to answer their yet-unborn children's questions about it once they have settled in the Promised Land. Twice now the story has been interrupted to address issues of no immediate importance.

Unfazed by this, the Israelites do as instructed. The night of the fateful final plague arrives, and across Egypt firstborn sons are struck down. Pharaoh calls Moses in desperation, demanding that he and his troublesome people leave forthwith. The Israelites exit in haste, carrying their freshly baked, but unleavened, bread. At this climactic moment the story is disrupted for a third time, as God spends seven verses teaching Moses and Aaron more rules about observing the Passover ritual in the future (Ex. 12:43–49).

After a brief return to the story, we come to the fourth and final interruption, the biggest of them all. Two-thirds of the next chapter is dedicated to rituals relating to the future remembrance of the Exodus (13:1–16). We learn about consecrating firstborn boys and beasts, observing Passover in the land, wearing *tefillin* as a regular reminder, and, again, answering our children's future questions:

> Should your son ask you tomorrow, saying, "What is this?" you shall say to him, "By strength of hand God brought us out from Egypt, from the house of slaves." (Ex. 13:14)

Once this long interruption is complete, we finally return to the urgency of the story: Pharaoh has a change of heart and takes up the chase.

How can this peculiar way of telling the Exodus story be explained? No Hollywood director would dream of such midscene interruptions. Why is dramatic tension sacrificed for educational interludes?

It must be that this is not simply an epic adventure, but rather a story told specifically to teach future generations how to live. *The educational imperative embedded in the story is not an interruption; it is the true intent of the story.* The narratives serve to illustrate this educational imperative. This is the Torah's essentially didactic approach: God's acts are recounted in order to teach us how to serve God in the future. The Exodus story is more of an inspirational instruction manual than an exact historical account. Thus, the truth of the story is contained in how we commit to remember it and learn from it, rather than focusing on the veracity of the narrative itself.

The Passover Haggada follows this approach. You might have expected its central text to be the account in the book of Exodus, but instead it chooses to focus on four verses from the book of Deuteronomy (26:5–8). They are a concise retelling of the Exodus story. Once the Israelites reached the Promised Land and began farming it, they were expected to bring the first yield of their fruit to God's House and proclaim these verses before a priest. This is the first full-fledged example of a verbal ritual in the Torah. The main body of the Haggada is a phrase-by-phrase analysis of these four verses, quoting excerpts from the book of Exodus to elucidate them. This all seems backward. Why choose the retelling in Deuteronomy as the primary text and treat the original account in Exodus as the secondary one? This only makes sense if how we retell the story is more important to us!

The educational imperative also helps us understand the miraculous nature of the Exodus story. The multiple miracles alert us to the absolutely shocking truth at the heart of this story: God can upturn even the greatest tyrant and give freedom to hopeless slaves. This idea is so radical, so utterly inconceivable, that the Torah must resort to fantastical descriptions to wake up the readers to the amazing truth. Fate is not fixed; the enslaved can be freed.

Years later, on the verge of entering Israel, Moses himself expresses his amazement at the Exodus:

> Has God ever tried to come to take Him a nation from inside another nation with trials, with signs and with wonders and with warfare and with a mighty hand and with an outstretched arm and with great terrors, like the Lord your God did for you in Egypt before your eyes? (Deut. 4:34)

The verse is positively dripping with incredulity.[20] After all, what method would you use to convey something too unbelievable to believe? Miracles are the way the Torah does this. As you consider the wonder of the miracle, you come to realize the enormity of the change that has taken place. The real miracle is God upturning the *political* order of the ancient world by freeing an enslaved people. This miracle is expressed in the narrative through the overturning of the *natural* order.

It was a startling talmudic statement that finally convinced me of Exodus's educational imperative:

> R. Yoḥanan said: It is as difficult to match a couple together as it was to split the Sea of Reeds.[21]

Initially, these seem incompatible. If you think that the whole point of a miracle is that (a) only God can do it, and (b) it is a break in the natural

---

20. God runs the gamut by assembling a sevenfold arsenal: trials, signs, wonders, battle, mighty hand, outstretched arm, and great terrors. This is emphasized by the seven-time repeated use of the Hebrew preposition *be* ("with").
21. Sota 2a.

order of things, then this comparison makes no sense at all. Granted, making a *shidduch* (match) between two people is not easy, but it is (a) well within the realms of human possibility, and (b) does not involve upsetting nature. However, if we understand a miracle as that which has the power to cause a radical change in human perspective and understanding, then indeed they are comparable. Helping two people find each other and fall in love requires the sincerity and vulnerability of all parties concerned. When a couple open their hearts to deep commitment, they are sacrificing some aspects of their individuality in order to become something more. This is the miracle of human relationships – that on the deepest level of awareness, we do not have to be alone.

The Talmud is comparing a matchmaker to God in the Exodus. A competent matchmaker readies people to embrace a new relationship. Similarly, the miracle of the splitting of the sea readied the Israelites to cross over and embrace a new relationship with God, "then they believed in God and in Moses His servant" (Ex. 14:31). And the awesome and wondrous nature of this event is meant to nurture similar feelings in us. We too can transform our view of the world and embrace a relationship with God. This may be why *Shirat HaYam*, the Song of the Sea, is recited daily in our morning prayers. Recalling this physical miracle serves as a constant reminder of the real psychological miracle – the profound capacity for human relationship.[22] Again we see the lasting power of the miracle is less in its execution and more as a force for education.

Literary Forms

How is the Exodus story told? From a historical perspective, the Bible contains several inconsistencies. The disparity between the books of Genesis and Exodus concerning the length of time the Israelites lived in Egypt, whether 400 or 430 years, has already been mentioned. Another example is the different number of plagues described in Exodus

22. There is a wonderful song in *Fiddler on the Roof* which sums up this approach for me. Motel the Tailor sings it to his beloved Tzeitel, when Tevye finally gives him permission to marry his daughter: "When Moses softened Pharaoh's heart, that was a miracle. When God made the waters of the Red Sea part, that was a miracle too! But of all God's miracles large and small, the most miraculous one of all...is the one I thought could never be, God has given you to me."

(7:14–12:30) when compared to shorter versions in the book of Psalms. In one psalm there appear to be eight or eleven plagues (Ps. 78:44–51),[23] and in another, seven or nine (Ps. 105:26–36).[24] Which of these texts is correct, and why do they not fully concur?

One response to these types of questions is to appreciate that a range of literary forms are employed by different books of the Torah and the rest of the Bible. The same event is portrayed differently depending on the context in which it appears and what it seeks to communicate. Thus, for example, the time span for the Israelites living in Egypt, was not meant to be a simple historical detail. Each, in its context, carries a different message. As Cassuto noted: "The numbers given in the Torah are mostly rounded or symbolic figures, and their purpose is to teach us something."[25]

In Genesis, God gives Abraham an impressionistic vision of the distant future. The figure of four hundred is used here, as in other places, to signify an unusually large round number that is beyond what a person could normally expect or even imagine. Hence, later, when Abraham is eager to buy a plot of land to bury his beloved Sarah, Ephron takes advantage of him and asks for an exorbitant *four hundred* shekels of silver (Gen. 23:15). Similarly, when Jacob hears that after many years apart his disgruntled brother is coming to confront him, Esau's entourage is *four hundred* men strong, which rightly terrifies Jacob (Gen. 32:6–7). Of course, it could be a coincidence that the same number occurs in all three instances, but more likely, the phrase *arba meot*, four hundred, is a literary motif of the book of Genesis that serves as an intimidatingly large number to challenge the patriarchs as they seek to live and fulfill God's will.[26]

---

23. Blood, gnats and frogs, caterpillars and locusts, hail and frost and thunderbolts, evil angels, pestilence, killing of firstborn.
24. Darkness, blood, frogs, flies and gnats, hail and flaming fire, locusts, killing of firstborn.
25. Umberto Cassuto, *A Commentary on the Book of Exodus*, trans. Israel Abrahams (Magnes Press, 1974), 86. He also presents his own understanding of the significance of the 430-year period.
26. Commentating on Genesis 15:13, Rashi calculates that it was actually four hundred years from the birth of Isaac until the Exodus. Thus, the four hundred motif touches the lives of all three patriarchs. See also Judges 21:12; I Sam. 22:2; and I Kings 22:6.

In Exodus, the specific number 430 seems less important than the fact that the phrase "four hundred and thirty years" is repeated in two consecutive verses (Ex. 12:40–41). This serves to emphasize the preciseness of God's predetermined plan. We are meant to understand that the Israelites were in Egypt *only exactly as long as God planned for them to be there,* not a day more, not a day less.[27] Ibn Ezra suggests that the "extra" thirty years was the period of time it took for the Israelites to cry out to God be saved. This also implies that the figure here reflects the drive of the Exodus context: God has geared up to save the Israelites and everything is following divine providence.

Meanwhile, the portrayal of the plagues in Psalms reflects a different literary form, a style reminiscent of the didactic poetry of the song of Moses at the end of the Torah (Deut. 32:1–43). In analyzing these texts, the traditional commentaries do not seek to determine the definitive version, but rather focus on all the distinct nuances and how they might add further dimensions to the awe-inspiring meaning of the plagues. Rabbi Hirsch comments:

> Every historic event of our past has far more than mere "factual" significance. Because of the truth which is proclaimed through every such act of God, it becomes a *mashal*… a maxim designed to serve as a pattern upon which to base our judgment.[28]

Likewise, the appearance of the ten plagues and splitting of the sea in the Passover Haggada differs greatly from that in the Torah. Instead of presenting straightforward accounts of each, the Haggada lists the plagues in the tersest possible way, choosing to then focus on a debate

---

The motif is also picked up in the Talmud. For instance, in Eiruvin 54b, Rabbi Preida had to repeat his lesson four hundred times to a particular student before he understood it. The exaggeration here highlights the responsibility of a teacher to ensure their lesson is comprehensible. See also Berakhot 28a, 31a, 51b, and Bava Batra 14a. Finally, note that four hundred is the largest single assigned number in the gematria system, signified by the final letter in the alphabet: *tav.*

27. *Mekhilta DeRabbi Yishmael* 12:42.

28. Samson Raphael Hirsch, *The Psalms: Translation and Commentary,* trans. Gertrude Hirschler (Feldheim, 1997), Book 3, 41.

between three talmudic sages as to which experience was the greater. R. Yossi the Galilean employs a pair of verses from Exodus as his proof texts (8:15, 14:31), while R. Eliezer and R. Akiva both use a verse from Psalms to make their cases (Ps. 78:49). Clearly, these rabbis are not seeking to uncover a definitive account. What engages them is the mining of biblical verses for ever deeper layers of significance. This shows us that the Haggada has a literary form all its own, which idiosyncratically selects phrases and verses from all over the Bible to retell the Exodus story in a thrilling and memorable way.[29]

With this perspective we can also address the problem of exactly how many Israelites left Egypt. As mentioned earlier, the Torah account indicates a figure in the millions, which is too large to be realistic. By revealing the literary symbolism in the census lists of the Israelite tribes in the book of Numbers, Joshua Berman suggests that neither these lists nor the precise size of the Israelite population that left Egypt were meant to be read literally.[30]

We will look at one further literary form in the presentation of the Exodus. The story is characterized by the multiple times Pharaoh speaks in response to Moses's pleas to release the Israelites (Ex. 5:2–9, 8:4, 21, 9:27–28, 10:8, 10–11, 16–17, 24, 28, 12:31–32). We also hear him speaking to the Israelite overseers (Ex. 5:17–18). In all these verses, the Torah seems to faithfully relay Pharaoh's words. The obvious question is this: Was Pharaoh speaking in Hebrew? This is highly unlikely.[31] Why would the supreme monarch of Egypt speak or even recognize the foreign tongue of a relatively minor people?

---

29. *Tzena Urena,* also called the "Women's Bible," is a sixteenth-century European Yiddish collection of midrashic texts woven into biblical passages to create a highly dramatized version of Torah, written for women more familiar with Yiddish than the Hebrew of the Torah. The version of the Exodus story in *Tzena Urena* would be the main one that many thousands of Jewish women would have known for hundreds of years. It too has its own literary form.
30. Joshua Berman, *Ani Maamin: Biblical Criticism, Historical Truth, and the Thirteen Principles of Faith* (Maggid, 2020), 45–52.
31. Indeed, medieval commentators such as Rashbam and Ibn Ezra infer from the phrase "heavy of tongue" (Ex. 4:10) that Moses lacked the fluency necessary to communicate with Pharaoh in his language.

The many biblical verses containing Pharaoh's speeches could be straightforward *translations* of his words from ancient Egyptian, but if they were, then we would expect them to be similar in style, rhythm, and expression to the multitude of hieroglyphic writings and inscriptions from that period. But they are not. Much more likely is that the Torah is not even trying to translate Pharaoh's pronouncements word for word.[32] Rather, they have been reworked to conform to the Torah's desired literary form for this context.

Pharaoh's script is sculpted to convey his essential character – that of an arrogant oppressor who is dismissive of any challenges to his authority and vindictive to boot. In their first encounter, Pharaoh is contemptuous of Moses's so-called god:

> Who is the Lord, that I should heed His voice to send off Israel? I do not know the Lord, nor will I send off Israel. (Ex. 5:2)

Later, he rants to the Israelite overseers, accusing them of laziness:

> Idlers, you are idlers! Therefore, you say, "Let us go sacrifice to the Lord." And now go work, and no straw will be given to you, but the quota of bricks you will give. (Ex. 5:17)

The Torah is blunt about the abusiveness of this tyrant. In repeating the word "idlers," his intransigence is forcefully conveyed. Robert Alter discusses the Bible's constant preference for dialogue over narration. This is one of several significant differences between ancient Greek literature and biblical storytelling.[33] Rather than lengthy scenic and character descriptions, the biblical text presents its stories through dialogue:

> In words each person reveals his distinctive nature... his ability to control others, to deceive them, to feel for them, and to respond

32. When the Bible *is* simply translating foreign words or phrases into Hebrew, it is overt about it, e.g., *yegar sahaduta* (Gen. 31:47) and *pur* (Est. 9:24).
33. Erich Auerbach, *Mimesis: The Representation of Reality in Western Literature*, trans. Willard R. Trask (Princeton, 2013), ch. 1, 3–23.

> to them. Spoken language is the substratum of everything human and divine that transpires in the Bible.[34]

The numerous conversations Pharaoh has with Moses are the way the Torah reveals the essence of their personalities. Pharaoh's dialect is not the primary concern here. This is not a formal public record of what was said. The verbal sparring of these opponents is meant to articulate their thoughts and feelings. Thus, a better sense of the inner life of the characters is revealed through this literary form.

In summation, the differing time spans of the Israelite sojourn in Egypt, the inconsistent numbering of the plagues, the size of the population that left, and the pronouncements of the pharaoh, are all examples of the distinctive fashion in which the Exodus story is presented. Michael Fishbane called it "a literary construct fusing saga and history." He continues:

> The exodus from Egypt was experienced as an event of divine redemption, during which ancient promises were realized and divine power confirmed. The transformative nature of this event in the lives of the ancient Israelites affected its recollection and literary formulation. For those who experienced it, no simple chronological report would do justice to the wonder of the divine intervention in their historical lives. Only the saga form would do, focusing selectively on specific events and people, endowing the encounters between the principal actors with a paradigmatic cast, and infusing historical process with the wonder of supernatural events.[35]

Egyptological Resonance

In 2010, I visited the *Ancient Egyptian Book of the Dead* exhibition at the British Museum. So began my long fascination with the texts and images of ancient Egypt. I never expected to find the exact Exodus story in hieroglyphic texts, but I was looking to understand Egyptian culture

---

34. Robert Alter, *The Art of Biblical Narrative* (Basic Books, 1984), 70.
35. Michael Fishbane, *Biblical Text and Texture: A Literary Reading of Selected Texts* (Oneworld, 2003), 64.

and beliefs and to see how they differed and contrasted with Judaism. My mandate came from the Torah:

> You shall not copy the practices of the land of Egypt in which you dwelled... nor shall you follow their statutes. (Lev. 18:3)

How can this biblical directive be fulfilled without some knowledge of the lives and practices of ancient Egypt?[36] A study of Egyptology provides this, and the results are remarkable. It turns out that there are intriguing resonances to be found between Egyptian writings and the biblical account of the Exodus.[37] These imply that aspects of the language and imagery in the biblical portrayal of the story deliberately contrast and pass judgment on Egyptian beliefs of the time. Here are three significant examples.

1. The mighty hand of God

God's "mighty hand" – *yad ḥazaka* – is a recurring phrase in the Exodus story. Throughout the Torah, it is only ever used in that context.[38] The related phrase "outstretched arm" – *zero'a netuya* – is also exclusive to God's conflict with Egypt.[39] When confronting the empires of Assyria, Babylon, and Persia, as well as Canaan and the other kingdoms in Israel's vicinity, the Bible does not use these phrases. This is because they are a specific response to Egyptian oppression.

The image of a pharaoh smiting his enemies with a mighty hand and outstretched arm is common in ancient Egyptian relief sculptures. The most likely pharaohs of the Exodus story, Seti I and Ramesses II,

36. Rashi comments on Leviticus 18:3 that "their statutes" refers to "their social customs and practices that have assumed the character of law... while R. Meir said these refer to the 'ways of the Amorites' [i.e., superstitious practices]." Some of these, it would seem, relate to the sexual prohibitions described in the rest of Leviticus 18.
37. See, for example, A. S. Yahuda, *The Language of the Pentateuch in Its Relation to Egyptian* (Oxford, 1933).
38. See Exodus 3:19, 6:1, 13:9, 14, 16, 32:11; Numbers 20:20; Deuteronomy 3:24, 4:34, 5:15, 6:21, 7:8, 19, 9:26, 11:2, 26:8, 34:12.
39. See Exodus 6:6; Deuteronomy 4:34, 5:15, 7:19, 9:29, 11:2, 26:8.

both appear in this pose.[40] The smiting motif can be traced back to the very first pharaoh and demonstrates the supreme power of the king at the very moment he crushes his enemies.[41] Thus, it is wholly fitting that the most commonly repeated phrases used to describe God's actions in the Exodus story are His "mighty hand" and "outstretched arm." More than likely, the Torah intentionally employed these anthropomorphisms to undermine Pharaoh's power. The message is clear: God is in charge here, not the king of Egypt. Joshua Berman calls this phenomenon "out-Pharaohing the Pharaoh."[42]

The imagery extends to the *zero'a* (shank bone) found on the traditional Passover Seder plate, which is also reminiscent of God's "outstretched arm." And the daily ritual of wearing *tefillin* – on arm and head – has its origin in God's "mighty hand" described in the Exodus story: "And it shall be for a sign to you upon your arm, and for a memorial between your eyes ... for with a *mighty hand* has the Lord brought you out of Egypt" (Ex. 13:9).[43]

2. *Pharaoh's heavy heart*

The heart of Pharaoh plays a crucial role in the Exodus story. The "hardening of Pharaoh's heart" as a metaphor for his defiance in the face of Moses's requests to free the Israelites is a constant refrain in the text. Following each of nine plagues we are told that Pharaoh's heart is hardened, and he will not let the Israelites go.[44] After the final, tenth plague he relents, but again, soon after the Israelites leave, "God hardened the heart of Pharaoh king of Egypt, and he pursued after the Israelites" (Ex. 14:8). In fact, we hear about the hardening of Pharaoh's heart twenty

40. Ronald Hendel, "The Exodus as Cultural Memory: Egyptian Bondage and the Song of the Sea," in *Israel's Exodus in Transdisciplinary Perspective: Text, Archaeology, Culture, and Geoscience,* ed. Thomas E. Levy, Thomas Schneider, and William H. C. Propp (Springer, 2015), 73.

41. See the five-thousand-year-old Narmar Palette, object EA35714 in the British Museum collection.

42. Berman, *Ani Maamin*, 54.

43. This is repeated in Exodus 13:16.

44. After the first plague, Ex. 7:23; after the second, Ex. 8:11; the third, Ex. 8:15; fourth, Ex. 8:28; fifth, Ex. 9:7; sixth, Ex. 9:12; seventh, Ex. 9:35; eighth, Ex. 10:20; ninth, Ex. 10:27.

times in the Torah. Though well known, the word "hardened" is not actually an accurate translation of the Hebrew. The Torah flips between two different words for what happened to Pharaoh's heart.[45] One is *yeḥezak libo,* which literally means "his heart was seized" (Ex. 7:13, 23, 8:15, 9:12, 35, 10:20, 27). The other is *hakhbed libo,* which literally means "his heart became heavy" (Ex. 7:14, 8:11, 28, 9:7, 34, 10:1). The Torah only ever uses these phrases for this king of Egypt. What is the particular purpose of this motif in the Exodus narrative?

One explanation lies in the *Book of the Dead*. The name refers to a genre of beautifully illustrated papyrus rolls containing religious texts and magical spells written in hieroglyphics, intended to protect a deceased Egyptian's hazardous passage through the afterlife. Defeating death was a major theme in Egyptian culture. Well-to-do Egyptians would commission such a papyrus to be placed in their tombs at the time of their death and mummification. They believed it would give them guidance and special powers to overcome the dangers of the underworld. Such rolls were in use for centuries, the first ones dating back to 1700 BCE, just a few hundred years before the Israelite Exodus.[46]

A significant scene that occurs in numerous versions of the *Book of the Dead* is known as "the weighing of the heart." The deceased's heart is in a jar and is being weighed on a huge set of scales against a feather, the symbol for *ma'at,* meaning truth and justice in ancient Egyptian thought. The jackal-headed Anubis checks the scales, and the ibis-headed scribe Thoth records the result. If the heart is not weighed down by any wrongdoing by its owner, then it will be as light as the feather and the deceased is allowed to pass into the afterlife. If not, the heart is eaten by Ammit, a terrible beast that sits at the ready by the scales.

Now we can understand the Torah's choice of words for Pharaoh's heart: "heavy" and "seized." They are a damning response to this

45. There is a third word used to describe Pharaoh's heart which does literally mean "harden," but it appears only once. Introducing the plagues, God said to Moses, "I will harden (*akshe*) the heart of Pharaoh" (Ex. 7:3). This usage might have been considered retribution for the "hard work" (*avoda kasha*) that the Israelites were forced to do in Egypt (Ex. 1:14, 6:9).

46. John H. Taylor, *Journey Through the Afterlife: Ancient Egyptian Book of the Dead* (British Museum Press, 2010), 55.

scene in the *Book of the Dead*. It is God who determines Pharaoh's fate, not the Egyptian deities. Pharaoh's cruelty weighs down his heart, tipping the scales, which leads to punishment from God. Since the heart reveals the morality of its owner, the *Book of the Dead* also talks of the Egyptian deities "seizing" the heart so that it works against its owner.[47] In the Torah, it is God who gradually begins to seize Pharaoh's heart so as to reveal his evil intentions.[48] The Egyptians, and no doubt many of the Israelite elders, would have been very familiar with this famous scene, and that is why the Torah overturns it so that the true orchestrator of events is revealed.

And there is more. Ammit, that beastly "Devourer of Hearts," had the head of a crocodile, the body of a lion, and the back end of a hippopotamus: the three largest and most dangerous animals known to ancient Egyptians. If she swallowed your heart in the underworld, your soul would be restless forever and you would die a second time.[49] So Ammit was their worst nightmare. The fourth of the ten plagues was called *arov*, which means "a mixture." Rashi suggests the plague was "a mix of different wild beasts that devastated the Egyptians."[50] But maybe *arov* was just one terrible beast made up of a mixture of animals, i.e., the dreaded Ammit. Hence, *arov* dramatically brought to life the sum of all the Egyptians' fears. Again, we see how the Torah appropriates Egyptian imagery, beliefs, and superstitions in order to proclaim God's superiority.

3. *Good vs. Evil*

The Exodus is not just a terrific tale, it is the foundational story of national Jewish identity. The redemption of the Israelite slaves from Egyptian oppression was a moral victory of right over wrong. And so, the Torah presents the clash between Moses and Pharaoh as a primal battle of good against evil, or in Hebrew, *tov* against *ra*.

---

47. Ibid., 162.
48. This explains why Pharaoh makes his *own* heart heavy in the initial five plagues but has his heart seized by God in the final five. As Maimonides explains, God is exposing Pharaoh's true desire, which was to prevent the Israelites from leaving (*Mishneh Torah, Hilkhot Teshuva* 6:3).
49. Taylor, *Journey Through the Afterlife*, 212–14.
50. Rashi's comment on Exodus 8:17.

Moses is actually named *tov*. When he was born his mother "looked at him and saw that he was good (*tov*) and hid him for three months" (Ex. 2:2). Any mother would have hidden her son to avoid the cruel Egyptian edict condemning Israelite baby boys to death (Ex. 1:22), so the *tov* here must imply more than just a pleasant appearance. The Talmud suggests that while Pharaoh's daughter later named him *Moshe* (Ex. 2:10), his mother had given him the name him *Tov* or possibly *Tuvyah* ("Good God"), or she foresaw the *tov* he would do as a prophet.[51] What is more, every mention of *tov* in the first half of the book of Exodus centers around Moses.[52] Additionally, the Talmud frames the entire narrative, from Exodus to Mount Sinai, with a fourfold homily of *tov:* "Let good come, and receive the good, from the Good, for the good ones."[53] This is explained as follows: Let Moses come, and receive the Torah, from God, for the Israelites.

Now if Moses is the embodiment of *tov* (good), then it would be fitting that his nemesis be the embodiment of *ra* (evil). And, in a delightful bilingual pun, we will see that he is. The prevalent opinion, as mentioned earlier, is that the pharaoh of the Exodus was Ramesses II. Ramesses means "born of Ra," Ra being the great sun god at the apex of ancient Egyptian worship. Ra's name in hieroglyphs is a circle with a dot in the center, representing the sun. The knowledge needed to decipher hieroglyphics was lost for centuries until Jean-François Champollion successfully decoded the Rosetta Stone in 1822.[54] Nevertheless, some widespread symbols always remained recognizable, and the sun was surely one of them. Indeed, one medieval rabbinic commentator interprets the word *Ra'amses* in the Torah as *ayin hashemesh*, the "eye of the sun."[55]

You will have noticed, of course, that the Egyptian name for the sun god is almost identical to the Hebrew word for evil – Ra corresponds

51. Sota 12a.
52. For instance, critiques about his leadership are framed in terms of *tov* (see Ex. 14:12 and 18:17).
53. Menaḥot 53b.
54. Andrew Robinson, *Cracking the Egyptian Code: The Revolutionary Life of Jean-Francois Champollion* (Thames and Hudson, 2018).
55. See Abraham ibn Ezra's comment on Exodus 1:11.

to *ra*.[56] This wordplay enables the Torah to signal its utter disdain for Egypt's premier deity. At one point, the book of Exodus is overt about this. Following Pharaoh's seventh refusal to release the Israelites, he adopts a sarcastic tone:

> May the Lord be with you when I send you off with your little ones! For evil is before your faces. (Ex. 10:10)

In other words, to the extent that Pharaoh was willing to release the Israelite children, to that extent may God be with them – which was not at all! But what does Pharaoh mean when he says, "For evil (*ra'ah*) is before your faces"? Rashi explains that Egyptian astrology identified a star called *ra'ah* as an omen of blood and slaughter, and that Pharaoh was threatening that this star would rise to meet them if they left Egypt, with dire consequences.[57] When the Israelites did leave, they walked through the night heading east, so they would have met the blood-red sun coming up over the desert. So it is possible that the *ra'ah* star was the rising sun. This then is a blatant use of the derogatory pun which equates evil with the Egyptian sun god.[58]

At the end of Moses's life, in his final speech to the Israelites, he expresses God's covenant in these stark terms:

> See, I have set before you this day – life and good, and death and evil…choose life. (Deut. 30:15, 19)

The commentaries say that acts of goodness promote life while wickedness courts death.[59] We see that the Torah concludes with a reiteration of the need for good to triumph over evil.

56. Evil, *ra*, in Hebrew is spelled with the letters *resh* and *ayin*, the same two letters with which the Hebraization of Ramesses begins. This is significant because a more appropriate spelling for a name beginning with *Ra* would be a *resh* and *alef*, not *ayin*, as in Ramoth (see Deut. 4:43).
57. Rashi's comment on Exodus 10:10, based on *Yalkut Shimoni* 392.
58. Gary A. Rendsburg, *How the Bible Is Written* (Hendrickson, 2019), 371–72.
59. Comments of Rashi and Sforno on Deuteronomy 30:15.

The mighty hand of God, Pharaoh's heavy heart, and the primal battle of good against evil are just three examples of a sustained Egyptological resonance to be found in the Exodus narrative.

The Cinematic Exodus

So how should we relate to the text of the Exodus today? We should not be so entrenched in the pursuit of historical verification that we lose the capacity to appreciate the nature of the Torah's unique account. It is a mistake to imprint modern sensibilities onto an ancient text. The Torah does not aim to give us a historical account of the Exodus; it has a very different set of purposes. As argued in this chapter, these include: educating its readers to remember this momentous experience by constructing a dramatic and miraculous narrative; employing various literary forms to convey symbolic and moral meaning; and appropriating phrases and images common to ancient Egypt in order to affirm the preeminence of God.

Reflecting on some of the cinematic portrayals of last century's world wars has deepened my appreciation of the profundity of the Exodus narrative. Consider, for example, Steven Spielberg's Holocaust film, *Schindler's List*; Christopher Nolan's World War II epic, *Dunkirk*; and Sam Mendes's World War I tale, *1917*.[60] In each case, the film is advertised as being "based on true events." What we see on the screen, though, is not a straightforward portrayal of actual incidents. Rather, each director evokes the atmosphere and drama of their subject. Screenplay, cinematography, soundtrack, and impeccable acting are all magically molded together to tell a compelling and memorable story.

After seeing *Schindler's List*, one survivor said to me, "It's a good film but it wasn't really like that, it was much worse, but better you shouldn't know." I was so taken by that comment. A "true" portrayal of the Holocaust would have been unwatchable. When it came to creating the three-stranded story of *Dunkirk*, Nolan was clear about his aim. He remarked that a movie cannot show you exactly what happened, but it can make you feel the experience. He believed that his responsibility as a filmmaker was to evoke deep emotion in his audience rather than give them a well-meaning history lesson. Mendes had a different focus in

60. These were released in 1994, 2017, and 2019, respectively.

1917. His grandfather was a military messenger in World War I, and the director wanted to create a very personal movie that paid tribute to him.

The Exodus narrative resonates with the directorial approaches of these three films. It portrays the bitter *magnitude* of the slavery, making it painful to read; it heaps on the *drama* through the clash of Pharaoh and Moses, the escalating ten plagues, and the sea-splitting finale; and it *personalizes* the story for the committed reader by teaching us how we should remember it in our own lives. Indeed, every Seder gathering is tasked with dramatizing the story for its participants, and rabbinic guidance is given as to the basic plotline we should follow: "Begin with *genut* (shame) and end with *shevaḥ* (praise)."[61] The Haggada is the script, and all present are the players in the evening's performance.

The profound truth of the Exodus story is that it was never meant to be a dry, academic history lecture. To restrict its credibility to scientific authentication misreads and misrepresents the text:

> When the sages ask, "Why was this written?" or "Why was this passage placed next to that?" their typical answer is not "Because that is how it happened," but "To teach you that..." ...Every nuance of the text is searched not for its correspondence with empirical actuality but for its halakhic or moral implications. For the sages, Torah is not an assemblage of facts but a series of rules and models of how Israel should live and thereby be sanctified. That is its genre and proper mode of interpretation.[62]

The Torah employs educational imperative, literary forms, Egyptological resonance, and so much more, to tell its amazing story. "There's nothing in the world more powerful than a good story,"[63] especially one that is passed down faithfully through the generations. Every Seder night we have the opportunity and privilege of retelling it in all its glory.

---

61. Mishna Pesaḥim 10:3.
62. Jonathan Sacks, *Crisis and Covenant: Jewish Thought after the Holocaust* (Manchester University Press, 1992), 225–26.
63. This quote comes from a speech in the final episode of the HBO TV series *Game of Thrones* (S8, E6: The Iron Throne). Tyrion Lannister says: "What unites people? Armies? Gold? Flags? Stories. There's nothing in the world more powerful than a good story. Nothing can stop it. No enemy can defeat it."

Part II
ETHICS

Chapter 5

How Can Slavery Be Condoned?

EXPLORING THE QUESTION

We drove out of New Orleans on a dusty road alongside the Mississippi River, traveling west for about an hour. My sister said we had to visit this place and insisted on taking us. I soon realized why. We arrived to find a collection of old buildings with huge grounds backing on to the bayou. This was the Whitney Plantation, an agricultural estate that kept and controlled hundreds of slaves from West-Central Africa for over a century. We were given a tour of the plantation, which had been transformed into a museum devoted to teaching about slavery and opened to the public in 2014.[1]

The tour began at the spacious Big House, a fine example of Spanish Creole architecture. Upstairs, we saw displays of the well-to-do lifestyle of the Haydel family, the plantation's owners. In stark contrast, we then visited the slave quarters, a series of dingy one-room cabins. Learning about the harshness of their everyday existence was heartbreaking:

> The African slaves cleared the land and planted corn, rice, and vegetables. They ran indigo processing facilities and later sugar

1. See https://www.whitneyplantation.org.

> mills. They built levees to protect dwellings and crops. They also served as sawyers, carpenters, masons, and smiths. They raised horses, oxen, mules, cows, sheep, swine, and poultry. Slaves also served as cooks, handling the demanding task of hulling rice with mortars and pestles. They performed all kinds of duties to make life easy and enjoyable for their masters. African female slaves raised their own children while caring for their masters'. Slaves often escaped and became marooned in swamps to avoid deadly work and whipping. Those recaptured suffered severe punishment such as branding with a hot iron, mutilation, and, eventually, the death penalty.[2]

Our guide looked at me and saw the *kippa* on my head. "You know what I'm talking about," he said. "Your ancestors were slaves three thousand years ago, but this happened to my people right here less than three hundred years ago, and we endured it for twice as long." In that moment, the shocking reality of slavery and its blight on history was brought home to me. All those many midrashic stories I had read, about the cruel treatment of the Israelite slaves in ancient Egypt, came to life before my eyes: backbreaking work, little rest, routine beatings, living in constant fear, and no hope of freedom.[3]

I could not help but see comparisons. By 1860 there were more than 330,000 slaves in Louisiana.[4] It was a "slave state" and New Orleans was a critical hub for the slave trade. The Torah called ancient Egypt *beit avadim*, not just a land that had slaves, but a "house of slaves." This biblical phrase, used uniquely to refer to ancient Egypt, indicates that slavery was essential to the nation's social and political structure.[5]

---

2. Ibrahima Seck, *Bouki Fait Gombo: A History of the Slave Community of Habitation Haydel (Whitney Plantation) Louisiana, 1750–1860* (Uno Press, 2014), 2.
3. See, for example, Numbers Rabba 7:1; *Midrash Lekaḥ Tov, Va'era* 7:17; Midrash HaGadol Exodus 2:11; and *Midrash Tanḥuma, Vayetze* 7 and *Shemot* 29.
4. R. Miller and D. Smith, *Dictionary of Afro-American Slavery* (Greenwood Press, 1988), 414.
5. The phrase occurs thirteen times in the Bible, and all refer to Egypt: Exodus 13:3, 14, 20:2; Deuteronomy 5:6, 6:12, 7:8, 8:14, 13:6, 11; Joshua 24:17; Judges 6:8; Jeremiah 34:13; Micah 6:4.

I learned about cultural comparisons too:

> The slaves brought to Louisiana strongly held onto their African culture and heritage as demonstrated in the retention of African personal names and naming practices.... It was quite usual for the slaves born in Africa and the Creoles to have at least two names: the Christian name given by the master and the African name they brought with them or which they gave to their children.[6]

This is reminiscent of the rabbinic tradition that the Israelites retained their own names and language, despite the constant suffering they experienced in Egypt.[7] These are both examples of cultural resistance in the face of dehumanizing slavery.

The guide then led us to a large square made up of a series of granite slabs, each containing long lists of names and dates. Called "The Field of Angels," it is a memorial dedicated to the 2,200 enslaved children who died in this district from 1823 to 1863. They died of diseases, drownings, and burns, many from the intense and dangerous production of raw sugar from sugarcane. Sadly, the memorial showed just the Christian name given to most of the children, and no specific place of origin, because their African name and homeland had never been recorded. This was how the slave owners robbed them of their identity. It is the bitter truth behind the vagueness of the contemporary ethnic term "African American."

My sister was right. I did need to visit the Whitney Plantation. The experience has had a lasting influence on myself and my family. In the shop, we purchased a book for our youngest about life as a child slave in Louisiana, and she read it a few weeks later on Pesach. I spoke about my trip in my classes before and during the festival, and many times since. I encourage people to visit this museum or one like it. I urge you as well.

The denial of freedom and brutal subjugation involved in human slavery and slave trading is abhorrent and unjust. It degrades people's humanity and causes lasting physical and psychological damage. This

---

6. Seck, *Bouki Fait Gombo*, 10.
7. Leviticus Rabba 32:5, *Tanna DeVei Eliyahu* 23:2, *Midrash Tehillim* 114:2.

lesson is an important reason for the centrality of the Exodus story in Judaism to this day. The first of the Ten Commandments states: "I am the Lord your God, who brought you out of the land of Egypt, out of the house of slaves" (Ex. 20:2). The message is clear. Just like our Israelite ancestors, no group or nation should ever be enslaved and denied their basic freedom. God saved us from that.

And yet, surprisingly, just a few weeks after they were rid of Egypt, among the first laws given at Mount Sinai was the permission for the Israelites to acquire slaves of their own (Ex. 21:2). How could the Torah legitimize slavery by encoding it in Jewish practice? Having been slaves themselves, how could the Israelites now become slave owners?

For nineteenth-century Christian slave owners in America, the Bible appeared so amenable to slavery that they confidently cited biblical verses to justify themselves. Some churches even sponsored slave ships from Africa. The Christianity of this period was pro-slavery, with much of early American religious rhetoric being entwined with owning slaves.[8]

The Torah gives instructions for the keeping of two kinds of slaves: Jewish and non-Jewish. Jewish slaves was forced to work without pay for six years, after which they were released, although they had the option of remaining for up to fifty years.[9] Meanwhile, non-Jewish slaves were bound for life and would be inherited by their master's children.[10] How could the Torah allow us to enslave our own people, never mind anyone else?

Some try to lessen the severity of the Jewish slave concept by arguing that the Torah's description is more akin to indentured servitude, because the work obligation is bound by a fixed period. Nevertheless, this was still a form of unpaid labor, and the Torah uses the very same terminology, *eved*, as it does for a non-Jewish slave.[11] Besides, why should a non-Jewish slave be treated differently, with no hope of ever being released?

---

8. Judy Zauzmer Weil, "The Bible Was Used to Justify Slavery," *Washington Post* (April 30, 2019), https://www.washingtonpost.com.
9. Exodus 21:2–6 and Rashi on 21:6.
10. Leviticus 25:46.
11. Rabbinic literature called the Jewish slave *eved ivri*, literally "Hebrew slave," as that term was used to introduce the laws (Ex. 21:2), while the non-Jewish slave was

Solomon Northup was kidnapped and sold into slavery in 1841. In the film adaptation of his memoir, *Twelve Years a Slave,* he remarks: "Slavery is an evil that should befall none."[12] In 1859, Charles Darwin referred to the urgent need to abolish slavery in North America as "the sacred cause of humanity."[13] President Abraham Lincoln wrote:

> He who would *be* no slave, must consent to *have* no slave. Those who deny freedom to others, deserve it not for themselves, and, under a just God, cannot long retain it.[14]

Four years later he issued the Emancipation Proclamation, which freed three and a half million African American slaves.

To condone any form of slavery at all calls into question the values of the Torah. How can it be legislated for in our most holy of books?

RESPONDING TO THE QUESTION

Rather than attempting to diminish the role of slavery in the Torah, we should recognize its centrality. The owning, trading, treatment, and attitude to slaves is a recurrent theme that cannot be ignored.

To begin with, Noah cursed his grandson for his son's disloyalty saying: "A slave of slaves shall he be to his brothers" (Gen. 9:25). Sarah told Abraham to evict Hagar saying: "Drive out that slave woman and her son, for the son of that slave woman shall not share the inheritance with my son, with Isaac" (Gen. 21:10). Joseph was sold into slavery (Gen. 37:27–28), and later his brothers offered themselves to him as slaves when he, now viceroy of Egypt, accused them of stealing (Gen. 44:9–10). The first half of the book of Exodus pivots on the slavery of

---

called *eved canaani,* literally, "Canaanite slave," because the Canaanites were the predominant nation living in the Land of Israel at the time of the patriarchs (Gen. 12:6) and the Exodus (Ex. 33:2).

12. Solomon Northup, *Twelve Years a Slave* (Penguin Classics, 2012). The multi-Oscar-winning film version was released in 2013.
13. Adrian Desmond and James Moore, *Darwin's Sacred Cause: Race, Slavery and the Quest for Human Origins* (Allen Lane, 2009).
14. Abraham Lincoln, Letter to H. L. Pierce, April 6, 1859. See www.abrahamlincolnonline.org/lincoln/speeches/pierce.htm.

the Israelites, and the second half, which takes place at Mount Sinai, soon introduces a host of slavery laws (21:2–11, 20–21, 26–27). More rules about slave ownership are presented in Leviticus (25:39–55), and these laws are reviewed and expanded upon in Deuteronomy (15:12–23, 23:16–17). Consequently, there are considerable portions of Jewish law dedicated to slave ownership.[15]

Why is slavery such a prevalent theme in the Torah? No doubt it is because this form of subjugation was an established norm in the ancient world:

> Slavery existed as a constant factor in the social and economic life of the Near East and Europe throughout the entire period of ancient history, differing greatly in intensity and effects according to time and place. Its validity as a system of labor was never seriously questioned. No attempt to abolish it was made by any ancient government.[16]

It was viewed as morally correct, too, because slaves were considered less than human:

> "It is clear that some men are by nature free and others are by nature slaves, and that for these latter, slavery is both expedient and right," Aristotle had declared in his *Politics* (350 BC) – to the approval of almost all Greek and Roman thinkers and leaders. In the ancient world, slaves and the working class generally had been considered creatures lacking reason, and therefore naturally fitted to dismal lives, as beasts of burden were to tilling fields. To hold that they might have rights and aspirations would have been thought by the elite to be no less absurd than to enquire into the mental state and level of happiness of a hammer or scythe.[17]

---

15. Nine chapters in Maimonides, *Mishneh Torah, Hilkhot Avadim*; and three long chapters in the *Shulḥan Arukh, Yoreh De'ah* (267–69).
16. William Linn Westermann, "Slavery: Ancient," *Encyclopaedia of the Social Sciences*, ed. Edwin R. A. Seligman (The Macmillan Company, 1930–1935, reissued 1937); http://www.ditext.com/moral/slavery.html.
17. Alain de Botton, *Status Anxiety* (Penguin Books, 2005), 48.

We will see that even though the Torah allowed for slavery, rather than simply accepting it the Torah tackled this pervasive practice by mounting a progressive attack upon it. This involved the institution of a range of biblical laws, elaborated upon in the rabbinic era, that actively deterred the slave trade, curtailed the exploitation of slaves, and demanded that slaves be treated with such respect that slavery would inevitably decline. Additionally, we will see how this process was fueled by Judaism's frequent recollection of the Exodus, its ubiquitous use of the word *eved*, and the establishment of the weekly Shabbat.

We will begin by looking at three aspects of the slavery suffered by our ancestors in Egypt and how the laws given to the Israelites at Mount Sinai were a response to this. These laws served to limit the mistreatment of slaves and progressively transformed the master-slave relationship. The first aspect addresses slave trading, the second the runaway slave, and the third the oppression at the heart of slavery itself. We will also briefly contrast these to the treatment of African slaves in Europe and America.

Trading in Slaves

It was the slave trade that first brought Joseph to Egypt. Although his brothers intended to sell him into slavery – "Come let us sell him to the Ishmaelites" (Gen. 37:27) – that was not what occurred. "And Midianite traders passed by and pulled Joseph up out of the pit, and sold Joseph to Ishmaelites for twenty pieces of silver, and they brought Joseph to Egypt" (Gen. 37:28). Through a close reading of the narrative, it can be shown that Joseph was actually resold four or five times to different parties before he finally ended up as a slave to Potiphar in Egypt.[18] This selling and reselling, which is mentioned again in a subsequent chapter (Gen. 39:1), serves to highlight the prevalence of the slave trade at the time.

The traveling bands of slave traders in Genesis are then eclipsed in Exodus by a much larger culture of institutionalized slavery. This is typified by the subjugation of the Israelites in the kingdom of Egypt:

18. Genesis Rabba 84:22.

> And they set over them forced-labor foremen so as to oppress them with their burdens, and they built store-cities for Pharaoh: Pitom and Ra'amses. (Ex. 1:11)

Sources confirm that as well as manual work and agriculture, slaves were needed for large-scale royal building projects.[19] The study of ancient Egypt has also shown that the chief source for the supply of slaves was the capture and enslavement of enemy soldiers, resulting from successful battles with foreign countries.[20] This might explain the roundabout way in which the Israelites were enslaved in the biblical account. Rather than worrying about the increasing population and power of the Israelites per se, Pharaoh argued that "if war breaks out, they may join our enemies and fight against us and leave" (Ex. 1:10). By warning that the Israelites might ally themselves with potential foreign attackers, Pharaoh preemptively recast them as treacherous enemies, providing the justification for enslaving them.

This culture of supply and trade in slaves prevalent in the land of Egypt was systematically minimized by the laws given at Mount Sinai. Israelite males could be legally enslaved in only one of two specific ways.[21] Either they had stolen something, and did not have the resources to repay, in which case the court had the right to force them into labor so that they paid their debt to society. Or, if they were financially desperate and facing nothing less than abject poverty, then the law permitted them to sell themselves into forced labor.[22] Additionally, to counter the likelihood of individuals ever reaching this level of poverty to begin with, the Torah also demanded:

> You shall not harden your heart or close your hand from your destitute brother. Rather, you shall open your heart to him; you shall lend him what he needs. (Deut. 15:7–8)

---

19. Rachell Shalomi-Hen, "Use of Semitic Slaves in Egypt," in *The Koren Tanakh of the Land of Israel: Exodus*, 7.
20. Sarna, *Understanding Genesis*, 214.
21. There was a different set of laws for the female Israelite slave.
22. Maimonides, *Mishneh Torah, Hilkhot Avadim* 1:1. In both cases, as mentioned, this was limited to a period of six years.

Buying slaves, both Israelite and non-Israelite, was also curtailed by prohibiting the coveting of another person's male or female slave. This was encoded in the last of the Ten Commandments (Ex. 20:14). The prohibition of pestering someone to sell you their slave or offering a high price was also understood to be included here.[23] Also, the Talmud expresses a distinct aversion to slave ownership.[24]

It can be argued that the Torah's restrictions were a very effective deterrent, because no mention of slave traders or any kind of slave market in the ancient kingdom of Israel appears in the Bible at all. Indeed, it is remarkable that there is scant reference to slaves in this entire period, which spanned well over five hundred years.[25]

Contrast this aversion to slave trading with what happened in medieval Europe. In 1452, Pope Nicholas V issued an order granting Portugal the exclusive right to trade with Africa and take slaves. The king of Portugal was given

> full and free permission to invade, search out, capture and subjugate the Saracens and pagans and any other unbelievers ... wherever they may be ... and place their persons into perpetual slavery.[26]

This was the birth of the transatlantic slave trade that lasted four hundred years. During that time, it has been estimated that some twelve million Africans were shipped across the Atlantic by slave traders.[27]

---

23. Ibid., *Hilkhot Gezeila VaAveda* 1:9.
24. Bava Metzia 60b.
25. Brief mention of slaves is given in Joshua 9:23, I Kings 2:39–40, 10:21, and II Kings 4:1, but note also the severe admonition and punishment given by God when the law of letting an Israelite slave go free after six years was not followed (Jer. 34:8–22).
26. *Dum Diversas*, a papal bull issued on June 18, 1452. I noted this down from a display at the Whitney Plantation Museum.
27. Ronald Segal, *The Black Diaspora: Five Centuries of the Black Experience Outside Africa* (Farrar, Straus and Giroux, 1995), 4.

The Runaway Slave

> You shall not hand over to his master a slave who escapes to you.... With you he shall he stay, in your midst.... You shall not mistreat him. (Deut. 23:16–17)

This is generally understood to refer to a non-Jewish slave who had escaped into the Land of Israel.[28] Offering asylum to runaway slaves was in direct opposition to the norms of the ancient Near East. There were laws to prohibit accommodating them and treaties between neighboring states which included extradition clauses for fugitive slaves.[29] Meanwhile, when a runaway slave arrived in Israel, they were given the status of a righteous convert and treated with special kindness because of the trauma they had endured.[30]

What motivated such a revolutionary law? It too could be seen as a response to the slavery of the Israelites in Egypt. In essence, the Exodus is a story of runaway slaves on a colossal scale. At Sinai these former slaves are inducted into a unique covenant with God, who promises to care for and protect them forever and to give them a country of their own. That is why, at the end of the Torah when the Israelites are about to enter the Land of Israel, Moses teaches them this law, that they in turn must protect and care for all future runaway slaves who enter their borders.

As before, we can contrast the Torah's approach with the severe punishment meted out to runaway slaves in eighteenth century Louisiana:

> The runaway slave...shall have his ears cut off, and shall be branded with the fleur-de-lys on the shoulder; and on a second offence of the same nature...he will be hamstrung, and be marked with the fleur-de-lys on the other shoulder. On the third offense, he shall suffer death.[31]

28. See Rashi on Deuteronomy 23:16.
29. I. Mendelson, "On Slavery in Alalakh," *Israel Exploration Journal* 5, no. 2 (1955): 65–72.
30. Maimonides, *Mishneh Torah, Hilkhot Avadim* 8:11, and *Guide for the Perplexed* 3:39.
31. Article 32 of the Code Noir promulgated in Louisiana in 1724, quoted in Seck, *Bouki Fait Gombo*, 107.

Cruelty to Slaves

The Torah shows us the moral fiber of the future leader of Israel by his reaction to the mistreatment of his enslaved brethren. According to the commentary of Rashi, when Moses saw an Egyptian taskmaster hitting an Israelite, he looked upon the downtrodden slave with great sympathy and recognized the lifetime of cruelty he had been subjected to.[32] Moses lashed out at the Egyptian so forcefully that he killed him. This extreme reaction revealed Moses's intense moral outrage. The lesson being taught here is that the cruelty caused by slavery is intolerable.

The legal restrictions placed by the Torah upon forced labor for a Jewish slave are also a response to what happened in Egypt. The book of Exodus twice uses the Hebrew word *befarekh* to describe the slavery:

> The Egyptians enslaved the Israelites *befarekh,* and they made their lives bitter...all the work they did was *befarekh.* (Ex. 1:13–14)

Rashi explains *befarekh* to mean "with harsh labor that crushed the body and broke it."[33] The law in Leviticus employs the very same term three times as the limiting factor in the treatment of a Jewish slave: "Do not subjugate them *befarekh*" (Lev. 25:43, 46, 53).[34] Maimonides provides us with a practical definition of *befarekh:*

> This is work that has no time-limit or work that is unnecessary and is assigned only so that the slave will not remain idle. Based on this our sages taught that a boss should not say, "Hoe under the vines until I return," because they have not set any time-limit. Rather the boss should say, "Hoe until this specific time or as far as this specific place." ...Even telling them to warm a cup of hot water when the boss does not need it is forbidden.[35]

---

32. Rashi on Exodus 2:11 ("and saw their burdens") and on 2:12 ("he turned this way and that way").
33. Rashi on Exodus 1:13.
34. Note that the two mentions in Exodus and the three in Leviticus are the only uses of the word *befarekh* in the Torah.
35. Maimonides, *Mishneh Torah, Hilkhot Avadim* 1:6.

We see that the work carried out by a Jewish slave must be worthwhile; they cannot be made to perform pointless or boundless tasks. The prohibition of *befarekh* makes the work conditions of a Jewish slave quite similar to modern workforce standards. Hence the Torah says:

> If your brother becomes impoverished and is sold to you, do not work him like a slave; he shall be with you like an employee. (Lev. 25:39)

The Talmud concluded that a Jewish slave had to be treated just like their master. They must be given the same food and drink as well as equally comfortable sleeping arrangements. Indeed, the sages said, "Anyone who acquires a Jewish slave is considered like one who acquires a master for themselves,"[36] to which Maimonides adds, "One must treat their Jewish slave like a brother."[37] This effectively subverted the entire master-slave relationship.

The treatment of a non-Jewish slave is in stark contrast to all this. They are allowed to be treated befarekh.[38] They can be handled harshly and forced to do unnecessary and unlimited work. Indeed, even though the Torah states that a non-Jewish slave must be freed if their master knocks out their eye or tooth (Ex. 21:26–27), this does not protect them from all physical harm:

> If a man hits his male slave or slave girl with the rod and they die under his hand, they shall surely be avenged. But if they will survive for a day or two, they shall not be avenged, for they are his property. (Ex. 21:20–21)

In other words, non-Jewish slaves may be beaten, but not to death. This Torah-permitted cruelty in the treatment of a non-Jewish slave is highly problematic. How can the Torah excuse treating a non-Jewish slave *befarekh*, i.e., in exactly the same way as our ancestors were treated

36. Kiddushin 20a.
37. Maimonides, *Mishneh Torah, Hilkhot Avadim* 1:9.
38. Ibid., 9:8.

in Egypt? An honest account of the Torah's attitude to slavery cannot ignore this.

We might suggest that the Torah privileges Jewish over non-Jewish slaves because the focus of the Exodus is on freeing one particular people from slavery and bringing them into a unique relationship with God. Nevertheless, it is difficult to comprehend how this could be the ideal situation. Returning to Maimonides, we find a better response that reveals a gradualist approach to upending the practice of slavery. At the end of his *Hilkhot Avadim* (Laws of Slaves), he writes:

> It is permitted to work a non-Jewish slave *befarekh*. But although this is the law, the quality of piety and the way of wisdom requires that one should be merciful and pursue justice and not make their yoke heavy upon the non-Jewish slave or distress them.... The sages of old would let them partake of every dish that they themselves ate.... The master should not humiliate them by hand or word, because the Torah law has delivered them into slavery, not humiliation. Nor should verbal abuse and anger be heaped upon them, but they should be spoken to softly, and their requests should be heard.[39]

Maimonides is teaching us that even though the laws pertaining to Jewish and non-Jewish slaves are theoretically distinct, in practice we must treat them both with compassion. There is no place for cruelty. Thus, despite the Torah statement that non-Jewish slaves are bound for life, Maimonides describes various ways in which rabbinic law enables their emancipation.[40] He concludes:

> This approach reflects the attributes of the Holy One, blessed be He, which we are meant to imitate, "for God's mercies are upon all His works" (Ps. 145:9).[41]

39. Maimonides, *Mishneh Torah, Hilkhot Avadim* 9:8.
40. Ibid., 9:6.
41. Ibid., 9:8.

In other words, we must be decent and kind to the Jewish and non-Jewish slave alike, just as we are to the slave and free person alike, for they are *all* God's works.

Remembering the Exodus

With these three examples – slave trading, the runaway slave, and cruelty to slaves – we have seen that the Torah purposefully details the slavery of our ancestors in Egypt in order to introduce a corpus of law at Mount Sinai that mitigates against ill-treatment of both Jewish and non-Jewish slaves, and emphatically promotes compassion. It would be simple to end the chapter here, as we have come a very long way from the normal understanding of slavery. Jewish law demands that a master must provide sustenance and accommodation for their slave on a par with their own. They must never be violent to them or humiliate them. They must listen to their grievances. It is never permissible to give a slave unnecessary or undefined work. They must be treated compassionately and justly at all times, and even the duration of their labor can always be limited. Given all these conditions, in what sense are they still really enslaved?

And yet to end here would be disingenuous because, despite the points made so far, the term "slave" is still somewhat applicable. The 2015 UK Modern Slavery Act states that anyone who "holds another person in slavery or servitude" or "requires another person to perform forced or compulsory labor" has committed a criminal offense.[42] An employee is free to walk out at any time, but a slave will be forced to remain and compelled to work. In that sense, the Jewish and non-Jewish slaves as described in the Torah are still slaves because they are not free to leave of their own volition or to refuse to work.

To address this issue, we need to look at another deeply ingrained biblical theme. Do you know how many times the Torah reminds us that God rescued our ancestors from Egyptian slavery? To make the point dramatically, the original plan was to reproduce every single verse here so you could read them all in full, but that would have covered several

---

42. https://www.legislation.gov.uk/ukpga/2015/30/section/1/enacted.

pages of uninterrupted text. Here, then, are just a few select verses which span the Torah:

> Remember this day, in which you came out from Egypt, out of the house of slaves. (Ex. 13:3)

> And they shall know that I am the Lord their God, that brought them out of the land of Egypt, that I may dwell among them; I am the Lord their God. (Ex. 29:46)

> For I am the Lord that brings you out of the land of Egypt, to be your God; you shall therefore be holy, for I am holy. (Lev. 11:45)

> For the children of Israel are servants to Me, they are My servants, whom I have taken out of the land of Egypt. (Lev. 25:55)

> I am the Lord your God who brought you out from the land of Egypt to be a God unto you; I am the Lord your God. (Num. 15:41)

> And you shall remember that you were a slave in the land of Egypt, and the Lord your God has taken you out from there... (Deut. 5:15)

> You shall remember that you were a slave in the land of Egypt; therefore I command you to do this thing... (Deut. 24:22)

All in all, the Torah recalls the Exodus from Egyptian slavery over forty times. These appear in a wide range of contexts and relate to numerous commandments:

- safeguarding the Shabbat (Deut. 5:15)
- observing Passover (Ex. 13:3, 14, 34:18; Deut. 16:1, 3), Shavuot (Deut. 16:12, 25:5–10), and Sukkot (Lev. 23:3)
- wearing *tefillin* (Ex. 13:16) and *tzitzit* (Num. 15:41)
- believing in God (Ex. 20:2)

- sanctifying God's name (Deut. 5:6, 29:24)
- keeping God's covenant (Lev. 22:32–33, 26:13, 45)
- not oppressing the stranger (Ex. 22:20, 23:9; Lev. 19:34; Deut. 10:19) or the widow and orphan (Deut. 24:18)
- supporting the poor (Deut. 24:22)
- worshipping in the Temple (Ex. 29:46)
- keeping kosher (Lev. 11:45)
- honesty in commerce (Lev. 19:36)
- not borrowing on interest (Lev. 25:37–38)
- keeping slaves (Lev. 25:42, 55; Deut. 15:15)
- not being arrogant (Deut. 6:12, 8:14)
- rejecting false prophets (Deut. 13:6) and idolatry (Deut. 13:7, 11, 29:15–17)
- teaching one's children the tradition (Deut. 6:21)

This is clearly a foundational theme in Torah and the motivation behind a wide range of Jewish practices to this day. The memory of the Exodus is a powerful prompt for ethical behavior and social responsibility because it reminds us of the unjust subjugation our ancestors endured. That in turn makes us empathetic, rather than just sympathetic, to people who are less fortunate than we are.[43] We identify with the stranger, the outcast, the menial worker, and the poor because we have a deep memory of being downtrodden in our own history. The Torah repeats and reinforces this memory on multiple occasions. "A nation's greatness is measured by how it treats its most vulnerable members."[44]

As we have already noted, slavery was a social norm in the ancient world. Rather than simply condoning it, the Torah presents laws that restrict the abuses it causes. But the Torah does more. By constantly reiterating the powerful theme of remembering the Exodus, it gradually conditions its adherents to see slavery itself as abhorrent

---

43. On this ethic of empathy, see Shalom Carmy, "'We Were Slaves to Pharaoh in Egypt': Literary-Theological Notes on Slavery and Empathy," *Hebrew Political Studies* 4, no. 4 (Fall 2009): 367–80 (Shalem Press).
44. The quotation is generally attributed to Mahatma Gandhi, though this has been challenged and similar versions are attributed to several people.

and to challenge its very existence. In a seminal essay, Rabbi Nachum Rabinovitch (1928–2020) wrote:

> Over time, as human knowledge increased, new scientific technological discoveries and technologies harnessed energies far more powerful than manual labor, thus contributing greatly to general welfare and wellbeing. Divine providence has thus brought about the elimination of slavery in almost every country. Blessed is the One who, through the light of His Torah, has given mankind understanding to recognize the Divine greatness ingrained in every human being. The abolition of slavery is in fact a partial realization of the ideals taught by the Torah, and it is clear to anyone who has studied a bit of the history of the West that the spread of Torah values was a decisive factor in this historical process.[45]

This understanding underpins the highly compassionate attitude to all slaves in Maimonides's legal presentation. The thrust of the Torah is the moral behavior that is planted in us because of the Exodus memory and nurtured through the practice of numerous mitzvot, making us passionate about human freedom and forceful advocates for both social justice and human dignity.

We will now look at two further ways in which the Torah seeks to dismantle slavery altogether.

From Slavery to Service

The purpose of the redemption was more than human liberty per se; it was the freedom to serve the one true God. This is clear from the demand that Moses made six times on God's behalf to Pharaoh when he refused to release the Israelite slaves: "Let My people go so that they may serve Me" (Ex. 7:16, 26, 8:16, 9:1, 13, 10:3).

Though the beginning of that demand ("Let My people go") has become a famous phrase, it never occurs on its own in the Torah. It is always coupled with the next phrase ("so that they may serve Me"). This

---

45. Nachum L. Rabinovitch, *Pathways to Their Hearts: Torah Perspectives on the Individual* (Maggid, 2023), 46.

makes it clear that the demand is for *freedom to* serve God, rather than just *freedom from* slavery.

The Hebrew for the phrase "so that they may serve Me" is just one word, *veyaavduni*, which has the three-letter Hebrew root E-V-D. This can be translated into English as either "service" or "slavery," depending on the context. The Torah calls the Israelites subjugated in Egypt *avadim*, which is universally translated as "slaves." Yet the very same term, when referring to the Israelites' relationship with God, is universally translated as "servants."[46] Why is this? Imagine a translation of Moses's demand to Pharaoh that read, "Let My people go so that they be enslaved to Me." Though perfectly accurate, it would be very jarring. It would imply that Moses was demanding that our ancestors be rescued from a human master only to be bound to a divine one – exchanging one form of slavery for another.

Now you could argue that the covenantal bond with God is indeed a form of slavery because it cannot be undone, the Master is all-powerful, and the hard labor of religious practice is commanded under threat of punishment. And yet no one thinks this way. Why? Because we understand slavery as subjugation to another human being, rather than to God. It makes sense to most people that no human has the right to bind another human in forced labor; but God is different. God is a higher being, the Creator who cares for all His creations, so service to God could never be termed slavery. Indeed, it is liberating: "I am Your servant... You set me free from my chains."[47] In which case, the question stands: Why does the Torah confuse things by using the same Hebrew word for slavery as for service?

It could be that the term E-V-D encompasses the full range of servile relationships – employee, servant, and slave – *on purpose*. In its various forms, the word-root occurs more than two hundred times in the Torah, and only a quarter of them refer to actual slavery. The rest are different forms of service to other humans and to God. This might

---

46. E.g., Leviticus 25:55. Note also that Moses is called *eved Hashem*, the "servant of God" (Deut. 34:5).
47. *The Koren Shalem Siddur*, 736, recited in the Hallel prayer. The verse is from Psalms 116:16.

very well be because the Torah sees all these different forms as part of a continuum. An employment contract contains rights and benefits for the employee, but it could also have clauses or penalties that turn them into a servant, or even, in extreme cases, a slave.

This is not to advocate for the philosophy, held by some extreme socialists, that all employment is slavery.[48] However, there are situations in which an employee can *fall into* slavery, for instance through debt bondage. This occurs when a person stuck in deep poverty borrows money and is then forced to work to pay off the debt. They eventually lose control of their employment conditions and their debt, becoming, effectively, slaves.[49] This is just one form of what is termed "modern slavery" and includes human trafficking, forced labor, descent-based slavery, child slavery, and sexual slavery.[50]

By using the same Hebrew root, E-V-D, the Torah ties together all forms of human labor, thereby teaching that restrictive laws are required for *all* these forms to ensure that the dignity of the employee, servant, or slave is always retained and respected. Though we often imagine the ancient world to be much more barbaric than our own, modern forms of slavery as well as abusive employment practices remain a major global problem. The fact that the Torah grapples with these very real challenges in a host of interrelated ways allows it to retain its effectiveness as a powerful ethical guide to this day.

Shabbat for All

A major element of Judaism that stands as a constant champion to the worker – whether employee, servant, or slave – is Shabbat. The origin of Shabbat is twofold. First, God rested on the seventh day from the work of Creation, sanctifying it for all time (Gen. 2:1–3; Ex. 31:17). Second, because the Israelite slaves had no respite from their harsh labors

48. Stephen Shenfield, "Is employment a form of slavery?" *World Socialist Party* (November 5, 2019) https://wspus.org/2019/11/is-employment-a-form-of-slavery/.
49. "What is bonded labour?" *Anti-Slavery International* [accessed 28.4.22] https://www.antislavery.org/slavery-today/bonded-labour/.
50. "What is modern slavery?" *Anti-Slavery International* [accessed 28.4.22] https://www.antislavery.org/slavery-today/modern-slavery/.

(Ex. 5:5), Shabbat was introduced to differentiate our work from that of the slave and, at the very same time, to include slaves in this law:

> The seventh day is the Sabbath of the Lord your God; in it you shall not do any work, you, nor your son, nor your daughter, nor your male slave, nor your female slave, nor your ox, nor your ass, nor any of your cattle, nor your stranger who is inside your gates; that your male slave and your female slave may rest as well as you. Remember that you were a slave in the land of Egypt, and that the Lord your God brought you out from there ... therefore the Lord your God commanded you to keep the Sabbath day. (Deut. 5:14–15)

A day of rest is essential for society not to be swallowed up by an unrelenting obligation to work and to subjugate workers. On that day, according to the Torah, there are no workers – employment, service, and slavery must all cease. All may partake of the Shabbat. By establishing the Shabbat in Jewish law, society is given a weekly reminder that *all* people are ends and not means, and that everyone has a right to freedom from labor.

Ancient Egypt was a hierarchical servant society, and our ancestors were at the very bottom. Shabbat is a weekly response to that painful memory. It enshrines the decent and moral treatment of workers, whatever their background or status.

Over time, the principles underpinning Shabbat have grown in influence beyond Judaism. In the wake of modern industrialization two centuries ago, labor unions were created and worker's rights in the UK began gaining recognition. In 1919, the International Labour Organization was formed by the League of Nations (the forerunner to the United Nations) to protect workers. And in 1948, the UN Declaration of Human Rights was adopted, which incorporates workers' rights.

Due to its Christian roots, shops in England used to be closed on Sundays, and trading was illegal. When this was reviewed by the British Government in 1994, the former Chief Rabbi, Lord Jakobovits, spoke about Shabbat in the House of Lords:

> The loss of the sabbath will deprive Britain of the last visible vestige of national spirituality and sanctification... at least on Sundays, even the streets proclaim that man doesn't live by bread alone; that the material quest for profit can be interrupted and that there is more to human happiness than the pursuit of wealth and of power over others. By closing our shops and workplaces we proclaim the equality of all men. The rich do not earn more than the poor. For once we do not measure all values in life by their material price.[51]

Do not forget that the establishment of Sunday as the day of rest, rather than Saturday, was a Christian innovation dating back to the council of Nicaea in 325 CE. The displacement of Saturday was a conscious rejection of Judaism. This makes the statement of Lord Jakobovits all the more astonishing. He clearly felt that the value of preserving a day of rest in British society eclipsed the painful memory of Christian supersessionism.

Considerations such as flexible hours for workers and convenience for shoppers ultimately led to an Act of Parliament that allowed Sunday trading, but with limited opening hours and exemptions for essential and time-sensitive services.[52] Although there are legitimate reasons why future legislation may abandon all restrictions on Sunday trading, Lord Jakobovits' impassioned plea still has value. How can a modern nation regularly remind its citizens that they are more than just materialist consumers in pursuit of wealth and power? The Jewish answer is Shabbat.

Slavery Today

Sadly, human slavery and trafficking have yet to be eradicated from our world. Constant vigilance is needed to ensure that workers in impoverished societies are not neglected or abused. Millions are subject to

---

51. Stephen Goodwin, "Inside Parliament: Lords Cherish Spiritual Roots: Peers Debate Sunday Trading – Jakobovits Says Sabbath 'Proclaims Equality of All Men,'" in *The Independent*, March 9, 1994.
52. www.legislation.gov.uk/ukpga/1994/20/contents.

Egyptian-like bondage to this day. The message of the Exodus will only be fully realized when these injustices are overturned. It has been argued that Jewish principles derived from the Torah challenge a human society still in desperate need of change.

Though Jews have been involved in the fight to end slavery, this has not always been the case. During the American revolution, there were religious Jews who owned African slaves like their Christian counterparts; and there were rabbis who gave justifications for this.[53]

In 1833, after decades of campaigning, the British Parliament passed the Slavery Abolition Act. Slave owners, however, demanded compensation for the losses they would incur as a consequence, and so a Slave Compensation Act was signed into law in 1837. Slave owners were paid approximately £20 million in compensation in over 40,000 awards for enslaved people freed in the colonies, but nothing was handed to the newly liberated people.[54] To finance the slave compensation package,

> Nathan Mayer Rothschild and his brother-in-law Moses Montefiore agreed to loan the British government £15m, with the government adding an additional £5m later. The total sum represented 40% of the government's yearly income in those days, equivalent to some £300bn today.[55]

Thus it was that two renowned British Jews facilitated the end of slavery in the UK. It was only in 2015 that the loan was finally paid off. For over one and a half centuries, generations of British taxpayers had been contributing to the huge slave owners' compensation package. The legacy of the UK's involvement in five hundred years of slave ownership and trading is still very much a current issue.

---

53. Adam Goodheart, "The Rabbi and the Rebellion," *New York Times,* https://opinionator.blogs.nytimes.com/2011/03/07/the-rabbi-and-the-rebellion/. And Jews were involved in many industries that supported the slave trade.
54. "Slave Compensation Act 1837," Wikipedia [accessed 27.4.22] https://en.wikipedia.org/wiki/Slave_Compensation_Act_1837.
55. Kris Manjapra, "When Will Britain Face Up to Its Crimes against Humanity?" *Guardian,* 29.3.18, last modified 10.11.21 www.theguardian.com/news/2018/mar/29/slavery-abolition-compensation-when-will-britain-face-up-to-its-crimes-against-humanity.

According to a 2019 Pew Research Center survey, the legacy of slavery still resonates for many Americans, too, with 63 percent believing it affects the position of black people in American society today, either a great deal or a fair amount.[56] As was highlighted in the summer of 2020, Black Americans continue to suffer institutionalized racism as a result of a long history of slavery. Even after it was finally abolished, slavery left in its wake a society that embraced decades of segregation and discrimination expressed in law, policy, and general culture.

Importantly, rather than condoning or ignoring slavery, the Torah tackled it head-on by establishing a range of laws that restricted the subjugation and exploitation of all types of workers, as well as improving their rights. Coupled with the constant reminders of the Exodus and the weekly observance of Shabbat, this general approach aimed to inspire a culture of dignity for all which might eventually lead to the demise of slavery altogether. In the words of Rabbi Jonathan Sacks, "The Torah did not abolish slavery, but it set in motion a process that would lead people to come of their own accord to the conclusion that it was wrong."[57]

The Torah's position continues to challenge modern forms of slavery and the mistreatment of workers. It recognizes that abusive practices will always surface in human society, so it is better to legislate against them than to naively hope they will simply disappear by themselves. Isaiah said that it was God's desire for us "to unlock the fetters of wickedness and break the slavery chain, to let the oppressed go free and shatter every yoke of slavery" (Is. 58:6).[58] This teaching should continue to guide us.

On Seder night we are called upon to reenact the Exodus and imagine what life might have been like as a slave in Egypt. I shut my eyes and remember the day we visited the Whitney Plantation outside New Orleans. It haunts me still.

---

56. Julianna Menashe Horowitz, Anna Brown, and Kiana Cox, "Race in America 2019," *Pew Research Center,* April 9, 2019, www.pewsocialtrends.org/2019/04/09/race-in-america-2019/.
57. Jonathan Sacks, *Leviticus: The Book of Holiness,* Covenant and Conversation (Maggid, 2015), 373.
58. The translation follows Ibn Ezra's understanding of this verse.

Chapter 6

Why Sacrifice or Eat Animals?

EXPLORING THE QUESTION

The Torah is packed with instances of animal sacrifice, all of which are welcomed by God. While Cain's offering was plant-based, Abel sacrificed animals "from the choice firstlings of his flock, and the Lord regarded Abel and his offering" (Gen. 4:4). When Noah left the ark and built an altar to God, "he took from every clean cattle and from every clean fowl and offered burnt offerings on the altar" (Gen. 8:20). God accepted Noah's sacrifices, resolving never again to flood the earth (Gen. 8:21). To confirm a covenant between them, God instructed Abraham to sacrifice "a three-year-old heifer, goat, and ram, and a turtle dove and young pigeon" (Gen. 15:9). Jacob too "offered sacrifices to the God of his father Isaac," which caused God to speak to him (Gen. 46:1–2). And all this is just in the book of Genesis. Why would God want these charred animals? What does sacrificial worship have to do with spirituality?

In the subsequent books of the Torah, the Israelites are given dozens of laws which formalized the place, process, personnel, and the myriad of particulars involved in sacrificing animals to God. In Exodus we read an extensive account of the construction of the Tabernacle, which contained a centralized sacrificial altar for daily use: "And this shall you offer on the altar: two yearling lambs each day, perpetually.

The one lamb you shall offer in the morning and the other lamb you shall offer at twilight" (Ex. 29:38–39).

In Leviticus we are introduced to the numerous regulations involved in preparing animals for sacrifice, as well as the different types of sacrifices and when they are mandated:

> This is the law for the burnt offering, for the grain offering, for the offense offering, and for the guilt offering, and for the installation offering and for the peace sacrifice, which the Lord commanded Moses at Mount Sinai. (Lev. 7:37–38)

The book of Numbers adds a large list of special animal sacrifices for Shabbat, Rosh Chodesh, and festivals (Num. 28:9–30:1) and, finally, numerous sacrifice-related laws are reviewed and elaborated in Deuteronomy, such as the paschal lamb (Deut. 16:4–7). Why is so much of the Torah dedicated to the slaughtering of animals for sacrificial purposes?

On the inauguration day of the Tabernacle, each tribe offered fourteen animals for sacrifice, over a hundred and fifty in all (Num. 7:12–83). One midrash imagines God regarding this as a paltry effort: "Are you honoring Me merely with this? Are you treating Me thus? I am King and Ruler of the world."[1] The excuse that desert travel precludes large-scale sacrifice was offered in response, but the import of the exchange is that God deserves better. This was achieved three centuries later at the inauguration of the Temple built by King Solomon in Jerusalem:

> King Solomon and all the community of Israel, who were assembled with him before the Ark, were sacrificing sheep and oxen in such abundance that they could not be numbered or counted.... Solomon offered 22,000 oxen and 120,000 sheep as well-being sacrifices to God; thus the king and all the Israelites dedicated the House of the Lord. (I Kings 8:5, 63)

Can you imagine the spectacle of slaughtering and burning this many animals?

1. *Midrash Tanḥuma, Naso* 15.

When the Jews returned to Jerusalem after the Babylonian exile, they were greatly diminished in number and had scant resources. Yet, at the inauguration of the restored Temple, they still managed to sacrifice "a hundred bulls, two hundred rams, and four hundred lambs" (Ezra 6:17). The sheer scale of the slaughter is again meant to impress, but to many modern readers it just comes off as gory, if not barbaric. Why did the formal worship of God require the death of so many of God's innocent creatures?

Surely, the many sections of the Torah concerning animal sacrifice are among the most alien to contemporary sensibilities. They come from a distant time when this form of worship was commonplace. The ancient Egyptians sacrificed animals to their gods; so did the Mesopotamian empires of Babylon and Assyria as well as the surrounding civilizations; later the Greeks and Romans did too. From a modern perspective, however, this feels primitive, cruel, and unnecessary. The average shul-goer finds it taxing to concentrate when the detail of ritual sacrifice becomes the focus of the weekly Torah reading. Combining the period when the Tabernacle was in operation with that of the First and Second Temples, it turns out that animal sacrifices were offered by our ancestors every day for more than thirteen centuries. Why was this the heart of ancient Judaism for such a long time?

Animal sacrifice cannot be investigated without also discussing meat consumption in general. This is because these two acts are intimately connected in the Torah. For most sacrifices, only select parts of the animal were burned on the altar, such as the kidneys, innards, parts of the liver, and the fats.[2] The rest, which was most of the meat, was eaten as food. Depending on the type of sacrifice, the meat was consumed by just the priest involved in the ritual, or by his family as well, or together with all the priests or the person who brought the offering and their family.[3] In reading through the book of Leviticus, you will find more verses dedicated to the rules of eating sacrificial meat than there are concerning the dietary laws (*kashrut*).

2. See, for example, Leviticus 3:3–5, 9–11, 14–16, 4:8–10, 26, 31, 7:3–5.
3. Leviticus 6:18–23; 10:14; Mishna Zevaḥim 5:5–8.

The relationship between sacrificing animals for ritual worship and eating animals for food is complicated by the fact that once the Tabernacle was built and dedicated, any time an Israelite wanted to eat meat, they were duty-bound to bring it first as a sacrifice:

> Every man of the house of Israel who slaughters a bull or a sheep or a goat in the camp, or who slaughters outside the camp, and does not bring it to the entrance of the Tent of Meeting to bring it forward as an offering to the Lord before the Lord's Tabernacle, it shall be counted as bloodshed ... and that man shall be cut off from the midst of his people. (Lev. 17:3–4)

This was how our ancestors ate meat for forty years in the wilderness on the way to the Promised Land: every meat meal began with a sacrifice.[4] From all these considerations, it is clear that any attempt to explain animal sacrifice must also involve the Torah's general permission to eat meat.

The fact that most sacrificial meat was for human consumption rather than burned up on the altar does help to explain the mass slaughter of animals at the inauguration of the First Temple. It enabled the fortnight-long feeding of the throngs of people who had come from far and wide:

> And at that time Solomon held a feast, and all Israel with him, a huge gathering, from the entrance to Hamath (in the north) to the brook of Egypt (in the south), before the Lord our God ... for fourteen days. (I Kings 8:65)

Considering the dramatic rise in the number of people choosing vegan or vegetarian diets in the last decade, the Torah's focus on sacrificing and eating animals seems outdated. Most major capital cities now have numerous vegetarian and vegan restaurants, and there has been a marked increase in plant-based products available in supermarkets. The many compelling nutritional, environmental, and moral arguments for a meat-free diet seem to be at odds with the Torah.

---

4. This follows the opinion of R. Yishmael in Ḥullin 16b.

Equally, the industrialization of meat production, which has enabled mass consumption on an unprecedented scale, also brings into question the proper and ethical treatment of animals. In the United Kingdom alone, some 7,000 cattle, 30,000 pigs, 40,000 sheep and two and a half million chickens are slaughtered for human consumption *every single day*.[5] Shockingly, over 20 percent is wasted and never eaten.[6] In the US the figure is even higher.[7] Many of the millions of chickens alive today are kept squashed together, each confined to an area about the size of a sheet of A4 paper, and will live for less than fifty days before being slaughtered.[8] As well as harsh and wasteful, meat consumption is a major contributor to climate change due to methane emissions. The carbon footprint from beef and lamb is more than all the other food groups combined.[9] Yet it appears that the human desire to consume meat outweighs concern for animal welfare and climate hazards.

The ethical treatment of animals is well developed in the Torah. Kept animals must be fed before their owners (Deut. 11:15).[10] Pack animals must never be hurt or overburdened (Deut. 22:4). Animals used for agricultural labor should not be muzzled (Deut. 22:10). Those

5. See "Monthly UK statistics on the number of cattle, sheep and pigs slaughtered," Department for Environmental, Food and Rural Affairs (DEFRA), published October 17, 2013, last updated March 10, 2022, www.gov.uk/government/collections/cattle-sheep-and-pig-slaughter; "Monthly statistics on the activity of UK hatcheries and UK poultry slaughterhouses," DEFRA, published June 27, 2013, last updated April 21, 2022, www.gov.uk/government/statistics/poultry-and-poultry-meat-statistics; and "Annual UK slaughter stats," Animal Clock UK, animalclock.org/uk/.
6. Malgorzata Karwowska, Sylwia Laba, and Krystian Szczepanski, "Food Loss and Waste in Meat Sector – Why the Consumption Stage Generates the Most Losses?" *Sustainability* 2021, 13 (11), 6227; https://doi.org/10.3390/su13116227.
7. Jean Buzby, Hodan Wells, and Jeffrey Hyman, *The Estimated Amount, Value, and Calories of Postharvest Food Losses at the Retail and Consumer Levels in the United States*, EIB-121, U.S. Department of Agriculture, Economic Research Service, February 2014.
8. Felicity Lawrence, "If consumers knew how farmed chickens were raised, they might never eat their meat again," *Guardian*, 24.4.2016, last modified August 18, 2018, www.theguardian.com/environment/2016/apr/24/real-cost-of-roast-chicken-animal-welfare-farms.
9. "Interactive: What is the climate impact of eating meat and dairy?" Carbon Brief, https://interactive.carbonbrief.org/what-is-the-climate-impact-of-eating-meat-and-dairy/.
10. See also Gittin 62a.

of different sizes and strengths should not be yoked together (Deut. 25:4).[11] Animals cannot be made to work on Shabbat (Ex. 20:10). Jewish law forbids forcing any animal to perform for fun, to fight for entertainment, or to be hunted purely for sport.[12] Animals must never be killed without justification, and when they are slaughtered for food, this must be carried out with minimal pain.[13]

The attitude to animals modeled by different characters in the Torah is also instructive. Two violent and immoral men, Nimrod and Esau, were both characterized as hunters (Gen. 10:9–10 and 25:27).[14] Conversely, Abraham (Gen. 12:16, 13:1–8), Isaac (Gen. 26:13–14), Jacob (Gen. 30:37–43, 31:18), and Moses (Ex. 3:1) were all shepherds who spent time tending to their flocks. Indeed, shepherding was seen by the rabbis as a great schooling for righteousness and leadership.[15]

Our patriarchs, however, had no problem with eating meat. Abraham served his guests calves (Gen. 18:7–8).[16] Isaac loved a well-cooked meat dish that his family made efforts to provide for him (Gen. 27:3–5, 8–9, 30–31). Joseph had a meat meal prepared for his brothers (Gen. 43:16). To be sure, there are several Torah laws that limit meat consumption. Eating blood and certain fats (Lev. 3:17) and the sinew of the hindquarter (Gen. 32:33) are all prohibited, as is mixing meat and milk (Ex. 23:19). And only select species may be eaten (Lev. 11:1–46). However, eating animals per se is an accepted practice.

In summary, why are the slaughter of animals for food and their offering as sacrifices such essential and interconnected elements within the Torah? What role did sacrifice play in our faith? Why were so many

---

11. See also Rashi's comment on this verse.
12. Avoda Zara 18b and Rashi, s.v. *kenigyon*; Leviticus Rabba 13:3. See also the responsa of Yechezkel Landau (1713–1793), the *Noda BiYehuda, Mahadura Tinyana, Yoreh De'ah* 10.
13. *Sefer HaḤinukh,* commandments 186 and 451.
14. According to midrash, Nimrod was responsible for the Tower of Babel (Ḥullin 89a), trying to kill Abraham, and waging war on Canaan (Eiruvin 53a), while Esau married unsuitable women (Gen. 26:34–35), aimed to kill Jacob his brother (Gen. 27:41), and, according to midrash, killed Nimrod (Exodus Rabba 63:13).
15. Exodus Rabba 2:2.
16. According to Bava Metzia 86b, Abraham served each guest the delicacy of a whole calf's tongue with mustard.

animals slaughtered for centuries? And, given the rise of meat-free diets coupled with the problems of the modern meat industry, why does Judaism still allow the consumption of meat?

RESPONDING TO THE QUESTION

The Torah has important things to say about the ethics of meat consumption today, and a fuller understanding of its attitude to sacrifice will aid in appreciating this. Perhaps we should begin by acknowledging that humans are omnivores because our anatomy and physiology enable us to eat both plants and animals. There is much evidence from the archaeological record that humankind ate meat from the earliest times.[17] Maimonides recognized this in his explanation of *sheḥita,* the kosher slaughtering of animals:

> The commandment concerning the slaughtering of animals is necessary because the natural food of man consists of vegetables and animal flesh, the best kinds of meat being those that are permitted to us. No physician is ignorant of this. Now since the necessity to have nutritious food requires that animals be killed, the aim was to kill them in a straightforward manner, as it was forbidden to torment them by cutting the throat clumsily, by poleaxing, or by cutting off a limb while the animal is alive.[18]

The omnivorous diet of humankind correlates with archaeological findings of animal sacrifices in most ancient civilizations. Eating parts of the animal was connected to the sacrificial procedure. There were also sacrificial rituals around meat eating in general. Grand theories and specific studies abound as to the symbolism and purpose of pagan sacrifice in relation to the gods being worshipped. In addition to sanctification and communion, these include the need to pay homage, secure favor, and appease the gods, as well as discerning their will.[19] Reviewing these in

---

17. John S. Allen, *The Omnivorous Mind: Our Evolving Relationship with Food* (Harvard University Press, 2012), 40–55.
18. Maimonides, *Guide for the Perplexed* 3:48.
19. Daniel Ullucci, "Sacrifice in the Ancient Mediterranean: Recent and Current

the context of the ancient Middle East can help identify the Torah's singular approach.

In ancient Egypt, homage and favor were maintained through the daily "feeding" of sacred figurines:

> Each morning the officiating priests would take the statue of the god or goddess from the shrine where it had rested overnight, remove the previous day's clothing and make-up, cleanse and dress the statue afresh. But above all, what gave the deity the strength to sustain the ordered world were the offerings supplied by the public: each day he or she was more than adequately fed.[20]

The function of the offerings was to secure divine power to protect and sustain the world and its inhabitants in good order. The gods of Mesopotamia were fed in similar ways at holy sites across the region:

> Already in the third millennium (BCE) the offerings of food and drink were very ample. In later times, the quantities that were supplied, day after day, to the temples in each city, became enormous: bulls and boars, scores of sheep and fowl, many hundredweights of bread, dozens of containers of wine and beer.[21]

Animal sacrifice by Egyptian priests for the sake of appeasement was graphically described by the fifth-century BCE Greek historian, Herodotus:

> They take the beast to the appropriate altar and light a fire; then, after pouring a libation of wine and invoking the god by name, they slaughter it, cut off its head, and flay the carcass. The head is loaded with curses and taken away.... The curses they pronounce take the form of a prayer that any disaster which threatens either

---

Research," *Currents in Biblical Research* 13, no. 3 (2015): 388–439.

20. Norman Cohn, *Cosmos, Chaos, and the World to Come* (Yale University Press, 2001), 24.
21. Ibid., 36.

> themselves or their country may be diverted and fall upon the severed head of the beast.[22]

At first glance these rituals would seem to resemble those in the Torah. Was the altar in the Tabernacle not "fed" with daily sacrifices too? Was the aim there not also to appease God and secure a good relationship?

To respond to these questions, we will examine three rabbinic interpretations as to the purpose of sacrifice in the Torah, which they understood to be significantly different from pagan practice. This will be followed by a discussion of how the Israelites gradually began to abuse sacrificial rituals, which leads to an account of Maimonides's perspective on idolatry and sacrificial worship. Finally, to address its contemporary significance, we will return to the Torah's connection between sacrificing and eating meat.

From Sacrifice to Offering

Through a simple but sustained change of terminology, the Torah established a clear distinction between its approach to sacrifices and what had gone before:

> Speak to the children of Israel and say to them: "When a person among you brings a *korban* (sacrificial offering) to the Lord..." (Lev. 1:2)

This is the first time the Hebrew word *korban* (plural, *korbanot*) appears in the Torah; it then continues to be the most common term for a sacrifice for the rest of the Torah, appearing a further seventy-seven times. Despite all the sacrifices in the books of Genesis and Exodus, *korbanot* are never mentioned. Cain's sacrifice was called a *minḥa* (Gen. 4:3–5), Noah's sacrifices were *olot* (Gen. 8:20–22), Abraham's replacement ram sacrifice was an *olah* (Gen. 22:13), and Jacob's sacrifices were *zevaḥim* (Gen. 46:1). The terms *olot, zevaḥim,* and *shelamim* for sacrifices occur frequently in Exodus (e.g., Ex. 24:5), but never *korbanot.* Only once the Tabernacle is up and running at the start of Leviticus is the word *korban*

22. Herodotus, *The Histories,* trans. Aubrey De Selincourt (Penguin, 2003), 2:39, 111.

introduced.[23] The Zohar explains how this new word encapsulates an essentially different approach to sacrifices:

> R. Ḥizkiya asked: What is the meaning of the term *korban*? R. Shimon replied: … It means "drawing near" [from the Hebrew root word K-R-V, "to draw near"], and refers to binding things together until they are unified, to make whole the Holy Name of God. Hence it is written, "a *korban* to the Lord" (Lev. 1:2) … this shows compassion, not harshness. … Hence God's name *yod-heh-vav-heh* is always used [when referring to sacrifices] and never the name *Elohim* [which implies judgment].[24] Said R. Ḥizkiya: I am glad to have asked this and received such an explanation.[25]

Clearly, to offer a *korban* is not an act of sacrifice. To "sacrifice" is to give up one thing of value for the sake of something else more valuable. When playing chess, for example, you might sacrifice a rook to capture your opponent's queen, or at one stage of your career you might sacrifice a work opportunity for the sake of your family. Similarly, pagans would sacrifice high-worth animals to placate their gods, who were of greater value to them. Offering a *korban,* on the other hand, meant something else entirely. It signified a desire to come near to God, to build a closer relationship or rebuild one if the person had sinned. A *korban* was a gift to express dedication and commitment.

Sacrifice always involved a transaction, a payment that had to be made for a worthwhile reward. Pagan sacrifice was straightforward and required no intense emotional investment, opening the door to selfish manipulation. Instead of serving the gods, it was possible to make the gods serve you. For example, in ancient Mesopotamia, "military aggression against another city could be justified as acting on behalf of the

---

23. See Rashi on Leviticus 1:1.
24. The four Hebrew letters *yod, heh, vav, heh* (sometimes rendered YHVH) is known as the tetragrammaton, the four-letter unpronounceable name of God. *Elohim* is the other often-used name for God, but literally means a judge (see Ex. 22:27) and is a more impersonal name for God, whereas *yod-heh-vav-heh* is the more intimate, personal name for God.
25. Zohar III:5a.

[local] city god; the assumption of power by an individual could be ascribed to his special selection by the deity.[26]

Conversely, says the Zohar, a *korban* was an end in itself, an honest offer of devotion; a gift, not a payment. The God of Israel cannot be bought: "For the Lord your God … shows no favor and takes no bribe" (Deut. 10:17). The slaughtering and burning of the animal expressed the passion and fire of a deep and intense relationship between giver and receiver. *Korbanot* were freely given offerings, not quid pro quo sacrifices.

Correspondence and Substitution

A second difference between pagan sacrifices and *korbanot* can be discerned in Nahmanides's explanation of the *ḥatat* offering, the *korban* that was brought for committing a sin unintentionally. He begins by showing the correspondence between aspects of the ritual for this *korban* and the sinful act itself.

> Deeds are accomplished through *thought, speech,* and *action,* therefore God commanded that when a person sins and has to then bring a sin-offering, they must lay their hands upon the animal to correspond to the wrongful *action*; confess their sin verbally to correspond to their wrongful *speech*; and burn the innards and kidneys in fire to correspond to the instruments of *thought* and desire in the human being. The animal's legs are also burnt since they correspond to the hands and legs of a person, which enable them to fulfill their actions.[27]

Thus, rather than trying to placate God so that they are not punished for their sin, the purpose of the *ḥatat* was to remind the sinner of what they had actually *done*. Through the person-animal correspondence, they had to relive the thought, speech, and action involved in the sin. This impressed on them the seriousness of their error. Nahmanides then reveals a further dimension to the ritual:

26. Gwendolyn Leick, *Mesopotamia: The Invention of the City* (Penguin Books, 2001), 147.
27. Nahmanides's comment on Leviticus 1:9.

> All this was done so that the person realized that they had sinned against their God with their body and their soul, and that it really would be fitting for *their* blood to be spilled and *their* body burned, were it not for the loving-kindness of the Creator, who instead took from them a substitute… the animal's life was in place of that person's life, and the major limbs of the offering were in place of that person's major limbs.

The sinner was meant to identify fully with the animal and appreciate that were it not for God's mercy, they would be the one being sacrificed. Their sin had removed their right to life, and watching the animal be offered as a *korban* in their place enabled them to experience the death they deserved in a vicarious manner. This intense ritual was their atonement (Lev. 4:31).

Finally, Nahmanides extends his thinking beyond the *ḥatat*: "And the reason for the *tamid*, the daily offering, was that it is impossible for the masses to continually avoid transgression." In other words, the regular daily *korbanot* were also meant to be constant reminders and warnings to all about the severity of sin.

Though this approach may not adequately justify the death of the animal to the modern mind, it does differentiate this ritual from its pagan equivalents. Rather than appeasing the gods, the Torah's *korbanot* were meant to humble the people. While the pagan ability to appease gave a measure of confidence and control, the experience of correspondence and substitution described by Nahmanides was set up to inspire a culture of self-reflection and obedience. The power of animal sacrifice was thus shifted from influencing pagan gods to influencing human beings. The Torah's approach was internally rather than externally directed.

Lifeblood

The Torah's treatment of sacrificial blood reveals a third difference from the pagan perspective. When an animal was slaughtered for a *korban*, it was essential that its blood was fully drained before any of its body parts could be burned on the altar. No blood was permitted, explained the talmudic sages, because nothing could be offered on the altar which was not permitted to be eaten by an Israelite.[28] And the Torah is very clear about not consuming blood under any circumstances:

> If any one of the house of Israel or of the strangers who reside among them consumes any blood, I will set My face against the person who consumes that blood, and I will cut them off from the midst of their people. For the soul of the flesh is in the blood. (Lev. 17:10–11)[29]

The flow of blood through the body is essential to life. This life force, or soul (*nefesh* in Hebrew), is what gives blood its sacred significance.

That is why, even though animal sacrifice was permitted, the blood always had to be separated beforehand. This entailed a four-step process. The animal was slaughtered (*sheḥita*), its blood received (*kabala*) in a sacred vessel, which was conveyed to the altar (*holakha*), where it was cast on its walls (*zerika*). The remainder of the blood was poured away at the base of the altar. The act of *zerika* is repeated ten times in the Torah.[30] It was judged to be the determining factor in validating an offering, rather than the subsequent burning of body parts on the altar.[31] What was the significance of *zerika*? Rabbi Samson Raphael Hirsch wrote:

> By means of blood, that medium which circulates throughout every part of the body, the soul regulates and directs the nerves and muscles which are only the organs of its activity. The ever-present blood in the body is the ever-present visible messenger in the body of the ever-present invisible directing soul. Hence it is the visible representative of the soul, and hence is most suitable to be the symbolic expression in offerings of elevating and devoting the soul to God.[32]

---

28. Ḥullin 90b, based on Ezekiel 45:15. Note that the Talmud here explains why offering *ḥeilev* (hard suet fat) was an exception to this rule.
29. See also Leviticus 7:26, 19:26; Deuteronomy 12:16, 23, 15:23.
30. Exodus 29:16, 20; Leviticus 1:5, 11, 3:2, 8, 13, 7:2, 17:6; Numbers 18:17.
31. See Zevaḥim 6a, 37b, 81b and Nahmanides's comment on Leviticus 6:3.
32. Samson Raphael Hirsch, *The Pentateuch, Vol. III, Leviticus,* trans. Isaac Levy

Rabbi Hirsch is saying that since "the soul of the flesh is in the blood," the blood of the sacrifice became a suitable symbol for the human soul in the *zerika* ritual. The casting of the blood onto the altar walls was a graphic representation of the elevation and cleansing of a person's soul, which led to their atonement: "for it is the blood that atones for the soul" (Lev. 17:11).[33]

Pagans also viewed blood as sacred, but for them this made it a potent gift for their gods. The blood was not drained from the animal. On the contrary, it needed to be burned and offered all together because the blood contained the life force that they wanted to pass on to their deities in order to fortify them. According to Rabbi Hirsch, the Torah had a very different approach. Blood had to be separated as a reminder of the sanctity of all life. Just as it could never be eaten, so it could never be offered up on the altar. Instead, most of it was poured away while a small amount was cast on the altar walls as a visual metaphor for personal purification. It symbolized the lifeblood of faith.

The Abuse of *Korbanot*

These three interpretations argue that the impetus of *korbanot* was the *psychological* effect that could be engendered in the person making the offering. It would have enabled them to experience a profound internal transformation, deepening their commitment to God.[34] However, these medieval and early modern rabbinic perspectives may well have been very far from the simple understanding of the general Israelite population in the First Temple period. And so, *korbanot* were susceptible to exploitation and inauthentic motivations. The story of these abuses and the attempts to rectify them are played out on the pages of the Bible, and into the rabbinic era.

The first major challenge was the struggle for centralized worship. From the moment *korbanot* were initiated in the Tabernacle, the Israelites

---

(Judaica Press, 1971), 470. See also Jacob Milgrom, *Leviticus: A Book of Ritual and Ethics* (2004), 18.

33. See also Exodus 30:10 and Leviticus 16:27.
34. See further, "Chief Rabbi, Lord Jakobovits' Essay on Animal Sacrifices in Judaism: Probings into a Psycho-Religious Drama," *United Synagogue Authorised Daily Prayer Book* (Revised Centenary Edition, 1998), 918–23; Joshua Berman, *The Temple: Its Symbolism and Meaning Then and Now* (Wipf and Stock, 2010), ch. 6.

were no longer permitted to sacrifice in any other location (Lev. 17:3–4).[35] This rule was respected during the wilderness years, when the Israelites camped in a tightly knit group surrounding the Tabernacle. However, once they settled in the Land of Israel, they began to sacrifice on *bamot* ("high places"), local hilltop altars, because a centralized Temple "had not yet been built for the Lord in those days" (I Kings 3:2). And even when the Temple was completed, the people still erected *bamot* across the country to serve their own interests.[36] This is supported by the archaeological record.[37] Prohibited forms of sacrificial worship involving both Levite and non-Levite priests were practiced in these places, and they were never fully eradicated.

Another essential problem was the wholesale waning of religious commitment and moral responsibility, despite the continued offering of *korbanot* in the Temple. We know of this because throughout that period the biblical prophets condemned the people for allowing *korbanot* to become hollow and meaningless rituals. Samuel reprimanded them for their disloyalty, Isaiah challenged their inauthenticity, Jeremiah dismissed them outright, and Micah criticized their grand gestures:

> Has the Lord as great delight in burnt offerings and sacrifices, as in obeying the voice of the Lord? (I Sam. 15:22)

> To what purpose is the multitude of your sacrifices to Me? said the Lord.... Bring your false sacrifices no more. (Is. 1:11–13)

> Your burnt offerings are not acceptable, nor are your sacrifices sweet to Me. (Jer. 6:20)

35. However, see Mishna Zevaḥim 14:4–10 for certain periodic exceptions and limitations.
36. See I Kings 14:23, 15:14, 22:44; II Kings 12:4, 14:4, 15:4, 35, 17:9, 11. The errant kings of Israel and Judah never blocked the building of *bamot*, and only two kings, Hezekiah and Josiah, made strenuous efforts to eradicate them.
37. Ellen White, "High Places, Altars and the Bamah," blogpost, *Biblical Archaeological Society*, 27 June 2020. See www.biblicalarchaeology.org/daily/ancient-cultures/ancient-israel/high-places-altars-and-the-bamah/.

> Will the Lord be pleased with thousands of rams, or with tens of thousands of rivers of oil? (Micah 6:7)[38]

To be sure, the prophets were not condemning the practice of offering *korbanot* itself; rather they attack it for becoming a substitute for goodness, morality, and respect for God:

> For I desire kindness not sacrifice; and the knowledge of God more than burnt offerings. (Hos. 6:6)

> I hate and despise your feast days, and I will not smell the sacrifices of your solemn assemblies.... But let justice roll down like waters, and righteousness like a mighty stream. (Amos 5:21, 24)

> For I did not speak to your fathers, nor did I charge them when I brought them out from the land of Egypt about matters of burnt offering and sacrifice. With this word did I charge them saying, Heed My voice and I will be your God. (Jer. 7:22–23)

These concerns recurred in the Second Temple period, prompting the sages to emphasize sincerity rather than size in the offering of *korbanot*:

> Whether offering a substantial sacrifice or a meager one; just as long as their heart is turned to heaven.[39]

Contrition in the one who offers the sacrifice was also praised in a highly dramatic way:

> R. Abba bar Yudan said: What God regards as unfit for sacrifice in an animal, God holds fit in a human being. In an animal, God regards as unfit one that is blind, or broken, or maimed,

---

38. See further, Abraham J. Heschel, *The Prophets* (Harper Perennial, 2001), 249–52.
39. Menaḥot 110a.

> or diseased...but in a human being God holds a broken and contrite heart to be fit for an offering.[40]

Ever since *korbanot* were first introduced, absolute clarity of intent was an essential element of the ritual:

> Anyone who has in mind a wrong thought while dealing with sacrifices transgresses a negative commandment, as it is written, "It is not his intention; it is rejected" (Lev. 7:18).[41]

Weaned Off Idolatry

Given the perennial problems with *korbanot,* it is possible to question their overall effectiveness. If they frequently failed to deepen religious conviction and they drew constant criticism from the biblical prophets, it seems difficult to comprehend why they were introduced in the first place. Maimonides responds to this challenge by presenting a radical reframing of the intended purpose of *korbanot*

For Maimonides, *korbanot* had a vital role to play in the Torah's robust response to the age-old problem of idol worship. Of the 613 commandments in the Torah, he determined that fifty-one of them dealt directly with the prohibition of idolatry.[42] He also explained how several more were instituted to oppose it,[43] and he determined that "most of the Torah's statutes (*ḥukim*), the reason for which is unknown to us, serve as a fence against idolatry."[44] Maimonides saw idolatry as an essential evil that was much worse than lackluster commitment, because it was a direct challenge to God's authority:

> Idolatry is equal to all the other commandments together... whosoever accepts idolatry denies the whole Torah, all the prophets... from Adam until the end of time.[45]

40. *Pesikta DeRav Kahana, shuva* 5, based on an interpretation of Psalms 51:19.
41. Maimonides, *Mishneh Torah, Hilkhot Pesulei HaMukdashin* 18:1; see also 15:3.
42. Ibid., *Hilkhot Avoda Zara,* introduction to the section.
43. Maimonides, *Guide for the Perplexed* 3:35.
44. Ibid., 3:49.
45. Maimonides, *Mishneh Torah, Hilkhot Avoda Zara* 2:4.

In opposition to this was the institution of *korbanot*. Maimonides explained that they were the secret weapon in the Torah's armory to fight idolatry. The practice of idol worship was pervasive in the ancient world, and centuries of slavery in the pagan culture of Egypt had taken its toll on the Israelites. Having lost much of their identity, they were mired in idolatry just like their masters.[46] They were considered to have sunk to the "49th level of impurity [out of 50]."[47] Even when God miraculously saved them at the splitting of the sea, many still clung to their idols to hedge their bets.[48] And despite hearing God at Mount Sinai, the Israelites still quickly slipped back into idolatry, worshipping a Golden Calf (Ex. 32:1–6). Clearly, kicking this habit was not going to be easy – hence the introduction of *korbanot*. This is Maimonides's thesis:

> The Israelites were commanded to devote themselves to the service of God... but the general custom in those days among all men, and the mode of worship in which the Israelites were brought up, consisted of sacrificing animals in temples which housed specific statues; to bow down to them and to burn incense before them.... So, it was in accordance with God's wisdom and plan... that He did not command us to give up and to discontinue all these manners of service. For to obey such a command would have been contrary to the nature of humanity, who generally cleave to that which they are used to....
>
> For this reason, God allowed these kinds of service to continue. God transferred to His service that which had formerly served as a worship of created beings, and of things imaginary and unreal, and commanded us to serve Him in the same manner: to build for Him a temple... to have an altar erected... to offer sacrifices to Him... to burn incense before Him. God forbade doing any of this worship for any other being.... By this divine plan the traces of idolatry were to be blotted out, and the truly great principle of our faith, the Existence and Unity of God, firmly

46. Ḥizkuni's comment on Deuteronomy 4:34, quoting Ezekiel 20:7.
47. Zohar Ḥadash, *Yitro* 39a.
48. Sanhedrin 103b, Rashi on s.v. *pislo shel Mikha*.

> established. This result was to be achieved without deterring or confusing the minds of the people by the abolition of the service to which they were accustomed.[49]

Banning every kind of sacrificial worship from the outset would have failed completely because it was culturally ingrained. The Tabernacle and *korbanot* were introduced to wean the Israelites off idolatry and to train them to worship the one true God instead. Thus, even though *korbanot* had their difficulties, they were still effective in distancing the people from the surrounding idolatrous practices.

The problem is that this approach seems to erase any essential religious significance for *korbanot* and reduces them to a pragmatic compromise. Do the many laws involved in *korbanot* have no timeless spiritual value? Aware of this challenge, Maimonides gave a compelling response. He compared the need to wean us off *korbanot* with the circuitous route that God led the Israelites on in the Exodus from Egypt:

> God did not lead them by way of the land of the Philistines though it was close, for God said, "Lest the people regret when they see battle and go back to Egypt"; so God turned the people round by way of the wilderness of the Sea of Reeds. (Ex. 13:17–18)

Slaves do not become soldiers overnight. Courage and independence take time to learn and take root. This, argued Maimonides, was God's approach to idolatry too. It is against human nature to abandon suddenly an embedded set of cultural attitudes and beliefs and to replace them with something new. Allowance must be made for people to adapt and learn to embrace a different perspective. Just as God took the Israelites on a roundabout route out of Egypt because that is all they could handle, so the Torah gradually guides its followers on a path toward correct worship, introducing certain laws that make the journey more manageable.[50]

---

49. Maimonides, *Guide for the Perplexed* 3:32.
50. Support for this gradualist approach can be deduced from Leviticus Rabba 22:8 and *Mekhilta DeRabbi Yishmael* 13:17.

It turns out that there is, after all, an inherent value to *korbanot* – their formidable educative power. This understanding complements the interpretations of *korbanot* presented earlier, which came from the Zohar, Nahmanides, and Rabbi Hirsch. They too were about bringing about a profoundly transformative mental change through symbolic representation and ritual.

Will *korbanot* be reinstated at some future time with the rebuilding of a Third Temple in Jerusalem? In his legal code, Maimonides is unequivocal this would be the case.[51] Some claim Rabbi Abraham Isaac Kook (1865–1935), the first chief rabbi of Israel, believed animal sacrifice would not return, but a thorough analysis of his writings seems to contradict this.[52] Though sacrificial rituals appear primitive to many modern readers, when placed in context and in proportion, it could be argued that they may yet have meaning and worth. We have seen that *korbanot* were valued for the deep psychological changes they could trigger. Might their visceral nature retain some ability to continue to do so today? And since *korbanot* were largely eaten, the amount burned up in obligatory sacrifice would be minuscule when compared to the shockingly large percentage of meat mentioned earlier that is discarded daily due to the excesses of modern consumerism.

Rather than imagining the consequences of a Third Temple, however, it is more instructive to see how Judaism actually coped when the Second Temple was destroyed by the Romans almost two thousand years ago, and animal sacrifice was suspended. The rabbis determined that the psychological impact of *korbanot* could still be accessed in two different ways. First, by studying their details and meaning:

> Whoever studies the *ḥatat* (sin offering) it is as if they offered a *ḥatat*, and whoever studies the *asham* (guilt offering) it is as if they offered an *asham*.[53]

---

51. Maimonides, *Mishneh Torah, Hilkhot Melakhim uMilḥemoteihem* 11:1.
52. A good online discussion can be found here: Ari Zivotofsky, *The Korbanot (OU Torah: Tzarich Iyun)*, https://outorah.org/p/33325/.
53. Menaḥot 110a.

Second, they determined that carefully reciting biblical and rabbinic texts concerning the *korbanot* as part of daily prayer could repair any breakdown in the relationship between the Jewish people and the Almighty:

> God said, "I have set the order of the *korbanot* so that as long as they continue to read it, it will be in My eyes as if they actually brought Me a *korban*, and I will forgive them."[54]

This is derived from the verse "Forgive all our sins... instead of calves we offer You our words of prayer" (Hos. 14:4).

These approaches further attest to the enduring educative power of the *korbanot*. Even contemplating them seriously is as effective as practicing them. As you will see, this is very helpful as we return to the issue of eating meat today.

Craving Meat

The Talmud rules that meat should not be consumed regularly, but only when one has a burning desire to eat it. "The Torah teaches proper behavior, that one should not eat meat except to satisfy a strong craving."[55] This is an unusual dietary law; a food should simply be permitted or prohibited. Why does craving matter here?

The law is derived from two consecutive verses in Deuteronomy that require careful analysis. The first is this:

> When the Lord your God enlarges your territory as He has spoken to you, and you say, "I shall eat some meat (*basar*)," because your soul craves (*te'aveh*) eating meat, then when your soul craves, you shall eat meat. (Deut. 12:20)[56]

54. Megilla 31b. These texts are recited each morning, toward the start of the prayer service. See *The Koren Shalem Siddur*, 42–53.
55. Ḥullin 84a.
56. See especially the comment of the Kli Yakar in which he concludes from the verse that meat consumption should not become habitual.

Notice the repetitive ping-ponging of two words here: meat, craves, meat, craves, meat. This is a literary device to accentuate the relationship between meat consumption and the psychological experience of intense craving.[57] The two words also occur together in an earlier story, in the book of Numbers. It concerns a rebellious element among the Israelites:

> The rabble that was in their midst felt a sharp craving (*taava*), and the Israelites also wept once more, and said, "Who will feed us meat (*basar*)?" (Num. 11:4)

Critical of these ravenous complaints, God sent a wind to carry a huge flock of quails from the sea into their camp:

> The meat was still between their teeth, it had not yet been chewed, when the Lord's wrath flared against the people, and the Lord struck a very great blow against the people. And the name of the place was called *Kivrot HaTaava*,[58] for there the people buried the people who had been craving. (Num. 11:33–34)

With the continued juxtaposing of "meat" and "craving," this episode seems to function as a precursor to the law in Deuteronomy, and the disdainful description of the insatiable Israelites communicates to us that craving meat to excess is wrong and dangerous. Returning to Deuteronomy, the second verse reads:

> If the place be far away from you that the Lord your God will choose to set His Name there, you may slaughter from your cattle and your flock that the Lord has given you, as I have commanded you, and you may eat within your towns when your soul craves. (Deut. 12:21)

---

57. The psychological factors involved in the craving for meat have recently become a significant area for academic research; see, for instance, Steve Loughnan, Brock Bastian, and Nick Haslam, "The Psychology of Eating Animals," *Current Directions in Psychological Science* 23, no. 2 (2014): 104–8.
58. The place name *Kivrot HaTaava* literally means "graves of craving."

This signals the end of the forty-year restriction in the wilderness, mentioned earlier, when the Israelites were permitted to eat meat only as part of a *korban*. The phrase "to set His Name there" refers to the central location chosen for offering *korbanot* in the Land of Israel. Initially this was the Tabernacle in Shiloh, and then later the Temple in Jerusalem.[59] The verse is pointing out that as the Israelites settled the land and spread across the country, most of them would no longer live near enough to this central location, making it impractical to offer a *korban* any time they wanted a meat meal. So, the verse introduces a concession to eating meat even without offering it as a *korban* first.

There is an important caveat to the concession: "You may eat within your towns *when your soul craves*." This implies that without the craving, you should not be eating meat at all when there is no *korban* involved. The Talmud derives two further restrictions from this verse:

> You might think a person is allowed to buy meat from the marketplace and eat it, so the verse says: "You shall slaughter from *your* herd and from *your* flock." And you might think a person is allowed to slaughter *all* their cattle and eat it, and *all* their flock and eat it, so it says "*from* your herd," i.e., not all your cattle, and "from your flock," i.e., not all of your flock.[60]

In other words, meat consumption should be limited to animals you already own, and you should not eat all of them. From the story of craving in Numbers and the restrictions in Deuteronomy, it is evident that eating meat just for its own sake is far from ideal. Meat eating was always meant to be part of the ritual of bringing an offering, with all the mental focus that entailed. To this day, *sheḥita*, the ritual method for slaughtering an animal to eat, is the same as that prescribed for slaughtering a *korban*. One is classified as *sheḥitat ḥullin*, "slaughter of non-sanctified animals," and the other *sheḥitat kodashim*, "slaughter of sanctified animals," but the method is identical.[61] This gives a clear indication that the Torah

59. Rashi's comment on Deuteronomy 12:9, based on Zevaḥim 119a.
60. Ḥullin 84a.
61. Ḥullin, the talmudic tractate about the laws of killing and eating kosher meat, and

always wants us to regard the consumption of meat within the broader context of bringing a *korban*.

Imagine if every time you wanted to eat a burger or a steak you first had to experience all the stages of the *korban* ritual – seeing the knife sharpened and checked to ensure minimal pain to the animal, watching the slaughter and the careful collecting of the blood, observing as the priests faithfully burned the meat on the altar and then divided up the rest. The encounter would have great psychological impact, and it would prevent you from taking the death of the animal lightly.

The way the Torah links slaughtering for a *korban* with slaughtering for food teaches us about how we should think about eating meat today. The lessons about *korbanot* from Nahmanides, Rabbi Hirsch, and others highlight the seriousness of taking an animal's life. The Torah's permission for us to satisfy our cravings for meat is clearly a concession, not an ideal; and the extent to which we eat meat must never go unchecked.[62] We should always be humbled by the sanctity of life.

Kosher, Caring, and Consumption

Does the Torah's permission to eat meat override all the animal welfare regulations discussed earlier? For instance, if animals are kept in poor conditions that cause them pain and stress, does this make them unkosher even before they are ritually slaughtered? Being precise, unkosher is the wrong terminology here. As long as the animals are not physically blemished, they can still be slaughtered and kosher. However, the issue here is the prohibition of *tzar baalei ḥayim*, "causing pain to live animals."

Rabbi Moses Isserles (the Rema, 1530–1572) states authoritatively that *tzar baalei ḥayim* does not apply if the animal is needed "for healing or other necessary purposes."[63] This includes slaughtering animals for life-saving medical research and for food. But how far does "necessary"

Zevaḥim, the tractate about the sacrificial Temple service for animals and birds, are to be found in the same Order of the Mishna, *Seder Kodashim*.

62. The Talmud (Pesaḥim 49b) states that an uneducated person should not eat meat. *Ben Yehodaya*, the commentary of Rabbi Yosef Ḥayim of Baghdad (the Ben Ish Ḥai), explains that one reason for this is because such a person will invariably yield to their cravings, so it would be better if they did not consume any meat at all.
63. See Rema's comment on *Shulḥan Arukh, Even HaEzer* 5:14.

extend? The Rema raises the question of plucking down, the soft layer of feathers close to a bird's skin, as it is ideal for insulating garments. He states that this is prohibited because plucking a bird for feathers while it is still alive is painful and cruel. Live-plucked down is a huge industry today, but Jewish law forbids it. It is not considered a necessity since thermal clothing can be manufactured in other ways.

This has implications for the appropriate treatment of animals in modern meat production. Animals today are often kept in cramped physical conditions while awaiting slaughter. Though the law of *tzar baalei ḥayim* does allow the slaughtering of animals for food, which is deemed necessary, it seems clear that treating them cruelly in the process is unacceptable. So, for example, the production of foie gras, by which ducks and geese are force-fed for extra fattening, is a contravention of *tzar baalei ḥayim.*[64] Animals need to be cared for and not mishandled on the way to slaughter. This is an important Jewish regulation for the modern abattoir to uphold.

The Talmud also tells a revealing story about R. Yehuda HaNasi.[65] A calf being led to slaughter broke away and hid its head in his cloak, trembling. "Go away," he said. "For this you were created." His lack of pity for the animal results in him being punished with years of physical ailments. His suffering only ends when, one day, he stops his servant from sweeping away some young weasels, saying, "Let them be," and quotes a verse from Psalms, "God's mercies extend to all His creatures" (Ps. 145:9). R. Yehuda was a leading figure in second-century Israel, so for the Talmud to recount a critical story about him in this way shows the extent to which unnecessary cruelty was condemned. We must never treat animals as mindless machines for producing meat.

In practice, Maimonides rules that it is enough for a healthy person to eat meat just once a week, on Shabbat. It is clear from his presentation that this is part of a lifestyle that emphasizes general restraint when it comes to consumption:

---

64. For a more in-depth halakhic and historical analysis of this issue, see Natan Slifkin, *Man and Beast: Our Relationships with Animals in Jewish Law and Thought* (Yashar Books, 2006), 200–205.
65. Bava Metzia 85a.

> An educated person should manage their financial affairs judiciously. They should eat, drink, and provide for their household in accordance with their funds.... The Sages have given direction as to the way to live. A person should eat meat only if they have a particular strong appetite for it, as it says, "If your soul should crave to eat meat" (Deut. 12:20). It is sufficient for a healthy person to eat meat just on one Shabbat to the next.[66]

Eating meat more than once a week is viewed more as a luxury than a necessity. The approach of Maimonides is rooted in the Talmud, which advised moderation for food, budgeting for clothing, and extra care and support for loved ones:

> A person should always eat and drink less than what is within their means; and they should dress in accordance with their means; and they should honor their family more than what is within their means.[67]

We now know that limiting meat consumption to once a week, if practiced on a large scale, would significantly reduce the demand for livestock and thereby considerably reduce the effects of climate change.[68] If we add what we have learned about the profound psychological impact of *korbanot,* and the restrictions on consumption due to craving and cruelty, then it is clear that the Torah has always urged us to care deeply for animals, pay close attention to slaughtering practices, and to consider thoughtfully how much meat we should eat.

---

66. Maimonides, *Mishneh Torah, Hilkhot Deot* 5:10.
67. Ḥullin 84b.
68. Bill McGuire, *Hothouse Earth: An Inhabitant's Guide* (Icon, 2022), 152; Joseph Poore and Thomas Nemecek, "Reducing Food's Environmental Impacts through Producers and Consumers," *Science* 360 (2018): 987–92.

Chapter 7

Is Collective Punishment Fair?

EXPLORING THE QUESTION

Just after 1 p.m. on Monday, August 26, 2019, Shai Ohayon was walking by the Segula junction in Petah Tikva when he was attacked. A man with a knife stabbed him three times and ran off. Magen David Adom teams quickly arrived to try to save Ohayon's life. They rushed him to the Rabin Medical Center, known as Beilinson, just a few minutes away, but he was pronounced dead soon after. Rabbi Shai Ohayon was married with four young children. He studied part-time in a kollel in Kfar Saba and worked to support his family. He was thirty-nine years old.

His murderer was Khalil Doikat, a resident of the Palestinian Authority–controlled town of Rujeib near Nablus. Doikat had been working on a building site near the junction, having entered Israel legally that morning with a work permit. Security forces swiftly apprehended him after the attack, and two weeks later he was charged at the Central District Court in Lod. The indictment stated that Doikat had planned to murder Israeli civilians or security personnel "for Palestine, the Palestinian people, the al-Aqsa Mosque, and for Allah." He had passed all the necessary background checks to obtain a work permit in Israel and was not associated with any terror groups. Doikat was forty-six years old with six children and was reported to suffer from some mental disorders.

In September 2020, the head of the IDF's Central Command, Tamir Yadai, signed an order for Doikat's family home to be demolished. Doikat's family petitioned the Israeli Supreme Court to cancel the order but in October the Court ruled two to one against the petition. The house was demolished on November 2, 2020.

The Israeli policy of house demolitions to fight terrorism is a controversial one but has firm legal authority.[1] In practice, house demolitions have been ordered only in response to lethal terror attacks. It has been estimated that about two thousand houses have been demolished in the last fifty years. Due to questions about its effectiveness, the policy was suspended temporarily in 2005, but following a resurgence of terror attacks in 2014, the policy was fully reinstated. Fifty houses have been either fully or partially demolished since then:

> The rationale underlying the house-demolition policy is that would-be terrorists might not commit attacks if they know that their actions would incur harm to the homes of their families, considering in particular the centrality of the home in Palestinian culture. Moreover... family members of terrorists would be more keen to "keep an eye" on potential terrorists in order to avoid the demolition of the family house (a consideration which may offset the social prestige enjoyed by families of so-called "martyrs" in Palestinian society).[2]

The house demolition policy appears to be an example of *collective punishment*. This is a type of retribution in which a group is made to suffer for the crimes of an individual or subgroup. Their family, friends, community, or even their entire society is punished collectively. Even though other members of the group might not have been involved in the criminal actions, the group is still held partially responsible. In

---

1. The policy is grounded in Article 119 of the Defence (Emergency) Regulations (1945) enacted by the British Mandatory Government in response to the Arab revolt in the then British-controlled Palestine.
2. Amichai Cohen and Yuval Shany, "House Demolition at the Israeli Supreme Court: Recent Developments," *LAWFARE* blogpost, January 14, 2019. See www.lawfareblog.com/house-demolition-israeli-supreme-court-recent-developments.

this case, the family of the terrorist is being punished for a crime they did not commit.

The counterargument is that demolishing a terrorist's house is justified because all those living in the home are in some way accessories to their illegal actions and therefore share some degree of responsibility. There is also data arguing for the effectiveness of the policy of house demolitions as a counterterrorism tactic when used selectively.[3]

History is filled with examples of rulers and governments meting out collective punishments to maintain order, protect society, or assert their authority:

> Although collective punishment is prohibited by international law, it is widely practiced throughout the world, including by the most democratic and liberty-minded countries. Indeed, no system of international deterrence can be effective without some reliance on collective punishment. Every time one nation retaliates against another, it collectively punishes citizens of that country.[4]

Economic sanctions are another form of collective punishment. According to the United Nations Charter (chapter 7), the UN Security Council has a mandate by the international community to apply such sanctions, but not military force.[5]

The moral justification and lasting efficacy of collective punishment continues to be intensely debated. How can a group be held accountable for the criminal act of an individual, an act of which they were unaware? Though unaware, might they be partly responsible through close association with the culprit? Must their punishment be proportionate to the crime? Can collective punishment be vindicated by its effectiveness as a deterrent? Does a recognition of collective responsibility detract from the principle of individual responsibility?

---

3. Efraim Benmelech, Claude Berribi, Esteban F. Klor, "Counter-Suicide-Terrorism: Evidence from House Demolitions," *The Journal of Politics* 77, no. 1 (2015): 27–43.
4. Alan Dershowitz, *The Case for Israel* (Wiley, 2003), 167.
5. "United Nations Charter, Chapter VII: Action with Respect to Threats to the Peace, Breaches of the Peace, and Acts of Aggression," United Nations [accessed April 28, 2022], www.un.org/en/about-us/un-charter/chapter-7.

The Torah contains several episodes involving collective punishment. In the story of Sodom and Gomorrah, Abraham challenged God's decision to punish the region collectively for their wrongdoing:

> Will you also destroy the righteous with the wicked? Perhaps there are fifty righteous inside the city... shall the Judge of all the earth not act justly? (Gen. 18:23–25)

God listened to Abraham's appeal, but only down to ten righteous people (Gen. 18:32–33); lower than that would still spell destruction, and that is what happened (Gen. 19:24–25).

Collective punishment is administered on an even larger scale in the Exodus narrative. This is evident from the last of the ten plagues:

> And every firstborn in the land of Egypt shall die, from the firstborn of Pharaoh sitting on his throne to the firstborn of the maidservant who is behind the millstones.... And it happened at midnight that the Lord struck down every firstborn in the land of Egypt, from the firstborn of Pharaoh sitting on his throne to the firstborn of the captive who was in the dungeon. (Ex. 11:5, 12:29)

Many Egyptians probably supported their king and participated in persecuting the Israelites, but did that necessitate the death of every single maidservant's and prisoner's innocent child? And did a six-hundred strong elite chariot division *all* have to be "drowned in the Reed Sea" (Ex. 15:4)[6] to thwart Pharaoh's stubborn refusal to release the Israelites?

After forty years in the desert, the Israelites were called upon to dispense collective punishment in conquering the land of Canaan. For blocking their passage, the kingdoms of Sihon and Og were annihilated, "until none was left remaining" (Deut. 3:3). Then the divine instruction was given that if the Israelites met resistance from a city in their invasion, they should "strike every male with the edge of the sword" and take the women, children, and animals as plunder (Deut. 20:13–14). An even

6. See also Exodus 14:7, 28. Pharaoh's obsession is evident from his dismissal of his advisors' dire warning: "Do you not yet know that Egypt is lost?" (Ex. 10:7).

harsher instruction was given for cities inhabited by one of the seven idolatrous nations in the region:

> You shall not let a soul stay alive. You shall utterly destroy the Hittites and the Amorites, the Canaanites and the Perizzites, the Hivites and the Jebusites, as the Lord your God has commanded you. (Deut. 20:16–17)[7]

Finally, an everlasting collective punishment was reserved for the Amalekites:

> Remember what Amalek did to you when you came out of Egypt, how he attacked from the rear… when you were faint and weary… So, when the Lord your God has given you rest from all your enemies around… you shall blot out the remembrance of Amalek from under heaven; you shall never forget it. (Deut. 25:17–19)

Was *every* member of the seven idolatrous nations irredeemably evil? And why should the Amalekites be held eternally responsible for the crimes of one generation of their ancestors? This all seems so heartless and unfair. The Torah is extremely forthright in its accounts of collective punishment, whether administered directly by God (against Sodom and Gomorrah, and Egypt) or divinely commanded (against the seven Canaanite nations and Amalek). Is this meant to be a policy model for how the Jewish people and the State of Israel should behave today? Given the highly questionable morality of collective punishment, why is the Torah so unremittingly insistent upon it?

RESPONDING TO THE QUESTION

Each of the biblical narratives outlined above – Sodom and Gomorrah, Egypt, Canaanite nations, and Amalek – has been analyzed by our talmudic and medieval sages in distinct ways, as they strove to make moral sense of the use of collective punishment. We will focus on the ethical considerations and important limiting circumstances they identify in

7. Ibn Ezra explains why the seventh nation, the Girgashites, are not mentioned here.

each of these four episodes. Then the issue of divine authority with respect to collective punishment will be considered. This will redirect the discussion to the analysis of two further biblical narratives in order to determine a reasoned Jewish perspective on this contemporary moral challenge.

Destroying Sodom and Gomorrah

The decision to wipe out the cities of Sodom and Gomorrah was the culmination of a long process. We first learn of Sodom's evil ways when Abraham separates from his nephew Lot (Gen. 13:13). The Talmud gives a detailed list of the many crimes of Sodom and Gomorrah, which can be read as a serial account of the gradual moral decline of their culture.[8] This fits well with the fact that it was only after two decades that God determined to punish them.[9] In that time, not only had Abraham rescued them from a foreign invasion, but he had settled nearby, monitored their regression, and, according to midrash, cared for those whom they had expelled.[10] So when God revealed to Abraham the plan for their destruction, Abraham should have gladly cheered on. But instead, he asked that they be spared. Why?

According to Rabbi Samson Raphael Hirsch, Abraham believed that a few righteous souls had the potential to reverse the fate of Sodom and Gomorrah:

> Abraham does not say, "perhaps there are fifty righteous *in* the city" but "*in the midst* of the city"... the city could be saved not for one who keeps to their own four walls, in haughty pride of their own superiority, who gives up on the masses and just looks on at their ruinous moral lapses, who thinks they have done quite enough if they save themselves and their own household.

---

8. Sanhedrin 109a–b recounts twenty stories of their cruelty, the final one being the shameless murder of a kind young girl who showed kindness to a beggar. This finally precipitates divine intervention.
9. We were told that Abraham is seventy-five years old just before we first learn of Sodom (Gen. 12:4), and that he is ninety-nine in the episode just before its destruction (Gen. 17:24).
10. See Genesis 14, Sanhedrin 109b, and Genesis Rabba 52:1.

> Such a person Abraham would not class as righteous, he would not consider that they had at all fulfilled the duty which lies on every good person in bad surroundings.... His righteous person is to be found "in the midst of the city" and in lively connection with everything and everybody. They never cease admonishing, teaching, warning, bettering wherever and however they can. They take everybody and everything to heart, they never despair, are never tired of trying, however distant the hopes of success may be.... For fifty of these Abraham dared to hope the whole might be spared.[11]

Just as the immoral culture of Sodom and Gomorrah had taken decades to spread, so too could it be gradually undone by a small but committed group. That was Abraham's hope. The key question was: How many good people would be enough to turn the tide?[12] Abraham bargained God down to just ten, for even such a small number, "in the midst of the city," could make a profound difference.

Whether or not those ten existed, the underlying assumption of this whole episode is that the culture of Sodom and Gomorrah had been created and bound together by the influence of its members on one another. This could have been positive or negative, but either way, it made them *collectively responsible* for how they eventually turned out. And this, in turn, implies that they were susceptible to the possibility of collective punishment. Social influencers knit together the fabric of a society and enable it to be viewed collectively. Thus, God's treatment of Sodom and Gomorrah was a direct consequence of the detrimental way in which they affected each other. Rabbi Hirsch reveals the story to be a lesson in the productive and destructive powers of collective responsibility.

---

11. Samson Raphael Hirsch, *The Pentateuch, Vol. I, Genesis,* trans. Isaac Levy (Judaica Press, 1971), 325–26, commenting on Gen. 18:24.
12. Maimonides discusses how one individual's change of heart could positively or adversely affect an entire city (*Mishneh Torah, Hilkhot Teshuva* 3:1–3).

Plaguing and Drowning the Egyptians

We know that Egyptian society was intensely hierarchal. It could be aptly represented by a pyramidal structure. On the top was the Pharaoh, the theocratic monarch; below him, a small group of court advisors; below them, a larger group of priests and scribes; then an even larger military leadership; then merchants and craftsman; then peasant farmers and herders; and at the very bottom, a large population of slaves and prisoners.[13] This chain of power and authority was a social order based on ancient Egypt's concept of *ma'at* (balance), which came from the gods and kept the world functioning in a harmonious equilibrium.[14] There was little social mobility because it was the accepted natural order of things that each stratum of society was fixed.

This might explain why the Torah's description of the tenth plague makes the point that it affected the most privileged firstborn in the land, Pharaoh's son, just as much as the firstborn of the lowliest of servants and prisoners. The plague served to upend the accepted hierarchy by treating the offspring of every stratum equally, thus exposing the injustice of Egyptian society. In fact, all ten plagues disturbed the pecking order by increasingly affecting every stratum of society. At first Pharaoh's magicians were able to shield him and themselves from harm, but eventually everyone succumbed (Ex. 7:11, 22, 8:14, 9:11). The plagues were the great equalizer.

This approach is reinforced by a rabbinic explanation as to why the firstborn of servants and prisoners also died in the tenth plague. They too were culpable, "because they rejoiced in the Egyptian decrees against the Israelites."[15] They had so internalized the hierarchical nature of Egyptian society that they were glad to look down upon another group less fortunate than themselves, rather than empathizing with their hardships. This perspective serves to make the collective punishment of the Egyptians more intelligible.

---

13. Joshua J. Mark, "Social Structure in Ancient Egypt," *World History Encyclopedia* (last modified September 21, 2017), www.worldhistory.org/article/1123/social-structure-in-ancient-egypt/.
14. Norman Cohn, *Cosmos, Chaos and the World to Come* (Yale University Press, 2001), 11–16.
15. *Midrash Tanḥuma, Bo* 7.

Meanwhile, the collective drowning of the Egyptians could be justified as a legitimate military maneuver to halt an imminent and potentially fatal attack. However, it was still recognized as a sad moment. The rabbis taught that the angels were about to break into song when God silenced them, declaring: "How dare you sing for joy when My creatures are dying?"[16] This teaches us that even in victory, we should be disturbed by the collective punishment our enemies suffer.[17]

The first-century rabbinic sage Samuel the Younger would often quote the verse "If your enemy falls do not rejoice" to warn people against such gloating, and rebuke them if they did.[18] This is one reason for the tradition of dipping a finger in the second cup of wine on Seder night and tapping it onto a plate when reciting each of the ten plagues.[19] It recalls the necessary but tragic suffering of the Egyptians as our ancestors gained their freedom.[20]

Conquering Canaan

The instructions Moses conveyed from God to the Israelites in the campaign to conquer Canaan had a caveat: "When you approach a city to do battle against it, you shall call out to it for peace" (Deut. 20:10).

The pursuit and acceptance of a peaceful surrender was always preferred to the disastrous alternative. According to Nahmanides, this applied to all the cities they confronted, even those inhabited by the seven idolatrous nations.[21] He quotes the Jerusalem Talmud: "Those [cities] who wish to make peace, let them come forward and make

---

16. Megilla 10b and Sanhedrin 39b.
17. Winston Churchill expressed this dramatically in the inscription that begins each of the six volumes of his monumental work, *The Second World War*: "Moral of the Work – In War: Resolution; In Defeat: Defiance; In Victory: Magnanimity; In Peace: Goodwill."
18. Mishna Avot 4:19, quoting Proverbs 24:17. Both Maimonides and Rabbi Obadiah Bartenura explain the Mishna in this way.
19. *Shulḥan Arukh, Oraḥ Ḥayim* 473:7.
20. For similar reasons, the practice is to recite only "Half Hallel" on the last six days of Passover. We curtail our joyous celebratory praise of God as we are mindful of the cost to human life (*Beit Yosef, Oraḥ Ḥayim* 490; *Yalkut Shimoni, Emor* 654).
21. Nahmanides on Deuteronomy 20:10. He disagreed with Rashi, who argued that the peace option was not available to the seven idolatrous nations.

peace; those who wish to leave, let them leave; and those who wish to make war, let them make war."[22] As it turned out, when the Israelites did invade, only one city chose to make peace, the inhabitants of a second decided to leave, and the remaining thirty-one cities of Canaan opted to wage war (Josh. 11:19–20, 12:9–24).

Thus, all but two of these cities were subject to God's instruction to wipe out all the inhabitants mentioned earlier, and this seems to be a prime example of collective punishment. The Torah gives the reason for their destruction: "So that they will not teach you to act according to all their abominations that they performed for their gods, so that you will sin to the Lord, your God" (Deut. 20:18). God's concern was the pernicious influence that the pagan worship and immoral practices of the Canaanite nations would have on the Israelites. Indeed, the Torah frequently speaks of their ethical failings.[23]

Importantly, the verse in Deuteronomy also implies that if they were to abandon idolatry and not influence the Israelites then they would be spared. This, in fact, is the understanding of the rabbis: "If they repented, they were not killed."[24] So even after overtures of peace had been rejected and war begun, if any individuals then rejected idolatry and accepted Israelite authority, then they would be allowed to live. It seems that many did, as evidenced by the fact that years later King Solomon levied taxes on these populations when he was building the Temple in Jerusalem (I Kings 9:15, 20–22).[25] Maimonides even adds that, based on the Torah's words "and you shall seek out and investigate" (Deut. 13:15), two wise Israelite emissaries would be despatched to an idolatrous city to warn them of the consequences of their actions and to encourage them to repent.[26] As with Sodom and Gomorrah, we see that the Torah recognizes the possibility of a small group influencing the masses in order to avert collective punishment.

---

22. Y. Shevi'it 6:1.
23. Exodus 23:23–33, 34:11–18; Leviticus 18:1–5, 24–30; Numbers 33:55–56; Deuteronomy 7:1–6, 22–26, 9:4–5, 12:29–13:1, 13:7–11, 18:9–13. See also Michael Hattin, *Joshua: The Challenge of the Promised Land* (Maggid, 2014), 176–83.
24. *Sifre* Deuteronomy 202.
25. This argument is given by Nahmanides in his comment on Deuteronomy 20:10.
26. Maimonides, *Mishneh Torah, Hilkhot Avoda Zara* 4:6.

Annihilating Amalek

God's unique command to wipe out the entire nation of Amalek appears to be even more extreme and unrelenting than any of the three narratives already discussed. However, Maimonides assigns Amalek the same status as the seven idolatrous nations in Canaan. Their mass destruction could thus not be considered until an overture of peace had been offered.[27] Similarly, giving individuals within such a group the opportunity to repent, as mentioned earlier, might be extended to the Amalekites too.

An alternative, historically based approach can be derived from the Talmud, which states: "Sennacherib, king of Assyria, came long ago and mixed up all the nations."[28] This refers to the mass resettlement policy employed by the Neo-Assyrian regime (ninth to seventh centuries BCE) in order to deter the nations it had conquered from dissent and to assimilate them into the expanding empire.[29] Since then, neither Amalek nor any other nation that the Israelites had faced could be identified.[30] Of course, this has prevented the possibility of collective punishment ever being applied to the Amalekite nation but, we must admit, this seems to rely on a technicality rather than addressing the questionable morality of collective punishment.

There is, though, an additional aspect to consider: Today we generally relate to national identity as a social and historical construct, rather than an innate biological trait. Though each nation has its own influential cultural traditions, we do not assert that every single person of that nation has a built-in national consciousness that completely determines their attitudes and morality.[31] Recognizing ourselves as autonomous

27. Ibid., *Hilkhot Melakhim uMilḥemoteihem* 6:1–4.
28. Berakhot 28a, based on Isaiah 10:13.
29. Gareth Brereton, ed., *I am Ashurbanipal, King of the World, King of Assyria* (Thames and Hudson, British Museum, 2018), 103.
30. Nachum Rabinovitch, *Responsa Melomdei Milḥama* (Maaliyot, 1993), 22–25.
31. Note, however, recent analyses of how various cultural groupings think in specific ways, for instance, Richard E. Nisbett, *The Geography of Thought* (Nicholas Brealey, 2003) and Jonathan Haidt, *The Righteous Mind* (Penguin, 2013). See also Daniel Goldhagen's disturbing *Hitler's Willing Executioners: Ordinary Germans and the Holocaust* (Abacus, 1997).

individuals who are capable of thinking and behaving independently is a recent phenomenon.

Until a few centuries ago, the populations of most kingdoms and empires were under the controlling authority of their rulers. They acted as one because they recognized the power of a small ruling family or class as a fact of life. Such autocracies and oligarchies were like the hierarchical society of ancient Egypt described earlier. This could be why the Torah commanded errant cities and nations to be punished collectively. The populations accepted their governors as superior and did not think to question their imperial or religious right to rule.

The loss of distinct national identities might be what the Talmud is driving at when it describes the mixing of nations policy of ancient Assyria. That empire was the very first to conquer the entire Middle Eastern region, spanning the fertile crescent from Egypt to Babylonia. This was subsequently achieved by the Persians, the Greeks, and then the Romans. The sheer size of these empires, containing so many different cultures, meant that it was even harder to establish a cohesive society. Indeed, ancient empires often had to stamp out local rebellions. Thus, the gradual demise of strictly deferential societies, which began with the resettlement and merging of nations and has ultimately made way for the modern culture of individualism, could explain why the ethics of collective punishment in the Torah seems so at odds with modern sensibilities.

Viewing a group of people as having a uniform identity that can justify collective punishment has not disappeared. Such bias continues in contemporary culture and is reinforced by popular literature and cinema. There are, for instance, no decent orcs in Tolkien's *Lord of the Rings*, and no elf is evil. Similarly, decades of American Westerns reassert the binary division between "goodies" and "baddies." Gradually, though, these simplistic divisions are being questioned. Every stormtrooper in the original Star Wars trilogy was irredeemably evil and could be killed with impunity by the plucky heroes, but in the recent sequels, one removes his helmet to reveal a human face and a personality capable of change. Similarly, as the Harry Potter saga neared its conclusion, J. K. Rowling revealed that members of the thoroughly wicked Slytherin house could in fact choose to be good.

Divine Authority

We have seen how rabbinic interpretation makes the collective punishment within these ancient narratives more palatable. Even so, lessons cannot be applied for the modern use of collective punishment because there is an essential difference. The punishments meted out in these Torah narratives come directly from God. It was God's decision to crush Sodom and Gomorrah in Genesis and the Egyptians in Exodus. And it was God's command in Deuteronomy that determined how the Israelites should treat the Canaanite and Amalekite nations.

Is it appropriate for us to replicate divinely instituted collective punishment? At first glance it might seems so, as the Talmud does endorse the principle of *imitatio Dei*, emulating God:

> What is the meaning of, "You shall follow after the Lord your God" (Deut. 13:5)? Can a person follow the Divine Presence?... Rather, the verse means for us to follow the *attributes* of God. Just as God clothed the naked [i.e., Adam and Eve (Gen. 3:21)]... so should you. Just as God visited the sick [i.e., Abraham after his circumcision (Gen. 18:1)]... so should you. Just as God comforted mourners [after Abraham's death (Gen. 25:11)]... so should you. And just as God buried the dead [i.e., Moses (Deut. 34:6)]... so should you.[32]

Notice, however, that all these examples are concerned with imitating the caring side of God. There is no notion of "because God drowned the Egyptians for enslaving the Israelites, so you should drown your oppressors," or "because God caused the earth to swallow up Korah and his followers, so you should bury alive the leaders of a religious rebellion." Only attributes of loving-kindness are appropriate for emulation.[33] Likewise, we are taught, "Become holy for holy am I, the Lord,

---

32. Sota 14a. See also Abba Saul's comment, "Just as God is gracious and compassionate, so you shall be gracious and compassionate" (Shabbat 113b).
33. Maimonides points out that all thirteen of God's divine attributes (Ex. 34:6–7), which are meant to be emulated, are based on mercy, except for one which relates exclusively to the eradication of idolatry (*Guide for the Perplexed* 1:54).

your God" (Lev. 19:2), holiness being another positive form of divine imitation. Hence, divinely instructed collective punishment should not directly inform human policy.

Additionally, even though the Israelites were given divine sanction to mete out collective punishment on the Canaanite nations, nevertheless, there was a stipulation. When Joshua was appointed to succeed Moses, God commanded that whenever Joshua found it necessary to go to war,

> he shall stand before Eleazer and inquire of him for the ruling of the *urim* before the Lord. By it shall they go out and by it shall they come in – he and all the Israelites with him, and all the community. (Num. 27:21)

Contained in the breastplate of the High Priest, the *urim* (also known as *urim vetumim*) was a miraculous device for revealing God's response to a particular request, especially a military matter.[34] Thus Joshua required specific divine confirmation every time he wanted to launch a military campaign that might inflict collective punishment, even though this policy was already authorized in principle.[35]

> The rabbinic texts appear to understand God as playing the role of the Commander-in-Chief, with the sole authority to decide whether or not Israel should go out to battle in any given situation.[36]

34. Exodus 28:30 and Yoma 73b.
35. An excellent analysis of the role of the *urim vetumin* in determining shared accountability can be found in Joshua Berman, "Collective Responsibility and the Sin of Achan," in *Radical Responsibility: Celebrating the Thought of Chief Rabbi Lord Jonathan Sacks,* ed. Michael J. Harris, Daniel Rynhold, and Tamra Wright (Maggid, 2012), ch. 3.
36. Daniel H. Weiss, "Do Biblical Commands Make People Violent?" in *Scripture and Violence*, ed. Julia Snyder and Daniel Weiss (Routledge, 2021), 38.

It should also be noted that "ever since the early prophets died, the *urim vetumim* was nullified";[37] thus the possibility of divinely legislated wars ended over twenty-five hundred years ago. All this confirms that collective punishment is the purview of God rather than humanity.

There are, however, two stories in which collective punishment was meted out by biblical heroes without any divine involvement whatsoever. An in-depth analysis of these disturbing narratives will shed light on their ethical dimensions and whether justification can be found for contemporary acts of collective punishment.

The Self-Righteous Revenge of Simeon and Levi

> You have brought trouble upon me – you have made me odious to the inhabitants of the land.... I am few in number, and if they join forces and attack me, I and my household will be destroyed. (Gen. 34:30)

These were Jacob's damning words to his sons Simeon and Levi on hearing that they had put to the sword all the men of an entire city – in order to rescue their sister Dinah from Shechem, son of Hamor, the prince of the region, who had raped and kidnapped her.[38] Later, on his deathbed, Jacob cursed their rage and the massacre it unleashed (Gen. 49:6–7). Nahmanides elaborates:

> Jacob became angry at Simeon and Levi when they killed all the men of the city because the brothers acted unjustly, for the men of the city had committed no sin against them at all.[39]

This would seem to be a prime example of the immorality of collective punishment. But despite Jacob's condemnation, Simeon and Levi still got the last word. They told their father, "Should our sister be treated like a whore?" (Gen. 34:31). Though the crude language betrays their

---

37. Mishna Sota 9:12.
38. The full story is told in Genesis 34.
39. Nahmanides on Genesis 49:5.

unresolved rage, its assertiveness attests to their confidence in the virtue of their actions. What then was their justification?

Maimonides explains that the prevailing Noahide law required Shechem to be punished for raping Dinah and that she be returned to her family, but because all the men of the city were negligent in enforcing the law, Simeon and Levi were obliged to administer the death penalty to them.[40] Nahmanides agrees that the death penalty was deserved, but claims that it was because the men of the city, like all Canaanites, were themselves immoral idolaters.[41]

These approaches find justification in the actions of Simeon and Levi by explaining how the men of the city were personally deserving of punishment. Though reasonable, both seem to downplay the brothers' reckless rage, Jacob's disapproving response, and the lack of any hint of righteous motive in the narrative. Nevertheless, they do expose an aversion to collective punishment. Maimonides and Nahmanides prefer the city's men to be guilty, rather than to view Jacob's sons as slaughtering the innocent.[42]

What led to this slaughter in the first place? Having abducted Dinah, the prince and his father approached Jacob to make a deal. Shechem was infatuated with Dinah, and so to resolve the situation Hamor proposed a merging of clans in which intermarriage and joint settlement would be mutually beneficial (Gen. 34:9–10).[43] Jacob was silent, but his sons agreed to the offer on one condition: if all Hamor's men would be circumcised, just as all Jacob's men were, "then we will

---

40. Maimonides, *Mishneh Torah, Hilkhot Melakhim uMilḥemoteihem* 9:14.
41. Nahmanides on Genesis 34:13.
42. Note, however, the Maharal (Rabbi Judah Loew of Prague, d. 1609) argues that Shechem's actions, coupled with the city's complicity, were effectively an act of war against Jacob and his family, allowing for a military response of collective punishment (*Gur Aryeh* on Gen. 34:13). But if so, then the previous comments concerning the need for divine confirmation in warfare would then apply here also.
43. Dinah's lack of agency in this story is disturbing for modern readers. It should be noted, however, that the Torah obliges a man who raped an unbetrothed girl to pay a heavy fine to her father and to marry her (Deut. 22:28–29), which Shechem offers to do at any cost (Gen. 34:11–12). In biblical society a woman in this predicament would be unmarriageable, so the law guarantees her social and economic security, if not her happiness.

become one people" (Gen. 34:16). The text says that Jacob's sons were acting "deceitfully" (*bemirma*) (34:13) because they really had no intention of merging clans; instead, they planned to rescue Dinah while Hamor's men were recovering from their circumcisions. But in their rage, Simeon and Levi preempted their brothers, descending upon the city to massacre all the men (Gen. 34:25).

There is an alternative approach that might explain the use of collective punishment in this case. Maybe the brothers really were open to the possibility of merging clans. This is not such an outlandish idea, as one midrash points out:

> When it says, "then we will become one people" (Gen. 34:16), the brothers meant the following: "If in truth and sincerity you will be circumcised then you will be accepted as one people with us." Our Sages have ruled: A non-Jew, or slave, that marries a daughter of Israel – their offspring are accepted as Jews.[44]

In other words, the merger was offered sincerely, as long as Hamor and his people would be equally sincere. This makes more sense – especially due to the pivotal role circumcision plays in the story. *Brit mila* was the supreme sign of God's covenant with Abraham and his descendants, so it is questionable if the brothers would really mess with such a sacred ritual and use it for a cheap ruse. It is much more likely that agreeing to be circumcised would prove an honest commitment to an ongoing joint venture. It was a test of trust, not a deception.[45]

If this is true, then what went wrong? Why did Simeon and Levi renege on the agreement? It is because Hamor and his people reneged first. You see, when Hamor and Shechem returned to their city to report about the potential merger, they presented it very differently from the actual conversation they had had with Jacob and his sons. There was no mention of Shechem's abduction of Dinah. Instead, they began by talking

44. *Midrash Seḥel Tov* on Genesis 34:16.

45. Indeed, Onkelos, author of the ancient Aramaic translation of the Torah, translates *bemirma* as *beḥokhmeta*, i.e., "wisely," implying that the brothers had acted wisely rather than deceitfully in order to check out the sincerity of their potential partners.

about trading opportunities, described the intermarriage as something they would control,[46] and only briefly mentioned circumcision before again talking business in an aggressive manner: "Their livestock, their possessions and all their animals, will they not be ours?" (Gen. 34:23). The speech was made publicly at "the gate of their city" (Gen. 34:20), so in all likelihood Jacob's sons heard about it, which would have signaled to them that Hamor was using his son's infatuation with Dinah as a commercial opportunity.

This was not a merger – it was a takeover, pure and simple.[47] Such deception would have infuriated Simeon and Levi as they felt their covenantal symbol had been abused, and so they took their swords to the city. Jacob was surely glad that the fake merger was revealed, but he was worried about the reputational fallout of Simeon and Levi's rash action.

This interpretation teaches us something new about collective punishment. The men of the city were not completely innocent because they had all agreed to be circumcised and were therefore in on the takeover bid. However, their leaders had given a false impression about the deal and this ultimately led to their collective downfall. The issue then becomes this: Collective punishment might be justified when all involved are partially responsible for the crime being punished, but does it also include instances when involvement was based on incomplete or incorrect information? This is often the case when a nation chooses to follow a leader but is not party to all the political decisions being made on its behalf. Are its citizens, then, still responsible for accepting this leadership and thus deserving of collective punishment?

King David Suppresses His Enemies

The first half of II Samuel chapter 8 tells of how King David expanded and secured his kingdom by defeating many of the surrounding enemies. In short order he subdues the Philistines in the southwest, Moab in the

46. Rashi on Genesis 34:16 points out that they switched who would have control of the inter-clan marriage arrangements from what they had presented to Jacob and sons (Gen. 34:9).
47. This approach is supported by the Talmud (Sota 22b) when it names the people of Shechem as one of seven types of posers who pretend that they are righteous.

southeast, Hadad-Ezer king of Zobah, and the Arameans in the north. They all become vassal states paying a regular tribute to Israel. But the single-verse account of vanquishing Moab stands out here for its cruelty:

> He [David] also defeated Moab; he then made them lie down on the ground and measured them off with a cord; he measured out two lengths of cord for those who were to be put to death, and one length for those to be spared; and Moab became a tribute-bearing vassal to David. (II Sam. 8:2)

First let us understand clearly what King David did. Having defeated Moab in battle and accepted their surrender, he then decided to slaughter two-thirds of their army. He does this dramatically by forcing them all to lie down on the ground in equal rows. He has three cords that each measure a third of the length of each row, which he uses to measure out two thirds of each row, i.e., two cord lengths, and then he has all those put to death.

This highlights the coldness of the account and brutality of his actions. David does not do this to any other army he defeats, only that of Moab. We are not told how many Moabite soldiers were slaughtered this way, but if their army was similar in size to others mentioned in the chapter, then it is likely that the death toll was over fifteen thousand. This is devastating. How could David, the beloved king of Israel and the author of so many of our sensitive psalms, have ordered this massacre?

The Talmud points out that David had a special relationship with Moab because his famous great-grandmother Ruth was a Moabitess: "Hence the popular saying: from the very forest itself comes the handle of the axe that will destroy it."[48] But David had an even more recent tie to Moab. Before becoming king, he had been forced to flee from King Saul, who was insanely jealous of the young warrior and wanted him dead. David's parents were also in danger, so he asked the king of Moab to protect them (I Sam. 22:1–5).

---

48. Sanhedrin 39b.

We never hear of David's parents again, and some midrashim suggest that the Moabite king had them killed once David had left.[49] This is one explanation as to why David cut down two-thirds of Moab's army: it was vengeful payback. Here then is another prime example of collective punishment meted out by man rather than by God. The Moabite soldiers had fought David in battle, but they were not involved in the death of his parents.

Rabbi Isaac ben Judah Abarbanel (1437–1508, Portugal) argues that David's actions served as a warning to Moab never to cross Israel again.[50] Could such a warning justify the collective punishment of the soldiers? Kings of that era were expected to assert their power brutally to ensure that their vassals would not attempt a rebellion. Moab did appear to remain a loyal vassal of Israel for a very long period, because there is no further mention of them until the battle with King Mesha of Moab over 130 years later (II Kings 3:4). David's ruthless punishment of Moab may have secured decades of respite from hostilities in which many Israelite and Moabite soldiers would have been killed. Thus, collective punishment might be acceptable if it acts as an effective deterrent preventing future casualties. Callous though it sounds, philosophers continue to debate the ethics of this kind of argument.[51]

The Zohar has a different approach. Through divine inspiration, David's choice of who should die miraculously fell upon only the Moabite soldiers who were already deserving of death for other (undisclosed) reasons.[52] It might be that the Zohar finds a long-lasting deterrent insufficient justification for cruel collective punishment, and therefore searches for an alternative to validate David's actions. Again, as with Simeon and Levi, we see rabbinic discomfort with punishing the many for the misdeeds of the few. Note also that the Zohar's approach relies on God, whom we must assume would never punish unfairly. Here again, collective punishment is reserved for God.

---

49. Numbers Rabba 14:1. See also *Midrash Tanḥuma* (Buber), *Vayera* 25.
50. Abarbanel's comment on II Samuel 8:2.
51. See, for example, Masahiro Morioka, "The Trolley Problem and the Dropping of Atomic Bombs," *Journal of Philosophy of Life* 7, no. 2 (2017): 316–37.
52. Zohar 3:190a–b.

There is a telling postscript to this story. Once David had secured the kingdom, what did he plan to do next? We know the answer because he told Solomon, his son and heir:

> My son, I wanted to build a House for the Name of the Lord My God. But the word of the Lord came to me, saying, "You have shed much blood and fought great battles; you shall not build a House for My Name for you have shed much blood on the earth in My sight." (I Chr. 22:7–8)

Rabbi David Kimchi, known as the Radak (1160–1235, France), explains in his biblical commentary that the phrase "much blood" was meant to include the innocent blood that David spilled during his lifetime because of his decisions. This would encompass the massacre of the Moabite troops. Radak points out that we never read anywhere in the Bible that God actually said this to David; we only learn about it when David tells his son. This, he suggests, might have been what David felt in his heart. David saw himself as undeserving of building a Temple for God because of all the blood on his hands. While he might have been justified in all the battles he fought and the people he killed, in his own mind David was not without sin. And, most importantly, the biblical text wants us to know this. This point is crucial to understanding the morality of collective punishment: *even if it can be rationalized, it still sullies those involved in doing it.*

The Jewish Spirit

Back in 1992 there was another instance in which the family home of a convicted terrorist was ordered for demolition by the IDF. In Bat Yam, Mohammed Alamarin had stabbed to death Helena Rapp, a fifteen-year-old girl. Then, too, there was an appeal to the Supreme Court by the terrorist's family not to destroy the house, but that order was upheld by the court, two to one. Justice M. Cheshin, who had delivered the minority opinion, did accept the legal basis for house demolitions, but argued against it in this case, referring to three biblical passages in support of his perspective.[53] First, he quoted a verse in Deuteronomy:

53. "HCJ 2722/92 – Alamarin v. IDF Commander in Gaza Strip." Decided June 14, 1992.

> Fathers shall not be put to death because of their sons, and sons shall not be put to death because of their fathers; a person shall be put to death for their own sin. (Deut. 24:16)

He then pointed out that this law was upheld by Amaziah, king of Judah, in the eighth century BCE:

> He slew his servants who killed the king, his father, but he did not put the sons of the killers to death, in accordance with what is written in the book of the law of Moses that God commanded him as follows: fathers shall not be put to death because of their sons, and sons shall not be put to death because of their fathers; a person shall be put to death for their own sin. (II Kings 14:5–6)

Finally, he quoted a vision from the prophet Jeremiah:

> In those days people shall no longer say: "Fathers have eaten unripe fruit and their sons' teeth shall be set on edge," but a person shall die because of their own sin. (Jer. 31:28–29)

These verses, Justice Cheshin wrote, epitomize the "Jewish spirit which has carried us on its wings throughout the generations, and on which we have suckled with our mother's milk." For him, the Jewish spirit is the morality of the Bible, which ultimately rejected collective punishment. Does this concur with the rabbinic tradition? The Talmud broached the issue by contrasting two other biblical verses:

> R. Yossi bar Ḥanina stated: Moses said, "God visits the sin of the parents upon the children and grandchildren" (Ex. 34:7),[54] but

---

VERSA: Opinions of the Supreme Court in Israel [accessed 28.4.22]: https://versa.cardozo.yu.edu/opinions/alamarin-v-idf-commander-gaza-strip.

54. Surprisingly, this phrase comes in the wake of Moses learning God's thirteen attributes of mercy. The phrase is almost identical to one occurring a few chapters earlier, in the Ten Commandments: "For I am the Lord your God, a jealous God who visits the sin of fathers upon sons to the third and fourth generations" (Ex. 20:5).

> then the prophet Ezekiel came and annulled this, as it says, "Only the soul that sinned shall die" (Ezek. 18:4).[55]

In other words, originally Moses was taught that God approved of collective punishment, but then, centuries later, the prophet Ezekiel declared instead that God would now only punish individuals for what they themselves did. R. Yossi's assertion that Ezekiel abrogated a Torah principle is startling. However, the foundations of Ezekiel's position can be found in the Torah itself. Recall, for instance, the verse quoted by Cheshin from Deuteronomy (24:16), which is patently opposed to collective punishment. Additionally, when God threatened to put an end to all the Israelites who had joined the coup led by Korah, Moses and Aaron said: "God of the spirits of all flesh, should one man offend and against all the community You rage?" (Num. 16:22). And God acquiesced.

Thus, although the Torah appears to express both points of view, it was not until Ezekiel that a conclusive position was firmly established. The Talmud reinforced the prophet by clarifying that "God visits the sin of the parents upon the children to the third and fourth generation" (Ex. 20:5) only "when the children retain their parents' sinful practices."[56] Otherwise the children are blameless. The conclusion is clear: the biblical ideal is individual rather than collective punishment. Justice Cheshin was correct in his characterization of the Jewish spirit.

In 2014, a group of eight human rights organizations petitioned the Israeli Supreme Court that the policy of house demolitions should be discontinued and made unlawful. Included was an argument that the policy violated fundamental principles of Jewish law. The petition was denied by the court unanimously. The full text of the case makes for fascinating reading, especially the in-depth discussion of relevant traditional Jewish sources.[57] Three key points were made by justices Rubinstein, Hayut, and Sohlberg. First, the policy is grounded on effective *deterrence* rather than

55. Makkot 24a.
56. Berakhot 7a. See also Sanhedrin 27b.
57. Case code: HCJ 8091/14. The ruling was written in Hebrew, but a (non-binding) translation is available. See *Hamoked: Center for the Defense of the Individual v. Minister of Defense* (December 31, 2014), https://versa.cardozo.yu.edu/opinions/hamoked-center-defense-individual-v-minister-defense.

collective *punishment*. Second, it is not illegal, under international law as there is an exemption for military need. Third, and crucially for our discussion, it is not a contravention of Jewish law because the policy allows for the destruction of *property* but not the taking of *human life*, which would be patently unlawful.[58] This distinction is essential: it is evident to all that Jewish law rejects administering any form of collective *capital* punishment.

Difficult Decisions

The parents of Helena Rapp will never get her back, and the children of Rabbi Shai Ohayon will never see their father again. Israel's policy of house demolitions cannot fix the past, but it can act as a deterrent for the future and result in the saving of more innocent lives. Although Israel's Supreme Court upheld the policy in 2014, Justice Rubinstein made an important final comment:

> The use of a tool the ramifications of which on a person's property are so grave, justifies a constant examination of the question whether it bears the expected fruit... therefore, I am of the opinion that State agencies should examine from time to time the tool and the gains brought about by the use thereof, including the conduct of follow-up and research on the issue, and to bring to this court in the future.[59]

When facing the evils of war and terrorism, difficult decisions need to be made. The best ethical path is not always immediately apparent and must be regularly revisited.[60] Even when there is the alternative option of using non-capital collective punishment, this grave decision should not be taken lightly, and careful reconsideration of the situation might lead to not carrying it out at all.

Several examples of collective capital punishment do occur in the Torah but, as we saw, those instructed by God are not something

58. See HCJ 8091/14; Sohlberg point 4 and Rubinstein points 24 and 27, respectively.
59. See HCJ 8091/14; Rubinstein point 28. See also Hayut point 6.
60. The ethics of military conflict are analyzed carefully in Michael Waltzer's *Just and Unjust Wars*, 5th ed. (Basic Books, 2015).

to emulate. Meanwhile, both King David and Jacob's sons Simeon and Levi took it upon themselves to mete out collective punishment. Though some rabbinic justification was given for their actions, we saw the recriminations and self-recriminations they suffered as a result, and how personal motives clouded their judgment. The moral cost of taking such actions can never be ignored. In the end it appears to be too much.

The damaging effect of delivering collective punishment is even implied by the Torah. When describing this kind of punishment for an idolatrous city, it says, "Thus the Lord will turn back from His blazing wrath and give you compassion, and be compassionate to you" (Deut. 13:18). In his Torah commentary, Rabbi Ḥayim ibn Attar (1696–1743, Morocco), known as the Ohr HaḤayim, explains that the phrase "give you compassion" was a special assurance by God that any cruelty generated in the Israelite consciousness through destroying an idolatrous city would be replaced with compassion.[61] This is a clear admission that meting out collective punishment is so psychologically harmful that it would require God's help to return those involved back to health. However, this divine assistance is limited to an occasion when the punishment was divinely endorsed in the first place. It cannot be relied upon in any other circumstances. Thus, the general administration of collective punishment should be strenuously avoided.

Ultimately, we saw the Talmud's conclusion as to the biblical standard: a person may only receive punishment for their own sin, never for anyone else's. Each of us is *individually* responsible for our own choices and accountable for our own actions.

61. Ohr HaḤayim's comments on Deuteronomy 13:18.

Chapter 8

Isn't Being the Chosen People a Little Bit Racist?

EXPLORING THE QUESTION

Equality has become a core principle of Western societies in our age. We expect everyone to have equal opportunity in making the most of their lives, and that all persons will be treated equitably by the law of the land. Discrimination against anyone because of their gender, age, race, appearance, religion, disability, or sexual orientation is accepted as wrong and offensive.

In the UK, this is enshrined in the 2010 Equality Act, which protects people from discrimination in the workplace and in wider society.[1] Discrimination against employees is also illegal in US federal law, and a more comprehensive Equality Act was passed by the US House of Representatives in 2021. The US perspective is, of course, founded on the 1776 American Declaration of Independence: "We hold these truths to be self-evident, that all men are created equal."[2] Nations across the

1. "Equality Act 2010 Guidance" *GOV.UK,* the UK Government website www.gov.uk/guidance/equality-act-2010-guidance.
2. Since its creation, the exact meaning of "all men" has been questioned. Though some have argued that it was meant to exclude women and children, it is generally recognized that, in its historical context, "all men" referred to humanity as a whole.

globe are gradually updating their anti-discrimination laws, addressing different forms of inequality on a selective or comprehensive basis.[3]

Given this common culture of non-discrimination, it is surprising that a form of elitist superiority appears to exist at the heart of Judaism. From a young age, Jews are taught that they are the "Chosen People." In the Torah blessings recited every morning are the words "Blessed are You, Lord our God ... who has chosen us from all the peoples and given us His Torah."[4] This special status is further detailed in the *Amida* prayer recited every Shabbat morning, "the descendants of Jacob whom You chose,"[5] and in the Musaf *Amida* prayer recited on Jewish festivals: "You have chosen us from all the peoples. You have loved and favored us."[6] Indeed, being "chosen" is a recurring theme in the book of Deuteronomy:

> And because God loved your fathers, He chose their seed after them and brought you out from Egypt. (Deut. 4:37)

> Not because you are more numerous than all the peoples did God desire you and choose you ... but because of God's love for you. (Deut. 7:7–8)

> Only your fathers did God desire to love them, and He chose their seed after them, chose you from all the peoples, as this day. (Deut. 10:15)

God chose the Jews out of love for us and our ancestors and, as a result, we are treasured by God:

This statement underpinned Elizabeth Cady Stanton's advocacy for women's rights, Abraham Lincoln's mission to abolish slavery, and Martin Luther King's demand for equality for African Americans.

3. "Equality and Non-discrimination," *United Nations and the Rule of Law* www.un.org/ruleoflaw/thematic-areas/human-rights/equality-and-non-discrimination/.
4. *The Koren Shalem Siddur*, 8.
5. Ibid., 486.
6. Ibid., 810.

> For you are a holy people to God your Lord; it is you God has chosen to be to Him as a treasured people, from all the peoples that are upon the face of the earth. (Deut. 7:6 and 14:2)[7]

Becoming God's "treasured people" (*am segula*) is first mentioned in the Torah in the introduction to the Revelation at Mount Sinai. On behalf of God, Moses told the Israelites:

> Now, therefore, if you will obey My voice indeed, and keep My covenant, then you shall be My own treasure from all the peoples; for all the earth is Mine." (Ex. 19:5)

Rashi explains that the phrase "for all the earth is Mine" comes to teach that, unlike the localized gods of the ancient world, each confined to its region or country of worship, the Israelite God is the Creator of all the nations of the world and is free to choose any of them to be His special treasure. Rashi then concludes with a disturbing statement, which he voices in God's name: "For in My eyes, and before Me, they [the other nations] are as nothing."[8]

The complete dismissal of every other nation at the very moment when an everlasting covenant between God and the Israelites was being established is an undeniable indication of the centrality of Jewish chosenness in the Torah. How can we explain this elitist ideology?

Expressions of God's special affinity with the nation of Israel can be traced back further, to before the Exodus from Egypt. God instructed Moses: "You shall say to Pharaoh, 'So said God: My firstborn child is Israel'" (Ex. 4:22). Rabbi Hezekiah ben Manoaḥ (1250–1310, France), known as Ḥizkuni, explained in his Torah commentary that all of the nations of the world are God's children, but the Israelites are God's most beloved firstborn because God had in mind to create them before any other nation.[9] This is yet another affirmation of Israel's preeminence

7. The Hebrew wording in the verses is almost identical.
8. Rashi's comment on Exodus 19:5.
9. Ḥizkuni's comment on Exodus 19:5.

and traces Jewish chosenness way back to the beginning of time, as a key element of Creation itself.

Unlike other countries, God also pays particular attention to the Land of Israel:

> For the land, which you enter to take possession of, is not as the land of Egypt, from where you came out, where you sowed your seed and irrigated it by foot, as in a garden of vegetables. But the land that you are going over to possess is a land of hills and valleys; it is watered from the rain of the skies. It is a land that the Lord your God cares for; the eyes of the Lord your God are always upon it, from the beginning of the year to the end of the year. (Deut. 11:10–12)

All year round, God will take special care of the Land of Israel, ensuring its bounty, for this is the country given to the Jewish people.[10] And to complement the "Chosen People," Deuteronomy repeatedly refers to a "Chosen Place," "the place the Lord your God will choose,"[11] which will be the central sanctuary and act as a rallying point for all the people in unified worship.

Our daily prayers also remind us of the special love, care, and attention that God has bestowed upon us. For instance, before the *Shema* come the words: "You have loved us with great love, Lord our God, and with surpassing compassion You had compassion on us."[12] This connection is closer than with the rest of humankind, as Rabbi Akiva used to say: "Beloved are humankind for they were created in God's image.… Beloved are Israel for they are called God's children.[13]

As a result, the idea of chosenness has always been a standard teaching within Jewish education, instilling pride and confidence in each new generation of Jewish children. But such pride can give way to

---

10. See, for example, Exodus 23:31, Numbers 27:12, 33:53, and Deuteronomy 1:8, 3:18, 8:10.
11. See Deuteronomy 12:5, 11, 14, 18, 21, 26, 14:23, 24, 25, 15:20, 16:2, 6, 7, 11, 15, 16, 17:8, 10; 18:6, 26:2, 31:11.
12. *The Koren Shalem Siddur*, 96.
13. Mishna Avot 3:14, referring to Deuteronomy 14:1.

arrogance and feelings of superiority, especially when that seems to be the inference from the biblical and liturgical texts quoted so far. Surely, there is a real danger of ethnocentrism, the strong identification you have for your own group that leads to feelings of rejection and stereotyping of other groups.

The principle of election, whereby one nation, Israel, was chosen for a special relationship with God, also led to animosity from the other religions that venerated the Bible. As Christianity grew, it advocated the doctrine of supersessionism whereby the church saw itself as *Verus Israel* ("the true Israel"), replacing the Jewish people's chosenness with its own:

> Western Christians have been particularly prone to the flattering belief that they are God's elect. During the eleventh and twelfth centuries, the crusaders justified their holy wars against Jews and Muslims by calling themselves the new Chosen People, who had taken up the vocation that the Jews had lost.[14]

The refusal of Jews to acquiesce to this replacement theology bred strands of Christian antisemitism. In a similar vein, the Islamic tradition saw itself as the most authentic expression of the monotheism begun with Abraham, superseding both Judaism and Christianity, which led to battles with both.

The European Enlightenment negated such pretensions of divine favoritism by forging universalistic ideals of reason and equality. The Jews, however, dared to double down on their distinctiveness and made every effort to remain a separate people. In the twentieth century this exposed them to intense and growing hatred. George Bernard Shaw was vociferous:

> Those Jews who still want to be the chosen race (chosen by the late Lord Balfour) can go to Palestine and stew in their own juice. The rest had better stop being Jews and start being human beings.[15]

---

14. Karen Armstrong, *A History of God* (Vintage, 1993), 68.
15. *The Literary Digest*, October 12, 1932.

The Nazi ideology of Aryan racial superiority viewed the Jews and their distinctiveness as an existential enemy, bent on world domination and thus in need of total eradication:

> The Jew will never spontaneously give up his march towards the goal of the world dictatorship... the Jewish people preserve the purity of their blood better than any other nation on earth. Therefore, the Jew follows his destined road until he is opposed by a force superior to him. And then a desperate struggle takes place to send back to Lucifer him who would assault the heavens.[16]

Such convoluted, sickening, and violent forms of antisemitism continue to this day, and Jewish chosenness is invariably exploited as a weapon in this hatred. So why hold on to such a potent idea that is prone to abuse?

There are clearly a whole host of challenging issues related to the idea of a Chosen People. Why would the *Adon Olam*, the Lord of the whole universe, choose to forge an eternal bond with one particular nation? That seems awfully limiting and parochial, and bound to antagonize every other nation. If God is the Creator of *all* people, how could He prefer *some* people more than others?

In our modern world where human equality and the recognition of individual rights is paramount, independent of color, creed, or any other distinguishing factors, how can Judaism continue to venerate a God who excludes 99.8 percent of the world's population from an intimate relationship? Isn't it more than a little bit racist to follow a faith that believes that God has chosen one race or group above all others?

RESPONDING TO THE QUESTION

The centrality of the Chosen People concept in the Jewish tradition cannot be overstated; yet its apparent opposition to modern sensibilities is especially vexing. So, in response, we will examine three different approaches to this complex issue. Though all are grounded in traditional sources, each represents a distinct stage in the understanding of what it

16. Adolf Hitler, *Mein Kampf*, Hutchinson's Illustrated Edition, trans. James Murphy (1939), 562.

has meant to be God's Chosen People. First, we will look at several allegorical rabbinic texts which analyze the question of exactly who chose whom; then we will face up to some disturbing Jewish notions of racial superiority from medieval Europe; and finally we will uncover the underlying purpose of chosenness and its continued importance for today.

Stage 1: Choosing God

As we have seen, there are multiple verses in the Torah that refer to God selecting the Israelites to be His Chosen People. However, it is intriguing that we find rabbinic sources which assert that God's choice was actually a response to the Israelites and their ancestors *choosing God.*

The process began with Abraham. God first appeared to him when he was seventy-five years old, telling him to leave his home and to journey to a foreign land to become a great nation (Gen. 12:1–4). The instruction seems to come out of the blue, as we have heard almost nothing about his early life (Gen. 11:26–32). Why then was he chosen to fulfill a divine mission?

The sages, sensitive to subtle nuances in the biblical text, fill in the gap and elaborate on Abraham's early years. We learn how he rejected his father's idolatry, and defied the regional despot Nimrod and almost lost his life, all the while gradually coming to comprehend the existence of the Creator.[17] This is what motivated God finally to approach him. Indeed, one midrash has it that God could only create the world once He knew that in the future there would be such a man as Abraham:

> The matter may be compared to a king who was planning a building project; but while digging to lay firm foundations, he found only swamps and mire. At last, he hit on solid rock, so he said, "Here I can build." Similarly, when God was about to create the world, He foresaw the sinful generation of Enosh, and the generation of the Flood, and said, "How shall I create the world when I see these wicked ones will rise and provoke Me?" But when God saw that Abraham would one day rise, He said, "Behold, I

17. See Genesis Rabba 38:13; Maimonides, *Mishneh Torah, Hilkhot Avoda Zara* 1:2. These accounts are discussed further in chapter 9.

> have found the solid rock on which to build and base the world." Thus, Abraham is called a *tzur* (rock) (Is. 51:1–2) and the people of Israel are called *tzurim* (rocks) (Num. 23:9).[18]

This story teaches us that it was the rock-solid monotheistic conviction of Abraham that inspired God to initiate the Creation project, confident that he could be relied upon to fulfill the divine mission. It was Abraham's choice of God that was the starting point, and not the other way around.

Abraham instilled this commitment to God in his son Isaac, who in turn passed it on to Jacob. All of Jacob's children shared that devotion, and they and their descendants became known as the "children of Israel," the foundation of the Jewish people. God responded positively to this loyalty, "God has declared His words to Jacob, His statutes and laws to Israel. He has done this for no other nation" (Ps. 147:19–20). A second allegorical midrash expounds these verses by responding to the question why God gave hundreds of commandments for the Israelites to keep, while requiring the other nations to observe only the seven Noahide laws:

> This can be compared to a king who had before him a well-laid table with all kinds of dishes on it. When his first servant entered, he gave him a slice of meat, to the second he gave an egg, to the third a vegetable, and so on. But when his son came in, he gave him all that was before him, saying, "To the others I gave only one portion, but to you I give all." Similarly, God gave the idolatrous nations only a few commandments, but when Israel arose, God said to them, "Behold the whole Torah is yours," as it says, "He has done this for no other nation" (Ps. 147:20).[19]

While this midrash seems dismissive of other nations, its intended focus is clearly the special relationship that God feels toward Israel. Though at Mount Sinai it is God who initiates the giving of the Torah to the

---

18. *Yalkut Shimoni, Balak*, 766:5.
19. Exodus Rabba 30:9.

Israelites, in a third pivotal midrash we learn that this only occurs *after* it had been rejected by the people of every other nation:

> At first God went to the children of Esau and asked, "Will you accept the Torah?" "What is written in it?" they said. God answered, "Do not murder" (Ex. 20:13). They replied, "Ruler of the universe, this goes against the grain. Our father [Esau] … led us to rely only on the sword because his father told him, 'By your sword you will live' (Gen. 27:40) – so we cannot accept the Torah."
>
> Then God went to the children of Ammon and Moab, and asked, "Will you accept the Torah?" "What is written in it?" they said. God answered, "You must not commit adultery" (Ex. 20:13). They replied, "Ruler of the universe, our very origin is in adultery, as it says, 'Thus were both the daughters of Lot with child by their father' (Gen. 19:36) – so we cannot accept the Torah."
>
> Then God went to the children of Ishmael. God asked them, "Will you accept the Torah?" "What is written in it?" they said. God answered, "You must not steal" (Ex. 20:13). They replied, "Ruler of the universe, it is our very nature to live off only what is stolen … of our forebear Ishmael, it is written, 'And he will be a wild ass of a man: his hand will be against every man, and every man's hand against him' (Gen. 16:12) – so we cannot accept the Torah."
>
> There was not a single nation among the nations to whom God did not go, speak, and, as it were, knock on its door asking whether it would be willing to accept the Torah. At long last God came to ask Israel. They said, "We will do and we will listen" (Ex. 24:7).[20]

This often-quoted midrash implies a strong critique of the other nations for their refusal to accept the Torah's moral constraints. Though, like the previous midrash, it may border on ethnocentrism, this misses the whole point of the allegory. It is about a lover trying to find a partner who is willing to receive what they have to give. Only with Israel does

20. *Sifrei*, Deuteronomy 343.

God experience an unconditional commitment. The fact that they do not ask any questions, unlike the other nations, is a sign of their suitability. The goal is the formation of a loving relationship in which we see God and Israel choosing each other.

A fourth midrash finds the origin of God's choosing Israel in their need to be rescued, time and again:

> Abraham was pursued by Nimrod, so God chose Abraham, as it says, "You are the Lord the God who chose Abram" (Neh. 9:7); Isaac was pursued by the Philistines, so God chose Isaac (Gen. 26:28).... Jacob was pursued by Esau, so God chose Jacob, as it says, "For God chose Jacob for Himself" (Ps. 135:4).... Moses was pursued by Pharaoh, so God chose Moses, as it says, "Moses His chosen one" (Ps. 106:23).... Saul was pursued by the Philistines, so God chose Saul, as it says, "See you him whom God has chosen" (I Sam. 10:24). Israel was pursued by the nations, so God chose Israel, as it says, "And God has chosen you to be His own treasure" (Deut. 14:2).[21]

Here we are told about a series of biblical heroes who needed rescuing, with each being saved because God "chose" them. This culminates in God choosing the children of Israel as a whole and, as a result, will always rescue them from any nation that threatens them. The story portrays God as a noble prince who never fails to come to the rescue of his beloved in distress. Notice, though, that each time, the dire straits of the beloved are a result of *their* choices to commit to God. Thus, Nimrod only chases Abraham *because* Abraham has rejected idolatry, etc. Here we see chosenness as a divine response to the vulnerability of Israel, both individually and collectively, for having chosen to follow God.

All four of these midrashim – and there are many more – serve to dramatize the deep and affectionate relationship between God and Israel. Through allegories and biblical quotations, each explores another aspect of that relationship. These are impassioned love stories, not objective

21. Leviticus Rabba 27:5.

accounts or conceptual presentations. In these dramas, the other nations are only mentioned as a foil in the divine romance with Israel.

Like all lovers, the partners feel that they are made for each other. This mutual affection is elegantly expressed in the renewal of the covenant at the end of the Torah: "You have proclaimed today the Lord to be your God.... And the Lord has proclaimed you today to be to Him a treasured people" (Deut. 26:17–18). The Talmud elaborates:

> God said to Israel: You have made Me the sole object of your love in the world, as it says, "Hear, O Israel, God is our Lord, God is One" (Deut. 6:4). And I shall make you the sole object of My love in the world, as it says, "And who is like Your people Israel, one nation on earth" (I Chr. 17:21).[22]

Lasting loving relationships are always exclusive. In fact, what makes the relationship special is that it is not shared with anyone else. The repeated rebuffs of the other nations in the biblical and rabbinic texts confirm this intense relationship between God and Israel.

One final midrash makes this eminently clear, justifying itself with a verse from Isaiah:

> God told Israel: You are a unique nation to Me, set apart from the nations of the world.... That is why it is written of them, "All the nations are as naught before God, as nothing and emptiness are they considered by Him" (Is. 40:17).[23]

The context of this verse is all-important. The northern kingdom of Israel had been destroyed, with ten tribes sent into exile. The downtrodden southern kingdom of Judah feared the same fate, so Isaiah desperately needed to find words of consolation. He had to reassure them that they were not abandoned and that God still cared for them. This is what you do for the one you love. You tell them no one else matters.

---

22. Ḥagiga 3a–b.
23. Leviticus Rabba 27:7.

God's relationship with Israel is the great love story of the Bible. Three times when chosenness is mentioned in Deuteronomy, God's love for our ancestors and for us is given as the reason (Deut. 4:37, 7:8, 10:15).[24] The Song of Songs is traditionally understood as the most vivid expression of this love.[25] When lovers are caught up in an embrace, it is not always apparent who is the initiator and who is the recipient. Both are both. Hence, say the rabbis, "We do not know if God chose Israel or if Israel chose God."[26] We are as much a choosing people as a chosen one. This loving mutuality is the first stage of the story of chosenness.

Stage 2: The Choicest People

The destruction of the Second Temple in 70 CE was the end of Jewish sovereignty for almost nineteen centuries. Though there was always a presence in Israel, Jewish communities spread and grew in Babylon, then into the Islamic lands and Christian Europe. At times they lived in peace and prosperity, but they also experienced prejudice and persecution and, in extreme cases, expulsion.

In this period, the concept of chosenness took on a new form, informed by two important sources. One was the *Kuzari,* a famous book of Jewish thought written by the physician, philosopher, and poet Judah HaLevi in twelfth-century Spain. The other was the Zohar, the foundational book of Jewish mysticism that appeared a century later, also in Spain, published by Moses de Leon. In both works we find striking expressions of a superiority of Jew over non-Jew.

In the *Kuzari*, HaLevi repeatedly describes an innate difference between Jews and gentiles: "God chose them as His people from all nations of the world and allowed His influence to rest on all of them" (1:95). This distinction, which applies to all Jews, is not just conceptual or idealistic; for HaLevi it exists on a physical level:

---

24. See an interesting discussion of God's love for Israel in Shira Weiss, *Joseph Albo on Free Choice* (Oxford, 2017), ch. 6, "The Choice of Israel."
25. Maimonides, *Mishneh Torah, Hilkhot Teshuva* 10:3.
26. *Sifrei,* Deuteronomy 312. See discussion in Ephraim Urbach, *The Sages: Their Concepts and Beliefs* (Magnus Press, 1979), 529–31.

> You know that from the primal elements gradually evolved metals, and then plants, and then animals, and then humankind, and then the treasure (*segula*) of humankind. The whole progression took place for the sake of this treasure. (2:44)

HaLevi gives the biblical phrase *am segula*, "treasured people" a racial quality. The Jewish people – men, women and children – are a different order of existence from the rest of humanity:

> The sons of Jacob were distinguished from other people by divine qualities, which made them, so to speak, an angelic caste. (1:103)

Does this preclude conversion to Judaism, or can the convert also gain these "divine qualities"? HaLevi's answer is surprising and further cements his view of the intrinsically biological nature of the Jewish people:

> Any non-Jew who joins us unconditionally shares our good fortune, without, however, being quite equal to us... because we are the treasure of humankind. (1:27)

In what way then is a convert not equal?

> Those who become Jews do not take equal rank with born Israelites, who are specially privileged to attain prophecy, while the former can only achieve something by learning from them, and can only become pious and learned, but never prophets. (1:115)

Jews, then, are superior from birth, a distinct species in nature, higher than all other forms of life, with prophetic powers, and positioned just below the angels.[27] If simply left unexplained, the undertones of HaLevi's approach are deeply concerning. But before broaching this, it is important

27. As Henry Slonimsky describes it, the *Kuzari* offers "an elaborate theory of an innate superhuman distinctiveness inhering in the Jewish people and amounting to a special soul-form... the climax towards which everything converges is the notion

to note similar ideas in the Zohar. In a presentation about the mystical component of sexual relations and birth, the Zohar also addresses the innate distinction between Jew and gentile:

> When coupling occurs below, the blessed Holy One sends a certain form – like a human visage – imprinted and engraved with an image (*tzelem*), poised above that union.... In that image the child will be created... as it is written, "God created the human species in His image" (Gen. 1:27). That image remains present with them until they issue into the world. Once they do, in that image they will grow.... Throughout the world, there is not a single union without an image. But as for holy Israel, this image is holy, entering into them from a holy place; whereas for the other nations, an image enters into them from those evil species, from the side of impurity. Consequently, a person must not mingle their image with the image of a gentile since one is holy and the other impure.[28]

That humankind was created in God's image is normally read as the great equalizer, but the Zohar uses it to differentiate between Jew and non-Jew because the "image" of each comes from the opposite place. One has a pure origin, the other impure. And this metaphysical distinction has physical ramifications. Sexual relations between Jew and non-Jew are essentially wrong because they merge opposing spiritual forces. The holiness of the chosen is sullied by impurity. A further distinction is made in death:

> Come and see the difference between Israel and other nations. Among Israel, when a person dies, they defile the whole house

---

of Election, and of the unique and supernatural character of the Jewish people and its history" (Slonimsky, "Judah Halevi: An Introduction," in *The Kuzari*, translated from the Arabic by Hartwig Hirschenfeld [Schocken Books, 1964], 25).

28. Zohar 3:104b.

> and the body is impure; whereas a gentile does not defile anyone else nor are they impure when they die.[29]

This is because, says the Zohar, when a Jew dies, their holy image leaves them, and so the body that is left becomes impure and can cause defilement. But a gentile was never holy in the first place:

> They are impure in all aspects of impurity: their image is impure, their spirit is impure. And since these impurities abide within them, they are entirely impure and it is forbidden to approach them. When they die, all these impurities depart from them and the body is left without defiling impurity.[30]

Although this perspective is based on a single talmudic opinion that was vigorously contested,[31] the Zohar brings in a metaphysical dimension, which has a significant practical consequence: Jews and gentiles should not interact *at all* because they are carriers of conflicting spiritual forces. This is a recurring theme in the Zohar and is described as a consequence of chosenness:

> Happy are Israel in that God has chosen them above all peoples, and for the sake of His love has given them true laws, planted in them the tree of life, and made His Divine Presence abide with them. Why? Because Israel are stamped with the holy impress on their flesh (circumcision), and they are marked as being His.... Therefore, all who are not stamped with the holy sign on their flesh are not His, and they are marked as coming from the side of impurity, and it is forbidden to associate with them.[32]

The implications for conversion to Judaism are even more extreme here than in Judah HaLevi's formulation, for now conversion courts

29. Ibid.
30. Ibid.
31. Yevamot 60b–61a, and see comments of *Tosafot* and Rosh there.
32. Zohar 3:72b–73a.

metaphysical conflict. The essential impurity of a non-Jew makes the process of them becoming a Jew either incomplete or impossible. One way out of this conundrum was to assert that all converts are actually in possession of a lost Jewish soul that was originally present at Mount Sinai, and received the Torah, but was only now finding its way back into the Jewish people.[33]

These ideas of the *Kuzari* and the Zohar, which imply a kind of racial superiority, were picked up in some later traditional Jewish writings.[34] How then to explain this disturbing strand of Jewish thought? Once again, appreciating the historical context is vital: Judah HaLevi was a teenager when the First Crusade erupted in 1096. In fact, his whole life was overshadowed by the relentless military conflicts between Christian and Muslim armies as they fought to control both Spain and the Holy Land. In one poem he wrote, "Whenever they fight their fight, it is *we* who fall.... The enemies battle like wild beasts."[35]

Pope Urban II urged the faithful Christians of Europe to join arms in liberating the city of Jerusalem from the so-called "Muslim infidels" who had conquered it more than four centuries earlier. But along the way, these crusaders encountered several Jewish communities. Caught up in religious fervor and taking advantage of an opportunity for easy spoil, they attacked them, murdering Jews in the thousands. "Whenever they fight their fight, it is *we* who fall." HaLevi had a point:

> Jews of Europe... witnessed shocking violence at the hands of the supposedly noble Crusaders. In the Rhineland, women, children and the elderly had been butchered in a sudden escalation of anti-Semitism.... Jews were paying the price for the refocusing of western Europe's manpower and attention towards the east. The bloodlust was directly linked to the idea that the Jews

33. Rabbi Hayim Joseph David Azulai (the Ḥida), *Medaber Kadmot*, 15. This is based on the phrase *ger shenitgayer*, "a convert who converts," Yevamot 97b. See also Shabbat 146a.
34. E.g., Rabbi Moses Hayim Luzzatto, *The Way of God* 2:4:1; Rabbi Shneur Zalman of Liadi, *Tanya*, end of ch. 1 and beginning of ch. 2, quoting earlier works.
35. As quoted in Henry Slonimsky's introduction to *The Kuzari*, 21.

were responsible for Jesus' crucifixion and that the land of Israel should be held by the Christians of Europe.[36]

Every year on Tisha Be'Av, Ashkenazi Jews still recite two *kinot* (laments) for the destruction of Jewish communities during the First Crusade.[37] Though Jerusalem was seized by the Christians in 1099, it was a huge ongoing effort to defend it, and more crusades followed. The Muslims under Saladin eventually recaptured it in 1187, which led to a retaliation by the three most powerful men in Europe: Richard I of England, Phillip II of France, and Frederick Barbarossa of Germany. Their campaign failed dismally, but Christian efforts to retake the Holy Land persisted until 1244. Thus, the end of 150 years of holy wars were still in living memory when the Zohar was published.

Given this horrendous backdrop, it is understandable how some Jewish thinkers came to the conclusion that Jews were racially superior in some essential way. The two dominant religions of medieval Europe were at each other's throats, killing each other in the name of God. To the Jews suffering under their hands, they must have seemed like crazed animals. Although many lived in peaceful coexistence, a number of Jewish communities had to endure centuries of economic restrictions, social controls, violent persecutions, and murderous mobs. Seeing their chosenness as a special feature that separated them from barbarous surroundings would have made perfect sense. No doubt it was also an inspiring source of strength, pride, and loyalty in the face of daily hardships.

These historical considerations go some way toward explaining how these ideas of superiority may have surfaced in the *Kuzari* and Zohar.[38] What is clear is that this notion of Jews being the "choicest people" was

---

36. Peter Frankopan, *The Silk Roads: A New History of the World* (Bloomsbury, 2015), 138.
37. One begins *Mi yiten roshi mayim*, "Would that my head were water, and my eye a fount of flowing tears," and the other begins *Evel a'orer*, "I shall arouse mourning" (No. 25 and No. 33, in ArtScroll *Kinot*, 270–77 and 316–19).
38. There is much more to be said about the influences of time and place on the *Kuzari* and Zohar. See, for example, Adam Shaer, *The Kuzari and the Shaping of Jewish Identity, 1167–1900* (Cambridge, 2012); Arthur Green, "The Zohar in Historical Context," in *A Guide to the Zohar* (Stanford, 2004), ch. 7, 86–98.

only one strand of medieval Jewish philosophy, and many disagreed. Additionally, there is no evidence of these ideas being translated into racially motivated violence at the time. Indeed, it could be argued that this second stage in the story of Jewish chosenness served as a very effective survival tactic. As we will now see, it was overtaken by a considerably different approach which has grown in significance in the modern era.

Stage 3: Chosen to Serve

With enlightenment and emancipation, the position of Jews in European society began to improve. As the absolute power of the monarchies waned, Jews like everyone else transitioned from being subjects to citizens. Citizenship brought obligations to the city or nation in which they lived, but it also granted rights and protections. Prejudice and persecution persisted, but Jews also began to see themselves more integrated into the societies in which they lived. With this new reality, the idea of chosenness was able to recapture a long dormant aspect, well-rooted in tradition, but now ready to flourish into a more empowering and universalistic understanding.

The nineteenth-century writings of Rabbi Samson Raphael Hirsch express this particularly well. Remember how Rashi interpreted God's pre-Revelation speech to Moses at Mount Sinai? He explained that the words "you shall be My own treasure from all the peoples; for all the earth is Mine" (Ex. 19:5) meant that God was highlighting the difference between Israel and the rest of humanity. While the people of Israel are God's "treasure," the other nations are "as nothing."[39] Eight centuries later, Rabbi Hirsch presents a strikingly alternate explanation. God's statement is not about the *difference*, but about the *similarity* between Israel and the rest of humanity. *All* nations come under God's jurisdiction. Thus, God was saying to the Israelites at Sinai:

> For this relationship you are to have with Me is really not exceptional. It is nothing but the beginning of the return to the normal condition which the world should bear towards Me. The whole of

39. Rashi on Exodus 19:5.

> humanity, every nation in the world, is really destined to belong to Me and will be ultimately educated by Me up to Me.[40]

Rabbi Hirsch sees the Jewish people as "early adopters" of the divine vision which had always been intended for humanity as a whole.[41] Reading "for all the earth is Mine" as a reference to God's global perspective can also be found in other modern commentaries, such as that of Cassuto, who explains the phrase as follows:

> I am not your God alone, but the God of the whole world; I am not like the gods of the land of Egypt whence you went forth, nor like the deities of the land of Canaan whither I am bringing you; these divinities, even according to their worshippers, have dominion over their own people only; whereas I am God of all peoples, "for all the earth is Mine," that is, all the peoples of the earth.[42]

With this global standpoint firmly established, God's speech continues with the crucial verse "You shall be to Me a kingdom of priests, and a holy nation" (Ex. 19:6). Rabbi Hirsch explains these two phrases – "kingdom of priests" and "holy nation" – as summarizing the special role of the Jewish people in bringing about God's vision. A "kingdom of priests," continues Rabbi Hirsch, means that

> each and every individual of you is to become a priest, in that all their actions are to be regulated by Me; to take the yoke of heaven faithfully on their shoulders and become a true priest who by their word and example spreads the knowledge of God and loyalty to God, as Isaiah expresses, "priests of the Lord you shall be called" (Is. 61:6).[43]

---

40. Hirsch on Exodus 19:5.
41. See, for instance, his commentary on Psalm 149: Hirsch, *The Psalms: Translation and Commentary,* Book Three, 492–95.
42. Umberto Cassuto, *A Commentary on the Book of Exodus,* trans. Israel Abrahams (Magnes, 1974), 227.
43. Hirsch on Exodus 19:6.

Rabbi Hirsch goes on to explain that a "holy nation" means that

> just as individually you are to appear priest-like, so is the impression which Israel as a nation is to make on the world to be one of holiness to God. You are to be a unique nation amongst the nations, a nation which does not exist for its own fame, its own greatness, its own glory, but the foundation and glorification of the Kingdom of God on Earth, a nation which is not to seek its greatness in power and might but in the absolute rule of the Divine Law – the *Torah* – for that is what holiness (*kedushah*) is.[44]

In Rabbi Hirsch's eyes, the Jewish people are commanded to be an entire nation of priests whose role is to spread the knowledge and law of God by living exemplary lives. Just as each nation has priests who teach and minister to the spiritual and ethical aspirations of a nation, so the Jewish people are to fulfill that role for all humanity. The "holy" aspect of the Jewish nation demands that their focus be on meaning and morals as opposed to fame and fortune. Observing the laws of the Torah will enable this focus to come to fruition.

Traces of this approach can be detected even earlier. In the sixteenth century, Sforno wrote that Israel's role was to "teach the entire human race to call in the name of God and serve Him."[45] And a lesser-known text from the thirteenth century foreshadows both Rabbi Hirsch and Sforno. The son of Maimonides, known as Rabbi Avraham ben HaRambam, asks why God told the Israelites at Mount Sinai, "You shall be to Me *a kingdom of* priests" rather than just "You shall be to Me as priests." God, he explains, was instructing them to be role models, just like distinguished kings. Effectively, God was saying: "You shall be, on My behalf, like kings for the world, as guides for them."[46]

This approach to chosenness completely upends the previous one of the "choicest people." How can Jews feel innately superior to others when their very role is to help others to become better, to become

44. Ibid.

45. Sforno on Exodus 19:6.

46. Avraham ben HaRambam, *Perush HaTorah l'Rabbeinu*, Exodus 19:6.

superior themselves? God chose the Jewish people to be a "treasure" in that they were tasked with sharing God's vision. Rather than chosenness being inward-looking and filled with self-congratulation, it is, in fact, meant to be outward-looking, filled with responsibility.

As previously mentioned, the Chosen People were given a chosen land. But this gift comes with conditions, due to the Torah's lofty expectations of Jews who live in the Land of Israel. In Leviticus, after presenting a long list of illicit sexual practices, God says:

> You shall keep My statutes and My laws, and you shall not do any of these abhorrent acts.... For the people of the land who were before you did all these abhorrent acts, and the land was defiled. Let not the land vomit you out for having defiled it. (Lev. 18:26–28)

Thus God's bestowal of the Land of Israel is conditional on appropriate behavior. Failing will lead to expulsion. The benefits of chosenness are contingent on serving God's vision.

Israel's responsibility to other nations is conveyed in the words of the prophet Isaiah:

> I the Lord have called you in righteousness and held your hand, and preserved you and made you a covenant for peoples and a light of the nations, to open blind eyes. (Is. 42:6–7)[47]

The Malbim explains the phrase "a light of the nations" as a religious charge: "You should enlighten them about faith, so that they do not walk in darkness, but come to recognize the unity of God."[48]

God's love for the Jewish people is displayed in the daily liturgy, "You have loved us with a great love,"[49] but this prayer then continues, "Instill in our hearts the desire to understand and discern, to listen, learn and teach, to observe, perform and fulfill all the teachings of Your Torah

---

47. See also Isaiah 49:6 for the phrase "a light of the nations."
48. Malbim on Isaiah 42:6.
49. *The Koren Shalem Siddur*, 96.

in love." In other words, God's love for the Jewish people comes with the expectation that they will strive to love God through their passionate commitment to keeping the commandments. Chosenness might be an honor, but it is also an awesome responsibility.

The immense nature of this responsibility can, at times, feel very unfair. In the musical, *A Fiddler on the Roof*, Tevye the Milkman cheekily says to God, "I know, I know. We are Your chosen people. But, once in a while, can't You choose someone else?" Tevye is giving voice to the hardships that the Jewish people have had to suffer as a result of being chosen for such an unenviable task. This arduous aspect of chosenness comes to the fore in the traditional attitude to conversion to Judaism:

> How do we go about accepting a genuine convert? ... We say to them, "Why would you want to become Jewish – don't you know that these days the Jews are belittled, disparaged, scorned, scattered, chased from place to place, and suffer affliction?" If they reply, "I know this, and I am not even worthy [to be part of it]" then we can accept them into the process.[50]

Notice that while the potential convert is challenged with the *drawbacks* of Judaism, the correct response is the feeling of *privilege* to be a part of such a nation. This illustrates the dual nature of chosenness. Indeed, in some Jewish communities today, a convert is referred to as "a Jew by choice."

There is however, one lingering aspect of superiority, even in this modern understanding of chosenness as "chosen to serve." It seems that you would still have to be Jewish, or become Jewish, to take a leading role in God's vision for the world. Is that fair? Judaism is not a proselytizing religion and there is no aspiration of mass conversion to the Jewish faith.[51] Does this imply that most of the world are destined to be only potential followers of Israel, but never to lead themselves? And today, even with global communications, there are millions of people who

---

50. Maimonides, *Mishneh Torah, Hilkhot Issurei Bia* 14:1, based on Yevamot 47a.
51. See, however, the opinion of R. Eleazer in Pesaḥim 87b, "The Holy One, blessed be He, exiled Israel among the nations only so that converts would join them."

have never encountered a Jew. Are they then excluded from God's special love? Can they not take part in a life dedicated to holiness as Rabbi Hirsch described? Maimonides addressed this issue when discussing the special role of the priests and Levites (*kohanim* and *levi'im*) to be the spiritual leaders of the Jewish people.[52] He wrote:

> Why did the tribe of Levi not merit to be given a land inheritance in Israel? ... This is because this tribe was set apart to serve God and to impart God's forthright paths and just laws.... Thus, the Levites have been set apart from the norms of the world: they do not wage war like the rest of Israel, they do not inherit land, nor do they compete personally through physical means.[53]

He then built on this idea in a most remarkable way:

> And not the tribe of Levi alone, in fact anyone at all, from across the globe, who is moved to dedicate themselves, whose mind comprehends the need to stand apart before God, to serve and to work to know God, and walk straight as God made them, to transcend the many thoughts in which others lose themselves; such a person becomes consecrated, a Holy of Holies. God is their portion and inheritance forever; and they will merit what this world has to offer them.[54]

I still remember my surprise when first reading these words. Despite living in a world of bitter and violent religious conflict, here was a twelfth-century rabbi recognizing the inherent capacity of every human on planet Earth to serve God in the most profound way, without even being Jewish. With effort, we are all capable. For him this was a clear outgrowth of his understanding of the Torah and rabbinic tradition. Maimonides was not

52. The priests were descendants of Moses's brother Aaron the high priest who was from the tribe of Levi. The priestly caste are a subgroup of the Levite tribe.
53. Maimonides, *Mishneh Torah, Hilkhot Shemitta VeYovel* 13:12.
54. Ibid., 13:13.

far away in space or time from Judah HaLevi, but he was a world away in his view of the chosenness of the Jewish people.

To be fair, this universalist perspective could always be found in the Jewish tradition, as is clear from this strident rabbinic statement. "I call heaven and earth to testify that whether heathen or Jew, man or woman, manservant or maidservant, the holy spirit rests upon a person only in line with deeds they do."[55] Ultimately, an individual's connection to God is not determined by religion, gender, or status, but only by the way they live their life.

Conclusions

Our road through chosenness has been a long and winding one. We began by focusing on the deep and loving special relationship that God is portrayed as having with the Jewish people. This mutual love, as evinced by the passionate commitment of the patriarchs, led to the assertion that the Jewish people and God chose each other. Or, to put it another way, the comeback to William Norman Ewer's famous comment, "How odd, of God, to choose the Jews," is, "Not so odd: the Jews chose God."

We then studied a strand of essentialist Jewish superiority found in some early medieval Jewish thinking and discovered why, given the harsh treatment of Jews at the time, this might have arisen and gained some acceptance. The Jews in some parts of medieval Europe looked at the religious powers of their time and saw barbarians. No wonder that some viewed themselves as superior, not only on a moral level but on a biological level too.

Finally, we reviewed the moment on Mount Sinai when God told the Israelites they were to be "a kingdom of priests and a holy nation." In the commentaries of scholars such as Rabbeinu Avraham ben HaRambam, then the Sforno, and later Rabbi Hirsch, we saw that this meant the Jewish people were given the role of being priests to the whole world. They were chosen for a particular purpose: to teach everyone about God and to model lives of morality and goodness that are inspired by God's Torah.

---

55. *Tanna DeVei Eliyahu Rabba* 9.

According to Rashi, the word for priest in Hebrew, *kohen*, has two definitions. It means both an "honored dignitary" (*sar*) and a person "in service" (*sherut*).[56] This reflects the dual nature of chosenness: it is both a great privilege *and* a great responsibility. I would simply add that it is a privilege *because* it is a responsibility. As Isaiah prophesied, "As for you, 'priests of the Lord' you shall be called, 'servants of our God' it shall be said of you" (Is. 61:6). To be of service is an honor in and of itself.

This might explain why God began His relationship with Abraham by giving him a job to do: leave where you are and what you know and join Me on a journey. God ended the first command to Abraham with the words "and in you shall all families of the earth be blessed" (Gen. 12:3). This expression touches on many of the facets of chosenness that we have discussed. Blessing comes when we learn to appreciate and feel valued by what we have been given as well as how we can share it with others and be of service.

The story of the chosenness of the Jewish people leads to a deep engagement of Jews with the world. That responsibility began long ago with the journey of Abraham. It is the very opposite of racism; it is a vision that believes in the potential of all peoples to seek and to find meaning, morality, and spiritual value.

56. Rashi's commentary on Exodus 19:6 and 28:3.

Part III
BELIEFS

Chapter 9

What Does It Mean to Believe in God?

EXPLORING THE QUESTION

Let me ask you a personal question: Has God ever spoken to you? Have you ever had a moment when you heard a voice from without that reached you within – one that you were completely certain was divine? A voice that told you what to do and utterly convinced you that this was a truth you needed to obey? Probably not.

There are few people today who claim God speaks to them directly, and the ones that do are generally regarded as unhinged. Some individuals claim to be modern-day prophets, but they largely remain on the fringe.

In the Bible, however, we read detailed accounts of many people who conversed with God. These prophecies had a life-changing effect on them and those around them. But this period is over. According to R. Yoḥanan, a third-century sage, "Since the day the Holy Temple was destroyed, the power of prophecy was taken from the prophets and given only to fools and children."[1] This is one way of expressing the fact that prophecy had lost its mainstream authority and acceptance. But this

1. Bava Batra 12b.

begs the question: If prophets could be taken seriously today, might that make it easier for us to believe in God?

When I ask people who doubt God's existence what it would take for them to truly believe, they say, "Well if God appeared to me or performed an obvious miracle, then of course I would be convinced." Their response comes from being confident that this is not going to happen anytime soon.

Those of us who do accept God's existence tend to talk about what we "believe" rather than what we "know." I *know* that the earth is round and that elephants are gray. I do not need to *believe* in the earth's shape or elephants' color, because these truths can be demonstrated. But because God is unobservable and undetectable, we think only "belief" is possible.

That is about as far as it goes for most of us. Once we realize that God is not going to show up, we either decide that God is not real and come to reject religious belief, or we choose to focus our attention on what accompanies belief instead, like living in a Jewish community and keeping the heart-warming traditions. Belief in God becomes a private matter that is hardly discussed. Synagogue turns into a place where we talk more to each other than to God. Without any real expectation of a response, prayer can feel more like an extended monologue than an intimate conversation.

Despite this, many people would like to have a deep connection to God, if they only could. If they could just meet God face-to-face or observe for themselves just one of the many miracles that our ancestors experienced in Egypt or at Mount Sinai, then they could be sure. They would know God and unreservedly commit to Judaism. There is a nagging worry that God might just be a figment of the imagination, and nobody wants to be taken for a fool. Rather than having to rely on belief, most of us would rather know for certain.

The truth is that even if we were granted such a meeting or experience, it still would not be enough. This is certainly the Torah's perspective because it's exactly what happened to the Israelites. They lived through ten plagues that devastated Egypt and watched a sea divide so they could walk through. As a result of those miraculous experiences, "they believed in God and Moses His servant" (Ex. 14:31). Then they were given manna from heaven and water from a rock, yet despite all these wonders, at the first sign of trouble they asked, "Is God in our midst or not?" (Ex. 17:7). What is more, not forty days after God put in a personal appearance at Mount Sinai and proclaimed the Ten Commandments, the Israelites were making a Golden Calf because they thought they had been abandoned by God and Moses.

Why were the miracles not enough? Why was divine revelation not enough? If even after marvelous displays and direct communication there is still a capacity for hesitation, what does it mean to know or believe in God?

Another concern to contend with when it comes to belief is the triumph of the modern rationalist age. In the past, people were convinced of the existence and power of God when a holy man gave them a prediction that came true, or when they observed an astounding coincidence, or when they had a rare or remarkable experience that defied explanation. The magical and mysterious were embraced as proof enough of the divine. Tales were told of miracle workers to reassure the masses of God's presence and influence. Biblical accounts of miracles aided the religious beliefs of the reader.

Today, however, proof lies firmly in the realm of reason and science. Logical arguments, physical evidence, and repeatable experiments are what persuade people of the truth of a matter. Magic, once treated as a glimpse of the divine beyond the physical, is now relegated to light entertainment. Rather than inspiring wonder, it smacks of trickery and illusion, and just leaves people wondering, "How did they do that?" The Bible's miracles are now beyond belief.

Science is the bedrock on which our modern world rests. Its successes in medicine, food production, communication, and countless other fields of human endeavor have transformed how we all now live. Can belief in God possibly reach this benchmark for proof? Is there a logic to God that is comparable to verifications of Pythagoras's theorem or the conservation of matter? How is belief in God to survive in today's supremely rational world?

Finally, there is the question of doubt. Should a Jew who is uncertain about God or even denies God's existence find a home in Judaism? The first of the Ten Commandments is to believe: "I am the Lord your God who brought you out of the land of Egypt, from the house of slaves" (Ex. 20:2).[2]

The first four of Maimonides's Thirteen Principles of Faith are to believe that God is the Creator of the universe, unique, non-physical, and eternal. The fifth, consequently, is that we should pray only to God. But how can a doubter or a nonbeliever pray? How can they fully embrace Jewish life when so much of it revolves around the synagogue, the house of prayer?

Observing the commandments is predicated on realizing there is a "commander." If there is no Divine Will demanding ethical behavior and ritual practice, why should these be kept? And without an all-seeing eye, what compels a person to avoid sin? Indeed, are you a "failed Jew" if you do not believe? Must doubts force you to the periphery of Jewish life or even lead to your eviction? Is there any point in Jewish practice without some basis in belief and understanding of God?

RESPONDING TO THE QUESTION

I have listened to so many people tell me about their doubts, and how they try to cope with them. Common methods include suppression, humor, distraction, compartmentalization, blind acceptance, the momentum of regular Jewish practice, relying on feelings of nostalgia, and the reassurance that comes from the faith of those they admire. But are those enough to sustain a Jewish life? Will "managing" your doubts be the most you can hope for? Or are there ideas that not only mitigate doubt, but pave a pathway to belief? Despite all the problems described, I do believe that we can all come to know God.

I have been encouraged to think about this a great deal. My rigorous academic background in science coupled with my role as a rabbi have led many serious people to my door to discuss their doubts and beliefs. They demand intellectual honesty and critical thinking. My having a foot in both rational and religious pursuits seems to reassure them

2. Although, strictly speaking, this verse reads as a statement rather than a commandment, it is understood traditionally as a mitzva; see Maimonides, *Sefer Hamitzvot*, Positive Commandments, no. 1.

that I will not merely fob them off with cheap certainties, spurious proofs, or clever but ultimately unsatisfying feel-good parables.

And so, after many earnest conversations, spirited walks, and coffee-fueled late nights, I have found some responses that make sense to me and speak to others. The contents of this chapter and the ones that follow reflect my broad approach to the nature of belief and some of the main aspects of what it means to be in a relationship with God.

We will begin here with the problems that Judaism has with belief based on miracles or logical proof, and then concentrate on a wholly different approach – an appreciation of the lifelong quest for God that is at the heart of Jewish belief, and how we can find God in the way we live.

It's a Miracle!

Although modern culture is dismissive of miracles, they still reinforce belief in God for many people. Wondrous occurrences, so the claim goes, violate the laws of nature, and these surely attest to a powerful force *beyond nature* that must be the cause, and that force is God. Furthermore, an abundance of oral and written accounts of miraculous incidents can be found in every religion, from their foundational texts and history to recent stories posted on websites and pamphlets pushed through your letterbox. These tell of inexplicable events that happened just at the right time or in response to a heartfelt prayer or acts of charity. Are miracles a convincing testimony to the presence of God?

David Hume, the eighteenth-century Scottish philosopher, provided four reasons to think that there has never been sufficient evidence to confirm a miracle.[3] First, "There is not to be found in all history any miracle attested by a sufficient number of men, of such unquestioned good sense, education and learning, as to secure us against all delusion in themselves." Second, because of "the passion of surprise and wonder arising from miracles," religious leaders can exploit them by spreading miraculous stories to inspire and influence the masses. Third, reports of miracles are generally to be found amongst "ignorant and barbarous nations" who may not be sophisticated enough to disbelieve fake testimony. And fourth, if every

3. David Hume, *An Inquiry Concerning Human Understanding* (Oxford, 2008), ch. 10, "Of Miracles," 79–95.

religion claims the truth of its own miraculous accounts as against those of other religions, how can all these miracles be true at the same time?

Hume's approach resonates with Maimonides who, centuries earlier, was very clear about the veracity and role of miracles in the Torah. When discussing the credibility of prophets, he pointed out that even the prophecy of Moses was not believed because of his miraculous exploits:

> The Israelites did not believe in Moses because of the wonders that he performed. Whenever anyone's belief is based on wonders, his heart has shortcomings, for it is possible to perform a wonder through magic or sorcery. Rather, all the wonders performed by Moses in the desert were performed by necessity, not to demonstrate prophecy. It was necessary to drown the Egyptians, so he split the sea and sank them. We needed food, so he provided us with manna.[4]

The Israeli philosopher Moshe Halbertal explains further:

> Maimonides thought that the basis of religious experience is not expressed in deviation from the natural order.… He therefore challenges the view that miracles and exceptions are the primary foundation of the religious attitude. The great miracles performed by Moses stemmed exclusively from the immediate needs of the Israelites; they served no real role in the lives of the believers.[5]

Thus, though biblical miracles are impressive, they serve a particular purpose in the narrative and are not theologically significant. From Maimonides and Hume we learn that stories of miracles to this day are susceptible to fallibility and fakery, so they should not be relied upon for religious belief.

---

4. Maimonides, *Mishneh Torah, Hilkhot Yesodei HaTorah* 8:1.
5. Moshe Halbertal, *Maimonides: Life and Thought* (Princeton, 2014), 128.

Proving God

Demonstrating God's existence has animated philosophers and theologians for centuries, but the writing of formal proofs came to the fore in the medieval period. Muslim thinkers such as Avicenna and Al-Ghazali, rabbinic scholars such as Rabbi Bahya ibn Paquda and Maimonides, and Christian theologians such as Anselm of Canterbury and Thomas Aquinas, presented reasoned arguments for God's existence within their respective faiths. Such arguments have been honed and discussed to the present day. For example, Bertrand Russell debated Father Copleston in 1948,[6] and in a populist fashion, Christopher Hitchens sparred with Rabbi Shmuley Boteach in 2008.[7]

Three of the most common proofs for God are the cosmological, ontological, and teleological arguments. "You can't get something from nothing" is the premise on which the cosmological argument is based. Our knowledge of the cosmos has shown us that nothing is the cause of itself, so the cosmos must have had a "first cause" or "prime mover" that brought it into existence, and that is what we understand as God. The ontological argument, meanwhile, is purely conceptual: we can conceive of nothing greater than God; it is greater to exist than to not exist; therefore, God must exist. Finally, the astonishing and irreducible complexity of biological organs, coupled with the astronomical positioning of planet Earth that makes it just right for life to emerge, and the fine-tuning of the fundamental physical constants of science, point to there being a supremely intelligent designer. This is the teleological argument, and it posits that this designer is God.

These three arguments come in many varieties, and their relative strengths and weaknesses continue to be debated.[8] At times I admit to

---

6. Bertrand Russell, *Why I Am Not a Christian* (Routledge Classics edition, 2004), 125–52.
7. "Christopher Hitchens and Rabbi Shmuley Boteach Debate on God" (2008), YouTube video, added by 92nd Street Y [online]. Available at www.youtube.com/watch?v=vnMYL8sF7bQ [accessed April 18, 2022].
8. For instance, see the entries of Bruce Reichenbach, "Cosmological Argument"; Graham Oppy, "Ontological Arguments"; and Del Ratzsch and Jeffrey Koperski, "Teleological Arguments for God's Existence," in *The Stanford Encyclopedia of Philosophy*, Edward N. Zalta, ed. (Winter 2021 edition),

having been swayed by one or another, though none in the end appear to be conclusive. These types of arguments are used in the campaign to strengthen Jewish belief, and with some success.[9] Although versions of such proofs can be found in medieval Jewish sources, they never became popular elements of Jewish teaching and were generally regarded as buttresses for belief rather than pillars of Jewish thought.[10]

Employing science and philosophy to refute such proofs is important to modern atheists in their mission to expose the folly of belief. If God's existence cannot be rationally or scientifically justified, they argue, then you would be a fool to believe. The problem is that the use of science for this purpose is highly questionable. One example is the use of "quantum fluctuations" to counter the cosmological proof. In the subatomic world of quantum mechanics, random fluctuations can produce matter and energy out of nothingness, so why not the whole universe? In other words, modern physics might imply that you really can get something from nothing, making God unnecessary as a first cause.[11] However, these fluctuations require a backdrop of gravitational and electromagnetic fields. Fluctuations need to occur within something, so they cannot be the cause of a universe coming from nothing.

It turns out that though the various proofs for God are disputable, so are their refutations. People new to these discussions often have the impression that modern thinking has dispelled the need for a Creator and that rejecting God is the only intellectually honest approach to take. But that is a huge mistake. Becoming an atheist is not a forgone conclusion

---

https://plato.stanford.edu/archives/win2021/entries/cosmological-argument/ https://plato.stanford.edu/archives/win2021/entries/ontological-arguments https://plato.stanford.edu/archives/spr2022/entries/teleological-arguments/. For an interesting list of proofs and their flaws, see the appendix to Rebecca Goldstein's novel, *36 Arguments for the Existence of God: A Work of Fiction* (Atlantic Books, 2010).

9. See for example: Lawrence Keleman, *Permission to Believe: Four Rational Approaches to God's Existence* (Targum/Feldheim, 1990), and Moshe Averick, *The Confused World of Modern Atheism* (Mosaica, 2016).
10. See J. David Bleich, *With Perfect Faith: The Foundations of Jewish Belief* (Ktav, 1983), 75–106.
11. This is the argument made in Lawrence Krauss, *The Universe from Nothing* (Simon and Schuster, 2012).

in the face of modernity. Scientists generally do not like their work being employed to refute theological arguments, because they appreciate that this is beyond the realm of their discipline. Valuable elements of proofs for God have successfully weathered multiple critiques.[12]

The upshot is that *it is not unreasonable to believe.* You are not a fool or crazy to believe in God. After spending much time wading through the vast literature on the subject, I have reached the conclusion that the refutations for God are unconvincing, even while the proofs themselves might not be wholly satisfying.

It is also essential to realize that even if you were to be convinced by one of these proofs, they still do not justify belief in a *personal* God. From the biblical perspective, God is mindful of each and every one of us:

> From the heavens the Lord looks down, He sees all humankind.… From His dwelling place He surveys all who dwell on the earth. God is the fashioner of the hearts of all, the discerner of all their actions. (Ps. 33:13–15)

The acceptance of a prime cause, necessary existence, or intelligent designer does not inevitably lead to a God who is intimately involved with humanity. Such proofs might make you a deist, but not a theist.

Beyond Proofs

There are deeper problems with trying to establish a scientific or philosophical proof for God's existence, for the whole endeavor is built on spurious assumptions. Physics, chemistry, and biology deal with the material world by analyzing and measuring its components in space and time. God, however, is not a physical being. Maimonides writes:

> The Torah is explicit that God does not have a body or physical form because it says, "The Lord is God in heaven above and on the earth below" (Deut. 4:39), and a physical body cannot be in

12. See for example, William L. Craig, *The Cosmological Argument from Plato to Leibniz* (Wipf and Stock, 2001), and Samuel Lebens, *A Guide for the Jewish Undecided* (Maggid, 2022), ch. 8, "Two Dozen (or so) Arguments for God."

> two places at once.... Nothing that happens to bodies happens to God...neither position nor measurement...and no placement in time."[13]

When recalling the revelation on Mount Sinai, Moses is careful to stress that God is empty of all physicality: "And you shall guard yourselves well, for you saw no image on the day the Lord spoke to you" (Deut. 4:15). The difficulty of comprehending this idea compels the Torah to describe God like a living creature, with a bodily form. We read of God's eyes (Gen. 38:7), ears (Num. 11:1), and legs (Ex. 24:10), as well as God's strong hand and outstretched arm (Deut. 26:8). Maimonides explains why the Torah employs physical descriptions of God:

> All these expressions relate to human thought processes which only understand physical imagery. The Torah speaks in the language of humankind. All such expressions are illustrative, as it says, "When I hone My flashing sword" (Deut. 32:41) – does God really have a sword? And with this sword does God kill? Rather, this is metaphorical, as are all such phrases.[14]

Thus, any attempt at a scientific verification of God is based on an erroneous assumption, for God is neither observable nor measurable.

Philosophical proofs for God, meanwhile, rely on argumentation methods such as inference, induction, and analogy. But, again, from a Jewish perspective, such logical demonstrations are not possible because God cannot be represented or conceptualized, and is incomparable. When Moses asked for God's name, the response was "I-Will-Be-Who-I-Will-Be" (Ex. 3:14). Said Isaiah, "And to whom would you liken Me that I be compared, says the Holy One?" (Is. 40:25). George Steiner, the acerbic novelist and philosopher, put it thus:

> Rigorously apprehended, the Mosaic God is inconceivable, incomprehensible, invisible, unattainable, in-human in the root-sense of

---

13. Maimonides, *Mishneh Torah, Hilkhot Yesodei HaTorah* 1:8, 11.
14. Ibid., 1:9.

> the word. He is blank as the desert air. If there is a Jewish theology, it is negative.... It condemns images and makes a blasphemy of imagining.[15]

The belief in physical or metaphysical proofs for God is tantamount to idolatry.[16] An appendix to the Zohar simply states, "No thought can comprehend You at all."[17]

Can we then say nothing at all about God? We even reinforce the absolute otherness of God by refusing to speak God's name. God is generally referred to as *Hashem*, "the Name," and in formal prayer today we are not meant to pronounce the letters that spell God's name, *yod-heh-vav-heh*, the tetragrammaton; instead we say *Adonai*, "My master."[18] This long-standing avoidance has been so successful that no one is even sure of the correct pronunciation.[19] Thus, every time we say *Adonai* or *Hashem* we are reminded of God's ineffability.

The *Kaddish*, one of our most beloved prayers that punctuates all our regular services, contains a paradoxical description of God. We say, "Blessed and praised, glorified and exalted, raised and honored, uplifted and lauded be the name of the Holy One, blessed be He," but then we immediately continue that God is, "*beyond* any blessing, song, praise, and consolation uttered in the world."[20] Which is it? Can God be blessed and praised or not? Through the dichotomy of giving blessing and praise while simultaneously recognizing their inadequacy, we express both our aspiration to relate to God and our inability to do so.

For the theologian Paul Tillich, even making the statement "God exists" is problematic:

---

15. George Steiner, *Errata: An Examined Life* (W&N, 1997), 58. This negative theology is described by Maimonides in his *Guide for the Perplexed* 1:58–59.
16. Sacks, *Crisis and Covenant*, 258.
17. *Tikkunei HaZohar* 17a.
18. Maimonides, *Mishneh Torah, Hilkhot Tefilla uVirkat Kohanim* 14:10. The Talmud discusses the tetragrammaton's hiddenness, and how rarely it was taught; see Kiddushin 71a.
19. Thomas Römer, *The Invention of God* (Harvard University Press, 2015), 30–32.
20. These words occur in all the various forms of the *Kaddish*; see, for instance, *The Koren Shalem Siddur*, 156, 178, 184, 197, and 1058.

> We can no longer speak of God easily to anybody, because he will immediately question: "Does God exist?" Now the very asking of that question signifies that the symbols of God have become meaningless. For God, in the question, has become one of the innumerable objects in time and space which may or may not exist. And this is not the meaning of God at all.[21]

Tillich described God not as *an* existence but as "being itself."[22] Although this description retains God's uniqueness, it seems to be incompatible with the notion of a personal God. For Tillich, "an awareness of God did not have a special name of its own but was fundamental to our ordinary emotions of courage, hope, and despair."[23] This does not chime well with the biblical description of a God who communicates with humanity and gave commandments to a particular people. And so, to gain an understanding of God rooted in Jewish beliefs, we must take a very different approach.

Seeking God

Maimonides opens his account of the laws prohibiting idolatry in an unusual way. Although writing a comprehensive legal code for Judaism, he begins this section with an elaborate story. He describes how the civilizations of old gradually came to embrace idol worship. With this background in place, he tells of the rejection of these practices by the young Abraham and how he embarked on a path to discover the true origins of existence. This story of Abraham's search is surprisingly detailed:

> While still an infant, his mind began to reflect. By day and by night he was thinking and wondering: How is it possible for the [celestial] sphere to continually revolve without having anyone to guide it?... He had no teacher or anyone to instruct him.

---

21. Mackenzie D. Brown, ed., *Ultimate Concern: Tillich in Dialogue* (London, 1965), 88.
22. Ibid., 46.
23. Karen Armstrong, *The Case for God: What Religion Really Means* (Vintage, 2010), 271. See also Robert Wright, *The Evolution of God* (Abacus, 2009), "Afterword: By the Way, What Is God?" 444–59.

> Rather, he was stuck in Ur of the Chaldees, among foolish idolaters.... But his mind was exploring and gaining understanding, until he attained the path of truth, apprehended the correct line of thought, and realized that there is one God who controls the sphere and who created everything.... Abraham was forty years old when he became aware of his Creator.[24]

In this account, Maimonides presents Abraham as the paradigmatic religious seeker. The purpose of this detailed narrative is to teach us that we too can follow such a path. Just as Abraham sought God over an extended period, so should we. The particulars of our search might differ from his, but the commitment to finding the "path of truth" for ourselves is modeled by our primary patriarch.

The Baal Shem Tov, the founder of Hasidism, asked: Why does the opening blessing of the *Amida* prayer describe God as "God of Abraham, God of Isaac, and God of Jacob" and not simply "God of Abraham, Isaac, and Jacob"? He explains that "Isaac and Jacob did not base their work on the searching and service of Abraham; they themselves searched for the unity of the Maker and His service."[25] Tradition is inherited, but belief needs to be acquired. Each of us can and must seek God for ourselves, in our own ways. The process is a lifelong quest, open to all.

Viewing religious belief as a quest clarifies what it means to fulfill the Ten Commandments, especially the first. Believing in the phrase "I am the Lord your God" is not a onetime binary decision – either you believe in God or you do not – rather, it is a journey of realization and discovery. As with the other commandments, such as observing Shabbat, honoring your parents, and not coveting, it is the work of a lifetime which requires constant effort. It is measured by the arc of your lived experience, not by occasional affirmations.

---

24. Maimonides, *Mishneh Torah, Hilkhot Avoda Zara* 1:3.
25. *Sefer Ba'al Shem Tov, Vayetze* 6:1; quoted in Martin Buber, *Tales of the Hasidim: The Early Masters* (Schocken Books, 1982), 48. The idea seems to be a development of the commentaries of Nahmanides and his contemporary, Rabbi Menaḥem Recanati (1223–1290), on Exodus 3:6, which describes God in this way.

Belief as quest can also shed light on the way God is described in the first commandment: "I am the Lord your God who brought you out of the land of Egypt, *from the house of slaves*" (Ex. 20:2). Belief requires breaking free from a fixed mindset and ending our slavery to ingrained ideas. When warning the Israelites against making any kind of idols, Moses said, "God brought you out from the iron's forge, from Egypt, to become God's people" (Deut. 4:20). Just as a forge rids a metal of its contaminants by gradually refining it, so the search for God involves constant refinement by moving beyond scientific or logic-based conceptions of God.

This search is expressed by the Hebrew term *lidrosh*, "to seek," which appears several times in the Torah with reference to God. In each case we find people engaged in a process of inquiry. Rebecca suffered a difficult pregnancy, and to find out why, "she went to seek God" (Gen. 25:22). At Mount Sinai, Jethro asked Moses why the Israelites stand around him all day long, and he replied, "For the people come to me to seek God" (Ex. 18:15). When preparing the Israelites to enter the land, Moses assured them that even if they falter and face exile, then "from there you shall search for the Lord your God, and you will find Him, if only you seek Him with all your heart and all your soul" (Deut. 4:29). And in describing the future Temple in Jerusalem, the national center of worship, the Israelites were told, "You shall seek out God's presence and come there" (Deut. 12:5). To this day, we come to synagogue to seek God.

The quest for God is a recurring theme in the book of Psalms too.[26] Its importance as an approach to belief can be seen in the way it bookends our daily morning prayers. As the service opens, in the verses recited after *Barukh She'amar*, we say: "Search out the Lord… seek His presence at all times" (I Chr. 16:11).[27] And as the service comes to a close, in the last verses of *Uva LeTziyon*, we say, "Lord, do not forsake those who seek You" (Ps. 9:11).[28] Every time we recite Grace after Meals, we include the verse "Lion cubs easily get weak and hungry, but those who

26. See Psalms 14:2, 22:27, 24:6, 34:5, 53:3, 69:33, 77:3, 105:4, 111:2, and 119:2.
27. *The Koren Shalem Siddur*, 64.
28. Ibid., 176.

seek the Lord shall lack nothing good" (Ps. 34:11).[29] With these words, we acknowledge the quest requires stamina and continuous effort; but it is worthwhile.

Finding God

What is involved in the quest for God? This is the focus of an impassioned and poetic essay by Rabbi Joseph Soloveitchik.[30] The launchpad for his analysis is one of the verses from Deuteronomy quoted above: "You shall search for the Lord your God, and you will find Him, if only you seek Him with all your heart and all your soul" (Deut. 4:29). But how is God to be found and in what ways are the heart and soul involved? Rabbi Soloveitchik describes two complementary forms of human consciousness: the "natural" and the "revelational."

In the search for purpose and meaning, people have always tried to make sense of the world by investigating every aspect of it:

> There is no hidden corner of the natural or spiritual world which man's consciousness does not peer into and scrutinize.... Flesh-and-blood man longs to escape from the straits of the limited, bounded, and contingent world and go out into the limitless, independent, wide-open spaces. This search is an act of transcendence.[31]

The project, which he calls our "natural consciousness," began at the dawn of human civilization and remains possible to this day. Yet there are limits as to how far natural consciousness can carry you. The intellectual pursuit of science and philosophy is not enough to have a sustained encounter with God for two essential reasons. First, searching for God by abstracting conceptional generalizations from reality is religiously unsatisfying: "He who relies only on the cosmological approach will

---

29. Ibid., 992. This is also recited every Shabbat morning, ibid., 414.
30. Joseph B. Soloveitchik, *And From There You Shall Seek,* translated from Hebrew by Naomi Goldblum (Ktav, 2008).
31. Ibid., 8.

end up ruined and faithless."[32] A second problem that frustrates our quest is moral weakness. Our immense capacity for selfishness and self-deception separates us from our Creator. If we could overcome our egotistical and wasteful preoccupations, we might gain the clarity needed to find God. However, this cannot be done alone, and may result in disappointment and confusion.

This leads to the second form of religious experience – God reaching out to humanity:

> God reveals Himself from above nature, from beyond the world bounded by time and space…bringing prophecies to human beings.[33]

However, this "revelational consciousness" can be overwhelming. It is why Adam and Eve hid in the Garden of Eden (Gen. 3:8) and Jonah ran away (Jonah 1:3). For when God communicates with humanity, it is not to satisfy our curiosity but to make demands of us:

> When God reveals Himself to man, He does so not in order to realize an intellectual, scientific goal – to tell him about the cosmic drama – but to command him and to give him the responsibility for keeping laws.[34]

Revelation breeds obligation. The high point of revelational consciousness was, of course, the giving of Torah at Mount Sinai; but, Rabbi Soloveitchik insists, the prophetic tradition is open to all:

> The confrontation between God and man, between the Creator and the creature, never ends; the discourse with God is constantly being renewed – in prayer, in transcendent thoughts, and in man's longing emotions.[35]

---

32. Ibid., 25.
33. Ibid., 29.
34. Ibid., 35.
35. Ibid., 134.

The God who spoke to Adam and Eve in the Garden of Eden "is still marching in the garden of history"; the God who told Abraham to leave his native land is still commanding us to leave our comfortable homes "and devote ourselves to a sublime aspiration"; and the God who set Moses on a path of leadership and redemption at the Burning Bush "has not disappeared; the bush is still burning, and God's voice from within it resounds in space, relaying the divine mission to all who fight to sanctify God's name."[36]

This brings purpose and meaning to each of us, for when we find God, we discover ourselves, our identity, and what it means to be human:

> The divine revelation lifts the individual up from the level of a living creature to the level of an intellectual, speaking being, from object to person, from a closed-off creature to an open one.[37]

These two forms of consciousness, natural and revelational, allow us to come face-to-face with both the "what" and the "why" of existence. The first shows us the way the world is, but the second teaches us the way the world could be. The first guides us to live practically and sensibly; the second demands that we live meaningfully and morally. Creation informs, but the Creator commands.

Rabbi Soloveitchik ends his essay with a loving description of what it means to be involved in the study of halakha, Jewish law, "the perpetuation of the *Shekhina* [God's Presence] and of the word of God."[38] For him, belief in God is a living relationship, expressed through a life-long engagement with Jewish tradition. So, in the end, the quest for God has the effect of changing us. While seeking God is to search for the meaning of life, finding God reframes this to living a life of meaning.

The Centrality of Relationship

In the decades since Rabbi Soloveitchik composed his essay, there has been considerable progress in several scientific fields. These developments can

36. Ibid., 135.
37. Ibid., 136.
38. Ibid., 139.

help us appreciate a key element of his thinking: the yearning for profound connection to our Creator as we try to fathom existence and ourselves. Findings in neuroscience, plant and animal biology, and quantum physics enable us to look at consciousness, life, and reality itself in new ways, which have important implications for belief in God.

Socrates said, "Know thyself,"[39] but, as it turns out, the only way to achieve this is through relationship with others. Dr. Daniel Siegel, clinical professor of Psychiatry at UCLA, developed the interdisciplinary framework of "interpersonal neurobiology."[40] As a result of extensive research into neurocircuitry, he has concluded:

> Mind, brain, and relationships are not separate elements of life – they are irreducible aspects of one interconnected triangle of being.... The mind uses the brain to create itself. As patterns of energy and information flow are passed among people within a culture and across generations, it is the mind shaping brain growth within our evolving human societies.... Relationships are woven into the fabric of our interior world. We come to know our minds through our interactions with others.... The brain is a social organ, and our relationships with one another are not a luxury but an essential nutrient for our survival.[41]

Self-knowledge and identity are only achievable and sustainable through experiencing interactions outside of ourselves. The mind sculpts the brain through these relationships with others. And just as relationships are vital to our psychological development, so too are they vital to our physical development. The trillions of microbes living inside and in relationship with the human body service our organs, maintain our health, and protect us from disease. For instance:

---

39. Motto inscribed on the temple of Apollo at Delphi, discussed by Socrates in Plato, *Charmides*, 164d–167a, and *Protagoras* 343b.
40. Daniel Siegel, *The Developing Mind: Towards a Neurobiology of Interpersonal Experience* (Guilford, 1999).
41. Daniel Siegel, *Mindsight* (Oneworld, 2020), 11, 63, 211, 261.

> Our gastrointestinal tract is home to more than a thousand different species of bacteria – plus minority populations of viruses and yeasts, as well as fungi and various other single-cell organisms.[42]

Learning about the plethora of microbes on and in us ultimately leads to a drastically altered sense of self:

> Even when we are alone, we are never alone. We exist in symbiosis ... different organisms living together. Some animals are colonized by microbes while they are still unfertilized eggs; others pick up their first partners at the moment of birth. We then proceed through our lives in their presence. When we eat, so do they. When we travel, they come along. When we die, they consume us. Every one of us is a zoo in our own right – a colony enclosed within a single body. A multi-species collective ...
>
> When we look at beetles and elephants, sea urchins and earthworms, parents and friends, we see individuals, working their way through life as a bunch of cells in a single body, driven by a single brain, operating with a single genome. This is a pleasant fiction. In fact, we are legion, each and every one of us. Always a "we" and never a "me."[43]

What then is the meaning of "self" if it cannot ever exist alone? Not only are the lives of animals and humans predicated on relationship, but all of life is. For instance, the "Wood Wide Web" is the nickname given to the mycorrhizal networks of fungi that connect individual plants, transferring water, nutrients, and minerals between them.[44] Research underground has revealed that trees of the same and different species trade carbon and other information through a mycelial communications

42. Giulia Enders, *GUT: The Inside Story of our Body's Most Under-Rated Organ*, trans. David Shaw (Scribe, 2015), 140.
43. Ed Wong, *I Contain Multitudes: The Microbes within us and a Grander View of Life* (Vintage, 2017), 3, 5.
44. Robert Macfarlane, "The Secrets of the Wood Wide Web," in *The New Yorker*, August 7, 2016, www.newyorker.com/tech/annals-of-technology/the-secrets-of-the-wood-wide-web.

network that is so vast it can extend hundreds of miles.[45] Plants do not exist individually; the Wood Wide Web is the living network of plant life.

Amazingly, the significance of relationship extends to reality itself. We know from modern physics that there are only four fundamental forces of nature governing every interaction in the universe. These forces describe the attraction and repulsion between all forms of matter, from huge planets to tiny particles. On the subatomic scale, matter obeys the laws of quantum mechanics. The theoretical physicist and writer Carlos Rovelli explains:

> The equations of quantum mechanics and their consequences are used daily in widely varying fields: by physicists, engineers, chemists, and biologists.... Yet they remain mysterious. For they do not describe what happens to a physical system, but only how a physical system affects another physical system. What does this mean? That the essential reality of a system is indescribable? Does it mean that we only lack a piece of the puzzle? Or does it mean, as it seems to me, *that we must accept the idea that reality is only interaction*?[46]

Rovelli's insight is profound: the relationships between elements of reality are more fundamental than the elements themselves. And so, we see that *on every level of existence*, from physical matter to plant life to animal bodies and the human mind, *everything* is continuously interacting, and these interactions are so complex that notions of separateness and self are secondary to the primal reality of relationship.

We could even say that *all reality is best expressed as relationship itself.* Nothing is disconnected and alone. Existence is an eternal dance of all there is, and we humans are plugged in on a neural, biological, and

---

45. Suzanne Simard, *Finding the Mother Tree: Uncovering the Wisdom and Intelligence of the Forest* (Allen Lane, 2021). See also Merlin Sheldrake, *Entangled Life: How Fungi Make Our Worlds, Change Our Minds and Shape Our Futures* (Vintage, 2021).
46. Carlo Rovelli, *Seven Brief Lessons on Physics,* trans. Simon Carnell and Erica Segre (Penguin, 2015), 18.

atomic level. This is expressed beautifully in a psalm we recite every morning, in which every constituent of reality praises God in concert:

> Hallelujah. Praise the Lord from the heavens, praise Him on the heights.... Praise Him, sun and moon, praise Him, all you stars of light.... Praise the Lord from the earth, sea monsters and all you deeps...the mountains and all the hills. Fruit trees and all cedars, wild beasts and all cattle...young men and also maidens, elders together with lads. Let them praise the Lord's name.... Hallelujah. (Ps. 148:1, 3, 7, 9–10, 12–14)

In this majestic cosmic vision, praising God represents the interrelationship of every aspect of reality, the symphony of all existence. We find God through recognizing the essentially relational nature of all reality.

The Talmud teaches that God's Presence, *Shekhina*, rests in relationship: when ten congregate to pray together, when three sit to judge together, when two meet to study together, and even when a person is alone the Divine Presence is with them when they engage in learning, for then they are reaching beyond themselves and becoming aware of their relational existence.[47] In each case, the sense of "togetherness" connects us with God.

The Dynamics of Relating to God

Given the relational nature of existence, believing in God cannot be understood as a passive emotion. It requires ongoing conscious awareness. This is difficult to maintain. The quest for God is challenging. Some days our efforts to engage in a religious experience will be incredibly meaningful, while other days it may be perfunctory at best. Maimonides compares our relationship with God to that of someone we love.[48] On occasion our feelings for them are deep and intense, but often they are just routine. In especially tough times we may even question whether we have a relationship with them at all, but in those moments the history we have together is what carries us through. And so it is with God.

---

47. Berakhot 6a.
48. See *Mishneh Torah, Hilkhot Teshuva* 10:3.

Hasidic thinkers use the Hebrew words *ratzo veshov,* "running back and forth," to express our dynamic relationship with God. This phrase comes from the enigmatic opening chapter of Ezekiel when the prophet had a vision of the mystical divine "chariot" with "angelic creatures running back and forth like the look of sparks" (Ezek. 1:14). The back-and-forth motion is a metaphor for the active and shifting nature of our connection to God.[49]

This is at odds with the way most of us generally think about religious belief. We tend to expect people to either believe in God or not, or just say they don't know. We might ask them: "Do you believe in God or are you an atheist or an agnostic?" But the truth is that we are not any of these consistently. They are not hard and fast categories. In life we move within and between them, traversing shades of devotion and skepticism, disillusionment and acceptance.

And so religious doubt and despondency are not suppressed in Judaism. On the contrary, the book of Psalms gives them a compelling voice:

> My God, my God, why have you forsaken me? (Ps. 22:2)
>
> Do not hide Your face from me… do not abandon me and do not forsake me. (Ps. 27:9)
>
> Why, O Lord, do you reject me, hiding Your face from me? (Ps. 88:15)

This biblical recognition of religious doubt should dispel any notion that there is something wrong in being a questioning Jew.[50] Rabbi Abraham Isaac Kook went further, arguing that skepticism may even uncover a deeper latent religious yearning:

---

49. See for example Rebbe Nahman of Breslov, *Likutei Moharan* I 4:9 and 6:4.
50. My teacher and friend, Rabbi Yehoshua Engelman, would often say: "If you doubt God then tell Him; work on the relationship. It's no one else's business."

> The self-same arguments and lines of thought which lead to the ways of God-denial, lead in their essence, if we search out their true origin, to a higher form of faith than the simple conceptions we entertain before the apparent breakdown.... Once a thought-form of this kind makes its appearance in the intellect, though at first it may raise doubts and superficially drive the divine light from the mind, at a deeper level it forms a most sublime basis on which to rest the concept of divine providence.[51]

Doubters are more concerned with their doubt than believers are with their belief. Take a moment to consider, if you will, why you are reading this book. Rabbi Kook might say that the desire to study a work about questioning beliefs implies that you are eager to reflect on your relationship with God, and that this could lead to a renewed and heightened faith.

One simple example of how belief in God is reinforced practically is the lexicon of traditional God-related responses we express in everyday Jewish life. When we hear something positive, we proclaim, *barukh Hashem* (Blessed is God); when we hope things will turn out well, we might say *be'ezrat Hashem* (With the help of God), or *Hashem yaazor* (May God help), or *Hashem yishmor* (God will protect); and when we hear of a bereavement, we accept it with the words *barukh Dayan ha'emet* (Blessed is the true Judge).

Instead of saying "good luck," "thank the stars," or "best wishes," expressions that seem to surrender our lives to fate, we call on God to acknowledge that our lives are founded on faith.[52] The English ideal of courtesy expects us to say "please" and "thank you," but in our tradition we also have the phrases "Please God" and "Thank God" so that beyond politeness we show our appreciation for the One who enabled all this

51. This is quoted in Aryeh Carmell and Cyril Domb, eds., *Challenge: Torah Views on Science and Its Problems* (Feldheim, 1988), 137. Note that Rabbi Kook only criticizes doubters who are "satisfied" with their doubts and are absolutely sure that they cannot be addressed. See Abraham Isaac Kook, *Igorot HaRaiyah, The Collected Letters of Rav Kook* (Mossad Harav Kook, 1965), Volume 1, Letter 20.
52. This is typified by the biblical book of Ruth in which the three primary characters – Naomi, Ruth, and Boaz – all invoke God in their opening words (Ruth 1:8-9, 16–17, 2:4).

to occur. Whether or not these responses were part of your upbringing, adopting some of them can make God more a part of your life.

Numerous concepts in the Bible and Talmud are described in terms of our dynamic reciprocal relationship with God. Protection: "I lift up my eyes to the mountains: from where will my help come? My help is from the Lord" (Ps. 121:1). Repentance: "Bring us back to You, Lord, that we come back to You" (Lam. 5:21). Mercy: "Anyone who is merciful to other creations will be treated mercifully from heaven."[53]

According to Rabbi Shlomo Wolbe (1914–2005), the verse "The Lord is your guard, the Lord is your shade at your right hand" (Ps. 121:5) is also responsive. It is as if God is saying to us, "Just as you are with Me, so will I be with you: if you open your hands and give charity, so will I open My hand."[54] Rabbi Wolbe bases this on a rabbinic interpretation of the famous verse in Micah:

> "God has told you, O Man, what is good, and what the Lord requires of you – only to do justice, love kindness, and walk humbly with your God" (Mic. 6:8). Instead of reading *im Elohekha* ("walk humbly with your God"), it should be read as *imkha Elohekha* ("walking humbly with you is your God"). This changes the meaning dramatically. Your acts of justice and loving-kindness will cause God to respond by "walking humbly with you."[55]

The blessings over learning Torah, recited each morning, also express our responsive relationship with God. We begin by blessing God who "has commanded us to engage in study of the words of Torah," and then we bless God "who teaches Torah to His people Israel."[56] So when we engage in learning, it is God who teaches us.

53. Shabbat 151b. See also 17a.
54. Shlomo Wolbe, "Hatznea Lekhet," in *The Blessings of Eliyahu* (Golders Green Beth Hamedrash Congregation, 1982), 5–6 (Hebrew section).
55. *Tanna DeVei Eliyahu Rabba* 28.
56. *The Koren Shalem Siddur*, 8.

Open to Relationship

In the dynamics of relating to God, there is another crucial element that needs addressing: openness. Rabbi Menachem Mendel Morgensztern, the fiery hasidic Rebbe of Kotzk (1787–1859), once said to a disciple:

> "Do you know where God resides?" And as the other gapes in astonishment, the Rebbe continues: "I'll tell you. He resides where He is allowed to enter."[57]

We need to "let God in" if we are to have a relationship. A modern expression of this openness can be found in the crisp and concise poem *Fun,* by musician and poet Leonard Cohen (1934–2016):

> It is so much fun
> to believe in G-d
> You must try it sometime
> Try it now
> and find out whether
> or not
> G-d wants you
> to believe in Him[58]

Cohen begins by declaring the innocent joy of faith: "It is so much fun to believe in G-d," and then moves quickly from a lighthearted suggestion "You must try it sometime," to an urgent insistence, "Try it now." This opens up the responsive relationship which is dynamic and uncertain: "and find out whether or not G-d wants you to believe in Him." I love how Cohen evokes the vulnerability and insecurity we feel when we open ourselves up to a relationship. Indeed, this is what makes it so valuable to us.

Note the hyphen in "G-d" appears in the original poem. Even when making simple marks on a page to signify God, Cohen wants to convey his reverence for divine otherness. At the same time, titling the

57. Elie Wiesel, *Souls on Fire and Somewhere a Master* (Penguin, 1987), 189.
58. Leonard Cohen, *Book of Longing* (Penguin Books, 2006), 49.

poem "Fun" brings a playfulness to the relationship. Maybe we should all write our own poems to and about God, for in the attempt to express our relationship, we give it more shape and meaning. This, in fact, is what much of Jewish prayer is: prose and poetry composed by our forebears over centuries as they attempted to characterize the relationship between our Creator and ourselves.

Let me summarize the journey taken. God's existence cannot be proven with miracles, physics, or metaphysics because God is indescribable and inscrutable. Abraham spent many years wondering about the world until he found a path to God. This is because belief is not binary (I do or I don't); it is a quest. In that search, God reaches out to find us through prophetic-like experiences which compel us to follow God's law, giving us purpose and meaning when we study and live by it.

Our relationship to God can be intensified by understanding the interrelated nature of all reality, even of our own self-perception. In finding ourselves, we find God. Regularly mentioning God in our responses increases our connection. There are ups and downs in this relationship. At times there is genuine closeness when the quest is won: "I sought the Lord and He answered me, and from all that I dread He saved me" (Ps. 34:5). And yet at other times there are feelings of abandonment: "My God, I call out by day and You do not answer, by night – no stillness for me" (Ps. 22:3). This is only natural. But in being responsive to God we are inspired to live more meaningfully and ethically. That is, if we let God into our lives.

One of my favorite hasidic stories is a fitting conclusion to this chapter. Through a simple child's game, it mourns our missed opportunities to engage in the quest for God:

> Rebbe Barukh's grandson, Yehiel, came running into his study, in tears.
>
> "Yehiel, Yehiel, why are you crying?"
>
> "My friend cheats! It's unfair; he left me all by myself, that's why I am crying."
>
> "Would you like to tell me about it?"
>
> "Certainly, Grandfather. We played hide-and-seek, and it was my turn to hide and his turn to look for me. But I hid so

well that he couldn't find me. So he gave up; he stopped looking. And that's unfair."

Rebbe Barukh began to caress Yehiel's face, and tears welled up in his eyes. "God too, Yehiel," he whispered softly. "God too is unhappy; He is hiding and man is not looking for Him. Do you understand Yehiel? God is hiding and man is not even searching for Him."[59]

---

59. Wiesel, *Souls on Fire,* 268. See *Toldot Yaakov Yosef, Parashat Bereishit,* analyzing Deuteronomy 31:8 about God hiding His face.

Chapter 10

How Is Arguing with God Even Possible?

EXPLORING THE QUESTION

"You'll believe a man can fly" was the tagline of the 1978 *Superman* movie, and I did. As a child I loved superheroes, especially the Man of Steel. The idea that a person with superhuman powers could be there in the nick of time to rescue people was enthralling. He embodied the message of doing what is right and putting yourself on the line for the sake of others. Though he was an alien from Krypton, he looked human, and so when he saved people, they could look him in the eye and say thank you. He was the face of justice and truth, and, for a time, I followed his adventures with excitement.

Superman's creators, Jerry Seigel and Joe Shuster, were two high school students in Cleveland. They were also children of Jewish immigrants. They published their new superhero in 1938, in the shadow of Nazism's rise. In 1940, two years before America joined the Allied powers, they wrote a story of how Superman could easily end World War II by capturing both Hitler and Stalin and dropping them off at the League of Nations in Geneva.[1]

1. Superman first appeared in *Action Comics* #1 in June 1938. The two-page spread, "How Superman Would End the War," appeared in *Look* magazine on February 27, 1940.

This fantasy fulfillment exemplified a problem I began to have with Superman: he was just too unbelievably powerful. Supersonic flight, laser eyes, amazing strength, and an impervious body made him hard to hurt and almost impossible to kill. That realization hampered my enjoyment of his exploits. I was less afraid of what would happen because I knew he was not in any real danger. Such was his power that the writers had to keep coming up with mightier villains to take him on. They looked off-planet and relied on world-threatening aliens from outer space, and, eventually, Earth's greatest hero was battling super beings from other dimensions and gods from alternate universes.

The only way to defeat Superman was to know his secret, his one weakness: exposure to Kryptonite. This "fatal flaw" resonates with the myth of Achilles' heel. When this ancient Greek warrior was only a child, his mother dipped him in the magical river Styx, making him invincible. Thetis had held Achilles by the heel, so that became his only weakness. The best way to ensure a dramatic narrative is for the hero to face a real threat, and a fatal flaw is ideal for this. Without that, the exploits of Superman and Achilles are less than compelling.

This brings me to God. God has no fatal flaw, and that is the whole point. We understand God to be all-knowing, all-powerful, and completely just. In a word, God is perfect: "God's way is perfection, the word of the Lord is pure" (Ps. 18:31). God cannot make mistakes because that would be an imperfection. God must always be right, could never be wrong, and thus would never change His mind: "God does not change, for there is nothing that could cause God to change."[2] The problem with this, though, is that key characters in the Torah not only challenge God, but, incredibly, God seems to listen and change His mind.

In Genesis, God told Abraham of the plan to wipe out Sodom and Gomorrah due to their sinful corruption, but when Abraham made a case for saving them, God conditionally agreed. In Exodus, God told Moses of the plan to wipe out the Israelites due to the sin of the Golden

---

Michael Chabon's novel, *The Amazing Adventures of Kavalier and Clay* (Random House, 2000), dramatizes this golden age of comics, telling how these young Jewish New Yorkers invented superheroes to wield the power they lacked.

2. Maimonides, *Mishneh Torah, Hilkhot Yesodei HaTorah* 1:11.

Calf, but when Moses made a case for saving them, God again acquiesced, and they were forgiven. How can this be? Doesn't it diminish God to think that persuasion could be effective? And was it not disrespectful of Abraham and Moses to argue with God at all? Why does the Torah contain such surprising stories? If God can be convinced, then surely His justice is not absolute. Heeding humans certainly dramatizes the Torah, but it defies belief in God's supremacy.

And what is more, the actions of Abraham and Moses were only the start of a Jewish tradition of challenging God spanning centuries. Jeremiah challenged God for allowing injustice:

> Why does the way of the wicked prosper?
> And why does every faithless traitor live securely? (Jer. 12:1)[3]

And in response to the shockingly unjust way he was treated, Job asked God:

> What have I done to You, warden of humanity?
> Why have You made me Your target? (Job 7:20–21)

Essentially, each of these biblical characters was presenting God with the same accusatory question: "You are acting unfairly. If You are good then how can You be so unjust?"

The rabbinic sages picked up this tradition and expanded on these biblical protests. The injustice of drought, childlessness, excessive punishment, and prolonged exile all warranted discussion.[4] The Talmud recognized that such challenges can even cause Jews to reject Judaism altogether. When a great sage of Yavneh, Rabbi Ḥutzpit, was executed by the Romans and his body dragged through the streets, it was all too much for Rabbi Elisha ben Avuya. "He said, 'Shall the mouth that produced pearls lap up dirt?' He left and began to sin."[5]

---

3. See also Jeremiah 11:18–23 and 18:19–23.
4. Anson Laytner, *Arguing with God: A Jewish Tradition* (Aronson, 2004), 41–101.
5. Kiddushin 39b. Note that despite becoming a heretic, some of Rabbi Elisha ben Avuya's teachings are still retained in tradition; see for example Mishna Avot 4:20.

By far the largest contribution to the tradition of challenging God occurs in the hundreds of protest *piyyutim* within Jewish prayer. Dating from the fourth century until after the Holocaust, these poetic rabbinic compositions rail against the painful plight of the Jewish people and present arguments to God in the hope of divine salvation. They include the *seliḥot* (penitences) recited before and during the High Holy Days and the *kinot* (laments) of the Fast of Av mourning Jerusalem's destruction.[6]

Arguing with God was also given a passionate voice by the hasidic masters of Eastern Europe in the eighteenth and nineteenth centuries. The Yiddish outbursts of Reb Levi Yitzchak of Berdichev during services are paradigmatic. He was a valiant fighter on behalf of his people whose protests evolved into open defiance.

> Once he remained standing at his pulpit from morning till night without moving his lips. Earlier he had issued a warning to God: "If You refuse to answer our prayers, I shall refuse to go on saying them." ...
>
> Another time he made a terrifying statement: "Know that if Your reign does not bring grace and mercy, *lo teshev al kissakha be'emet,* Your throne will not be a throne of truth." ...
>
> [And he once said:] "You order man to the aid of orphans. We too are orphans. Why do You refuse to help us?"[7]

Then there is the well-known story of Auschwitz inmates who put God on trial for allowing the systematic annihilation of His people.[8] Though in equal measures shocking and audacious, this episode is the culmination of a long tradition of challenging God to be just. And so today, in the wake of a global pandemic that has killed millions, especially the elderly, should a faithful Jew not also question God? If, as the sages teach, "there isn't a single blade of grass that does not have a heavenly

6. Laytner, *Arguing with God,* 127–76.
7. Wiesel, *Souls on Fire,* 88–90.
8. Elie Wiesel, *Against Silence: The Voice and Vision of Elie Wiesel,* selected and edited by Irving Abrahamson (Holocaust Publications, 1965), 112–13.

force to drive it and say to it, 'Grow!'"[9] then God cannot but be ultimately responsible for Covid-19.

Most religions allow for requests of their deity, but only in Judaism is arguing with God put on a pedestal, recurring in multiple biblical, rabbinic, hasidic, and liturgical texts. But does the very act of protest not deny God's perfection? God's greatness would seem to be compromised if He can be challenged by His creations for not acting justly. And is it not childish to hope that just because we oppose God, our plea deserves accommodation?

Of course, in comparison to God, Superman is just a naive fantasy of a superpowered fight for justice, and yet it seems that impassioned human protest is God's kryptonite, His fatal flaw. In sum, the Jewish tradition of religious defiance negates divine faultlessness, is susceptible to infantilizing belief, and seems to mock the notion of an all-just and almighty God whose commands should be obeyed unquestionably.

RESPONDING TO THE QUESTION

Clearly, when it comes to protest, the portrayal of God in the Torah needs explaining. Our approach will be to examine the narratives in which Moses and Abraham challenge God's justice, and to uncover a surprising common motif and discuss its pivotal role in the Torah. Focusing further on Abraham will allow us to see how our relationship with God is balanced by the opposing attitudes of defiance and obedience. The way in which these ideas have permeated Jewish prayer will then be discussed, as well as their impact on more recent history, from Hasidism to the Holocaust. Ultimately, this will lead to a better understanding of the rightful place of protest in contemporary Jewish faith.

Moses Protests

The climactic moment of God's revelation at Mount Sinai comes crashing down when shortly afterward the Israelites turn to worship a Golden Calf: "They offered up burnt offerings...they ate and drank and rose

9. Genesis Rabba 10:6.

up to play" (Ex. 32:6).[10] God is infuriated and informs Moses of His response:

> I see this people and, look, it is a stiff-necked people. So now leave Me be, that My anger may flare against them, and I will put an end to them, and I will make you a great nation. (Ex. 32:9–10)

Fed up with this fractious people, God wants to wipe them out and start again with Moses. But Moses chooses to intercede on their behalf. First, he questions God's decision by describing the bad optics that will result:

> Why, O Lord, should Your anger flare against Your people that You brought out from the land of Egypt with great power and with a strong hand? Why should the Egyptians say, "For evil He brought them out, to kill them in the mountains, to put an end to them on the face of the earth?" (Ex. 32:11–12)

Then Moses demands forgiveness for the Israelites and reminds God of His promises to their ancestors:

> Turn back from Your flaring anger and relent from the evil against Your people. Remember Abraham, Isaac, and Israel Your servants, to whom You swore … "I will multiply your seed like the stars of the heavens, and all this land that I said I will give to your seed, they will inherit it forever." (Ex. 32:12–13)

Remarkably, God listens: "And the Lord relented from the evil that He had spoken to do to His people." (Ex. 32:14). Why did God cave in on the spot? Moses was not saying anything new. God must have been cognizant of the consequences of ending the Israelites and rebooting with Moses. What made Moses so convincing?

The entire thrust of the episode is transformed when you consider why God uttered the phrase "So now leave Me be" even before

---

10. Rashi describes it like a bacchanalian party.

Moses had begun to challenge Him. The midrash compares this to a king who was angry with his son. When the father was about to beat him, he called out, "Leave me be so I can hit him!" The son's mentor overheard and realized that the king was hinting that he wanted to be stopped, and so the mentor rushed in to plead for the boy, and the king instantly relented.[11] Similarly here. God did not want to wipe out the Israelites, so hinted to Moses to intercede. It was God who was pleading to be interrupted in order to encourage Moses to plead for his people.

This reading is supported by the structure of the text itself. Twice we find the phrase "And God spoke to Moses" with no intervening response (Ex. 32:7, 9).[12] This was a prompt for Moses to speak up. Moses's protest persuaded God because it was what God wanted to hear in the first place. All along, God was managing the proceedings.

The threat of annihilation also empowered Moses to reassert God's commitment to fulfilling the ancestral promise. That is why Moses restated God's plan to make the Israelites a great nation and give them a permanent homeland. God was not fearful of looking weak in Egyptian eyes – the aim was to empower Moses to reaffirm the purpose of the Exodus. And once he did this, God was ready to back down immediately.

Moreover, God's threatening stance provoked Moses to plead for forgiveness. Rather than talking down a wrathful God from destroying the Israelites, Moses was taking up God's cue to ask for compassion.[13]

The importance of God's forgiveness is developed further as the narrative continues. When Moses reascended Mount Sinai to receive a second set of tablets, God taught him an appeal process that would

---

11. Exodus Rabba 2:9. Another version of this also appears in Berakhot 32a, where many aspects of Moses's argument with God are investigated.
12. Rabbi Hirsch points out that the two words for "said" are different. The first is *vayedaber*, which has a more formal connotation, and the second is *vayomer*, which is softer and more open.
13. Even the way Moses initiated his response by questioning God's anger – "Why, O Lord, should your anger flare up?" – seems to be based on the way God responded to Cain's anger at his rejected offering, "Why are you angry?" (Gen. 4:6). This too implies that God is the instigator of how these conversations should play out.

always lead to forgiveness. This entailed proclaiming God's thirteen attributes:

> The Lord, the Lord! God, compassionate and gracious, slow to anger, and abounding in kindness and truth, keeping kindness to a thousand generations, forgiving iniquity, rebellion and sin, but does not acquit the guilty. (Ex. 34:6–7)

There would always be consequences for sin – indeed, the people directly involved in worshipping the Golden Calf were punished, but all the rest were forgiven and, according to Rabbi Yoḥanan, God reassured Moses that, "whenever Israel sin, let them say this prayer before Me and I will forgive them."[14]

Moses did just that the following year in another major protest story. The people had now left Sinai and sent spies ahead to check out the Land of Israel. But they returned with a damning and insidious report that caused the Israelites to erupt in regret: "If only we had died in the land of Egypt!" (Num. 14:2). They were about to stone their leaders when God appeared, halting the insurrection (Num. 14:10). God said to Moses:

> How long will this people despise Me, and how long will they not trust Me.... I will strike them with the plague and destroy them, and I shall make you a nation greater and mightier than they. (Num. 14:11–12)

Note the similarity to the Mount Sinai episode. Once more God is fed up and wants to begin again with Moses. This time, however, no hint is necessary. Moses knows exactly what to do. He immediately responds, just as he did at Sinai:

> The Egyptians will hear that through Your power You brought up this people from their midst...yet You would put to death this people? ...The nations that heard of Your fame will say,

14. Rosh HaShana 17b.

> "Because of the Lord's inability to bring this people to the land that He swore them, He slaughtered them in the wilderness." (Num. 14:13–16)

Again, we see that God's threat gave Moses the opportunity to reassert the aim of the redemption, to bring the Israelites safely to the Promised Land. And, as before, Moses asks for forgiveness, but this time, he is in possession of the formula that cannot fail:

> May the Lord's strength be great, as You have spoken, saying, "The Lord is slow to anger and abounding in kindness, forgiving iniquity and rebellion, but does not acquit the guilty." (Num. 14:17–18)[15]

And God accepts Moses's words as expected: "And the Lord said, 'I have forgiven, according to your word'" (Num. 14:20). The spies and this generation of Israelites are then punished, but the Israelites survive as a people, just as God promised.

These two episodes exemplify the argument motif in Torah. This process is made up of four stages: God threatens destruction, the people's advocate protests, God forgives, and God passes judgment only on the guilty. It turns out that rather than denigrating God, protest seems to be what God wanted all along. "Said the Holy One, blessed be God, to Moses, 'Moses, you have given Me life with your words.'"[16] Note also Moses's response when God proposed to rebuild a nation starting just from him. In both episodes, Moses completely ignores the offer, focusing instead on defending his people. This too is what God expects of leaders.[17]

The rabbinic sages understood the argument motif to play a vital role in the ongoing relationship between the Jewish people and God. They instituted that at times of hardship and in recalling past tragedies,

15. A number of commentators, including Nahmanides, explain why Moses lists only some of the thirteen attributes.
16. Berakhot 32a, interpreting God's phrasing, "as I live," in Numbers 14:21.
17. Moses was praised for advocating so vociferously for his people. See Deuteronomy Rabba 11:3.

prayers should incorporate this motif. Thus, the Torah readings on all public fast days and the many *seliḥot* prayers contain key verses from these episodes, when Moses petitioned God on behalf of the people. In the Sephardi traditions and in many communities in Israel a version of this is recited every day, save Shabbat and festivals.[18]

Back to Abraham

The original and more extensive version of the argument motif can be traced back to a well-known story in Genesis. God said to Abraham:

> Because the outcry of Sodom and Gomorrah has become great, and because their sin has been so grave, I will go down to see whether this outcry before Me deserves their destruction, or if not, I will know. (Gen. 18:20–21)

As with Moses, God informed Abraham of intended mass destruction. However, unlike in the case of Moses, the inhabitants of the cities under threat were not Abraham's people. Nevertheless, he does not remain silent:

> And Abraham stepped forward and said, "Will You really wipe out the righteous with the wicked? Perhaps there may be fifty righteous within the city. Will You really wipe out the place and not forgive it for the sake of the fifty righteous within it… Far be it from You! Will not the Judge of all the earth not act justly?" (Gen. 18:23–25)

The sages characterized this interaction as a dramatic confrontation:

> Rabbi Yehuda said: Abraham stepped forward for battle.… Rabbi Neḥemia said: He stepped forward to reconcile.… The Rabbis said: He stepped forward to pray.… Rabbi Elazar said: Abraham

18. *Mishna Berura* 134:1, *Kaf HaḤayim* 134:1.

> declared, "Whether it be for battle, for conciliation, or for prayer, I am coming!"[19]

This midrash makes it clear that Abraham is challenging the justice of God's decision. And yet, incredibly, God is entirely unfazed by this and immediately compromises: "Should I find in Sodom fifty righteous within the city, I will forgive the whole place for their sake" (Gen. 18:26).

Abraham persists, asking if forty-five are enough to save all. God concedes yet again and so the back-and-forth continues. Abraham asks for forty, then thirty, then twenty, then ten, and each time God agrees, but after ten God departs and Abraham can go no further.

At first sight, even more than with Moses, this exchange seems to disregard God's authority. Abraham is audacious and demanding, accusatory and relentless in his campaign. Despite all this, though, God never reprimands him. There is no indication that Abraham is behaving inappropriately or is in any way wrong to address God in this manner. I am struck by Abraham's candor each time I study this episode.

God's composure is more understandable when we notice that before He speaks to Abraham, the Torah revealed His thinking to us:

> Shall I conceal from Abraham what I am about to do? For Abraham will surely become a great and mighty nation, and all the nations of the earth will be blessed through him. For I have become acquainted with him so that he may direct his children and his household after him to keep the way of the Lord by doing what is right and just. (Gen. 18:17–19)

With Moses, we had to infer how God urged him to protest, but here God's thinking is clearer. God *wants* Abraham to be the progenitor of a significant nation, so Abraham needs to be able to handle the huge responsibility this entails. He must be able to do battle for its survival against all odds. He must be willing to make a stand even if the chance of success is extremely slim. For this, we learn, is "the way of the Lord," to do "what is right and just" at all costs. In fact, forms of the Hebrew

19. Genesis Rabba 49:8.

word for doing what is right, *tzedek*, occur seven times in Abraham's argument with God. This is a literary device to indicate the underlying theme of Abraham's protest – the fight for a fair and just outcome.[20]

This argument motif, begun by Abraham and then taken up by Moses, transforms our understanding of God in the Torah. God is not presented as an aloof, perfect being that can never be questioned. On the contrary, our biblical heroes challenge God and hold God to account with impunity, which in no way diminishes God.

To reference a contemporary image, it is as if the Torah casts God as a boxing coach, training his students to be prizefighters for doing what is right and just. Abraham and Moses, our foremost Jewish leaders, are given the opportunity to spar with God and practice their craft, emboldened with a powerful sense of moral responsibility. God celebrates when they score points against Him because this makes them better leaders, more able to do battle in the name of what is right and just for their own people and for others too. God coached Abraham by telling him, "Do not be afraid" (Gen. 15:1) and "walk in front of Me" (Gen. 17:1). And God spent time training Moses for his mission to Pharaoh, arming him with miraculous signs (Ex. 3:1–4:17). The Torah portrays God as a dedicated mentor to both of them.

God also taught them the rules of engagement; this is the bond of *brit*, covenant. Abraham's protest over Sodom and Gomorrah occurs immediately after God commits to an eternal covenant with him and his descendants (Gen. 17:1–14). Similarly, Moses's protest at Mount Sinai occurs in the wake of the establishment of the national covenant when Moses "took the book of the covenant and read it in the hearing of all the people, and they said, 'All that the Lord has spoken we will do and we will heed'" (Ex. 24:7). Thus, both Abraham and Moses knew for sure that they were bound in a relationship with God that could not be broken. Being within the framework of a covenantal relationship boosted these leaders' ability to argue with confidence.

20. The seven occurrences are Genesis 18:23, 24 (twice), 25 (twice), 26, 28. The literary device is known as *mila manḥa*, the "guiding word," also called *Leitwort*. See Yonatan Grossman, "Study of Biblical Narrative, Lecture #11: *Leitwort*," Part I, https://torah.etzion.org.il/en/leitwort-part-i.

Two additional elements of the argument motif occur in the episodes with Abraham and Moses. First, there is always mention of Israel becoming "a great nation," *goi gadol* (Gen. 18:18; Ex. 32:10; Num. 14:12). This reminds the reader of the purpose of these protests: to forge the nation and its defenders. Second, the combined elements of God's judgment and forgiveness always play a role. God's judgment leads to a degree of punishment, but there is always an element of forgiveness too. Sodom and Gomorrah would have been forgiven if there had been enough righteous residents. Only the revelers in the Golden Calf episode were punished, while Moses was taught how to attain forgiveness for the rest. Similarly, the Israelites were judged for their initial rejection of the land. Along with the spies, all the adults of that generation were punished, but as a nation they were forgiven, and their children were able to continue on to Israel.

We see, then, that divine judgment is God's innate way of doing what is "just" (*mishpat*), while divine forgiveness is God's innate way of doing what is "right" (*tzedaka*). These two must work in combination. Without forgiveness, God's judgment is not right and just. God empowered both Abraham and Moses to fight for a combination of *tzedaka* and *mishpat*. It has already been mentioned that God knew Abraham to be a man who does what is "right and just" (Gen. 18:19), and, in a fitting parallel, it says of Moses in the penultimate chapter of the Torah: "He carried out the *right* way of the Lord, and God's *just* acts for Israel" (Deut. 33:21).[21]

Now we can appreciate why arguing with God in the Torah is not only possible but necessary for the physical survival and moral development of the Jewish people. Human protest is an articulation of *tzedaka* and *mishpat* – doing what is right and just. These attributes establish rather than diminish God's perfection: "The Rock, His work is whole, for all His ways are just … right and fair is He" (Deut. 32:4).

21. Moses is not mentioned by name here but, Rashi and other commentators state that it refers to him.

Argument vs. Acceptance

If arguing with God is so valued in the Torah, how does this square with the undeniable importance of conformity, which makes up the everyday practice of Judaism? We are duty bound to accept God's laws, not argue against them; to live them, not protest them. The expected norm is respectful obedience, not moral defiance.

This apparent contradiction can be resolved by noticing an incredible irony. The person who initiated arguing with God's will turns out to be the very same person who came to exemplify the acceptance of God's will. The supreme act of submission to be found in the Torah is undoubtedly Abraham's readiness to sacrifice his son (Gen. 22:1–19). Known as the *Akeida*, or the Binding of Isaac, this famous story is usually understood as a lesson in devotion.

When Abraham was instructed to abort the sacrifice, the angel told him: "For now I know that you fear God, because you have not held back your son, your only son, from Me" (Gen. 22:12). With this act, Abraham came to exemplify the servant of God who displays obedience even in the face of the strongest personal feelings. The problem is that Abraham now appears to be somewhat of a contradiction. How could the man who protested the destruction of the sinful cities of Sodom and Gomorrah not challenge God when told to sacrifice his own innocent offspring? Why did he take God to task in one case but just accept the task in another?

To respond to this, we first need to address the shocking nature of the *Akeida* itself. To the modern mind, it is morally outrageous. What kind of God commands the killing of a child? How could God have ever asked this of Abraham? How could a father lift a knife to his son? And why does such an ethically suspect story even appear in our holy Torah? To some readers, Abraham's absolute obedience here is more disturbing than the question of arguing with God. But both, as you will see, are fundamental.

The sages sought to make sense of the *Akeida* in various ways: God never intended the test to be completed; Abraham misunderstood the command; or he chose to suppress his feelings; he knew Isaac would be saved somehow, and so on.[22] Despite these justifications, the harshness

22. Taanit 4a; Genesis Rabba 56:8, 10.

of the experience is still palpable. It was suggested that Sarah's death soon after (Gen. 23:2) may have been due to shock, sadness, or disappointment.[23] Azariah, the first-century rabbi, said it was unnatural for a parent to kill their child.[24] One medieval commentator even asked, "How could the Lord command such an abomination to be done?"[25]

The most meaningful explanation for me comes from Maimonides, who addresses the *Akeida* as a parable. He explains that when the angel says, "For now I know that you fear God," it cannot mean that until now God did not know and had set the trial to find out the extent of Abraham's devotion. Of course, God already knew, for God is all-knowing. Rather, the lesson was for us to acquire the angel's perspective so that *now we know* what reverence for God truly entails. Maimonides writes:

> The aim of all the trials mentioned in the Torah is to teach people what they ought to do or believe. Concerning the act which forms the trial, it is as if the purpose is not the accomplishment of the act itself; but rather its purpose is to be a model to learn from and be guided by.[26]

Maimonides is saying that the intent of the story is its lesson, not the event itself. A principal goal of the entire Torah, he argues, is to teach reverence for God.

Though Abraham protests vehemently against God in one narrative and yet displays devout reverence for God in another, this is not a contradiction. Both are essential aspects of how we interact with God. *There is a time for argument and a time for acceptance.* God invited Abraham to question the destruction of Sodom and Gomorrah, while the *Akeida* was a direct instruction demanding to be obeyed. One was a dialogue while the other was a directive. The challenge is in finding

23. Leviticus Rabba 20:2.
24. Genesis Rabba 56:5.
25. Hannah Kasher, "'How Could the Lord Command Such an Abomination to Be Done?' – Rabbi Joseph ibn Caspi's Critics on the Binding of Isaac," *Et-Hadaat* 1 (1997): 38–46 [Hebrew].
26. Maimonides, *Guide for the Perplexed* 3:24.

the balance, knowing which is appropriate in any given situation. The strongest evidence for this is that these two episodes both occur *in the very same sedra,* only three chapters apart. By having them both read out on the same Shabbat morning in synagogue, our tradition is pressing us to contrast the two and manage the delicate balance between them. This only adds to the subtlety and intensity of our relationship to God. We must be reverent enough to follow faithfully, but close enough to argue ardently, and still always thoughtful enough to work out when each is appropriate.

Influencing Prayer

It is important to realize that both these stories involving Abraham have profoundly influenced the daily morning liturgy. However, the way they each appear is surprising and gives us insight into the central role of petition in our daily devotions.

Abraham's clash with God over Sodom and Gomorrah led to the establishment of the daily morning *Amida,* the silent standing prayer at the high point of the service. Though Abraham's protest failed because the cities did not contain enough righteous citizens to unseal their fate, nevertheless, he did not concede. On the morrow, the day set for the destruction, "Abraham arose early in the morning to the place where he had stood before God" (Gen. 19:27). He was returning to the site which overlooked the doomed cities, where he had argued with God.[27] Sforno writes: "Since Abraham had failed to find justification for them in terms of strict justice, he thought to plead for compassion on their behalf."[28]

Clearly, Abraham had not given up. His presence on the scene was a last-ditch effort to challenge God's verdict; he was still hoping for an eleventh-hour reprieve. Abraham's final stand is the origin of the morning *Amida*. The Talmud teaches, "Abraham instituted the morning *Amida*

27. This is clear when comparing Genesis 18:16 and 19:28.
28. Sforno on Genesis 19:27; the Radak concurs. Others propose that Abraham returned because he did not know if indeed there were enough righteous citizens (Rashi) or to pray for the safe rescue of his nephew Lot from Sodom (Rif on *Ein Yaakov* to Berakhot 6b).

prayer, as it says, 'Abraham arose early in the morning to the place where he had stood.'"[29]

Two key points can be drawn from this. First, in the *Akeida* the Torah also uses the phrase "Abraham arose early in the morning" (Gen. 22:3), and so this second episode is often mistakenly thought to be the origin of the morning *Amida* rather than the first one. After all, it is a little surprising that a story about arguing with God was understood by the rabbis to be the inspiration for the daily morning *Amida,* instead of a far more conservative story of submission to God. The point, then, is exactly the opposite. The morning *Amida* is not a prayer of acceptance and devotion but rather one of petition and confrontation.

This leads to the second point, that the Hebrew word for "had stood" in the Torah is *amad,* which is the root of the word *Amida* itself. In other words, to recite this *Amida* is to "make a stand," just as Abraham did. We are thus reminded, every day, to be aware of the suffering of other nations, as well as our own, and to appeal to God to be merciful. And, being at the start of the day, this cannot but spur us on to find practical ways to contribute to alleviating this suffering during our day. The Talmud also learns the general principle of fixing a regular place to pray from the fact that Abraham returned "to the place he had stood before God."[30] This further emphasizes the need to never give up this challenge, but to return to it daily, every time we pray, thus guiding us to act for others.

The *Akeida* has also found its way into the morning liturgy. There is a tradition to recite the entire episode daily,[31] so it is now printed in many prayer books after the morning blessings.[32] Though, as discussed, the episode testifies to Abraham's supreme commitment to God, it is employed for a very different purpose in prayer, as is clear from the rabbinically authored passage inserted as a postscript:

29. Berakhot 26b.
30. Berakhot 6b.
31. *Shulḥan Arukh, Oraḥ Ḥayim* 1:5.
32. *The Koren Shalem Siddur,* 32–35.

> Master of the Universe, just as Abraham our father suppressed his compassion to do Your will wholeheartedly, so may Your compassion suppress Your anger from us, and may Your compassion prevail over Your other attributes.[33]

This statement requires careful reading to notice the subtle switch-around it expresses. Abraham's loyalty is lauded because he "suppressed his compassion" but, in response, we ask God that "Your compassion suppress Your anger." So instead of idealizing the suppression of compassion, the prayer switches to promoting the suppression of anger. Indeed, it then says, "May Your compassion prevail over Your other attributes." Before our eyes this postscript has transformed the lesson of the *Akeida*. Rather than learning, as Abraham did, to be unquestionably devoted to God by suppressing our feelings of compassion, the *Akeida* has been reframed as a petition text on our behalf. It has been flipped into an appeal to God to "suppress Your anger" and, as the postscript continues, "deal with us, Lord our God, with the attributes of loving-kindness and compassion."[34]

In the hands of the sages who constructed the daily morning liturgy, these two biblical episodes in which Abraham appears take on new meaning. The starkly contrasting stories of argument and acceptance have both been adapted to focus on the respectful but insistent petitioning of God. This, again, testifies to the intimate relationship that we express in our prayers. We are reverent *to* God as well as reasoning *with* God. This has a powerful effect on the human psyche. When encountering challenges, we can appreciate why they are happening and, at the same time, not accept them as inevitable. We can still constantly find ways to face up to them and overcome them. To react like this is to follow in the footsteps of both Abraham and Moses in their pursuit of doing what is right and just, inspired by God.

---

33. Ibid., 34. A version of this also appears at the end of the *Zikhronot* section of the Rosh HaShana Musaf prayer.
34. The basis for this appears to be Genesis Rabba 56:10.

Tears of a Strained Relationship

We have explained that the argument motif is ever present in our regular liturgy. Nevertheless, in periods of dire need, the tradition of protest has found even more intense expression. After centuries of European persecution, the rise of Hasidism played an important role in this. That is why there are numerous examples of grappling with God to be found in the hasidic tradition. The responses of judgment and forgiveness that make up God's way of being right and just occur here, in dramatic and unrestrained ways. A story from the founding father of Hasidism powerfully demonstrates this:

> "Do you know who rescinded the celestial decree that would have unleashed catastrophe unto our people?" the Baal Shem asked Rebbe Nahman of Horodenko. "I'll tell you. Neither I nor you, nor the sages, nor the great spiritual leaders. Our litanies, our fasting were all in vain. We were saved by a woman, a woman of our people. This is how it happened: She came to the synagogue, tears running down her face, and addressed the Almighty: 'Master of the Universe, are You or are You not our father? Why won't You listen to your children imploring You? You see, I am a mother. Children I have plenty of: five. And every time they shed a tear, it breaks my heart. But You, Father, You have so many more. Every man is Your child, and every one of them is weeping and weeping. Even if Your heart is made of stone, how can You remain indifferent?' And," the Baal Shem concluded, "God decided she was right."[35]

In the world of hasidic tales an unnamed Jewish mother, drenched in tears but inspired by her ancestors Abraham and Moses, can challenge God, and win. Such is the familiarity she has with her Maker. The Talmud says, "Though the gates of prayer may be closed, the gate of tears

35. Wiesel, *Souls on Fire*, 43–44. This tale might have been inspired by the story of Hagar weeping as her son was dying, until God intervened (Gen. 21:15–19).

is never closed."[36] In another aphorism we learn that God collects these tears and never fails to account for them:

> Anyone who sheds tears over a decent person, the Holy One, Blessed be He, counts their tears and places them in His treasury, as it is stated, "My sorrow you Yourself have counted out, place my tears in Your bottle; are they not in Your counting?" (Ps. 56:9)[37]

In the nightmare of the Holocaust, this intensely personal and passionate way of talking about God reemerged but was strained almost to a breaking point.[38] One extreme example was the parable written by the survivor and scholar David Weiss Halivni (1927–2022). He boldly reimagined the aphorism about collecting tears:

> When the sound of the closing of the door, after the first child was shoved into the crematorium, reached heaven, Michael, the most beneficent of angels, could not contain himself and angrily approached God. Michael asked, "Do You now pour out Your wrath upon children? In the past, children were indirectly caught up in the slaughter. This time they are the chief target of destruction. Have pity on the little ones, O, Lord." God, piqued by Michael's insolence, shouted back at him, "I am the Lord of the Universe. If you are displeased with the way I conduct the world, I will return it to void and null."
>
> Hearing these words, Michael knew that there was no reversal. He had heard these words once before in connection with the Ten Martyrs. He knew their effect. He went back to his place, ashen and dejected, but could not resist looking back sheepishly at God and saw a huge tear rolling down His

36. Berakhot 32b; Bava Metzia 59a. This is the theme of *Ne'ila*, short for *Ne'ilat She'arim*, "the closing of the gates," the final prayer service on Yom Kippur. E.g., "Open us a gate at the time of the locking of the gate, for day is passing" (*Koren Yom Kippur Mahzor* [2012], 1148).
37. Shabbat 105b.
38. See, for example, Elie Wiesel, *Night* (Hill and Wang, 2006), 34; Yaffa Eliach, *Hasidic Tales of the Holocaust* (Avon, 1982), 190–91, 250–51.

> face, destined for the legendary cup which collects tears and which, when full, will bring the redemption of the world. Alas, to Michael's horror, instead of entering the cup, the tear hit its rim, most of it spilling on the ground – and the fire of the crematorium continued to burn.[39]

In this story the tears being collected are not human; they come from God. The angel Michael has asked for pity on the children, and though refused, he catches God crying.[40] But the tears are no longer filling the cup of redemption; they are just spilling on the ground. In other words, they make no difference at all. The suffering has become meaningless. To Weiss Halivni, the pain and horror of the Holocaust did not bring redemption any closer; it was all in vain.

How can we make sense of such a perspective that flies in the face of faith? This heartbreaking imagery is what happens when the circumstances are so terrible that they appear irredeemable, when hope is overwhelmed by despair. After the war, many Jews gave up on God. In the shadow of the death camps, the Jewish tradition of protest had become so intense, so extreme, that it reached crisis point. Why argue if God does not listen? If the worst can happen, *and it did,* then why keep up the challenge?

Back to Isaac

This relates to one of the worries with which this chapter began. The possibility of arguing with God can, when overstretched, diminish our view of God, and this in turn can lead to a rejection of faith. When forgiveness is not forthcoming, when expectations are not met, then many become disillusioned. Despite this, God wants us to answer back in the face of injustice and to petition for forgiveness. What then prevents us from despairing when we experience severe tragedy?

---

39. David Weiss Halivni, *The Book and the Sword: A Life of Learning in the Shadow of Destruction* (Farrar, Straus and Girou, 1996), 3.
40. There are also examples of God crying in rabbinic literature; see Lamentations Rabba, *Petiḥta* 24 and 1:1.

Why play out this drama at all? What is the ultimate purpose of the argument motif?

One response to this issue comes from an audacious story in the Talmud in which the themes of justice, despair, and forgiveness all play a part.[41] In the future, it says, the Jewish people will inevitably sin and deserve punishment. When this time comes, God will ask the patriarchs in heaven to defend their descendants. However, when God says to Abraham and Jacob in turn, "Your children have sinned against Me," they each will respond, "Sovereign of the Universe, let them be wiped out for the sanctification of Your Name!" Unsatisfied with their dismissive replies, God will then turn to the last remaining patriarch:

> God will say to Isaac, "Your children have sinned against me." But Isaac will answer God, "Sovereign of the Universe, are they *my* children and not *Your* children? In their commitment to You they said 'we will do' before 'we will listen' (Ex. 24:7) and You called them, 'Israel my son, my firstborn' (Ex. 4:22), and now they are my sons and not Your sons?"

Isaac is both informal and accusatory, which is quite surprising given the previous responses of both his father and his son. But Isaac is only just getting started. The Talmud continues:

> [Isaac then said:] "And after all, how much have they really sinned? How long does an average person live, seventy years? Well, subtract the first twenty, for which You do not punish, and there remain fifty. Then subtract twenty-five for nights, and there remain twenty-five. Subtract another twelve and a half for prayer, eating, and toilet breaks, and there remain just twelve and a half in which to sin. Now if You will shoulder all that, then great, but if not, then let half be on me and half on You. And should You say that they must all be on me, then fine, after all, I offered myself up before You didn't I?"

41. Shabbat 89b.

Isaac's petition is forthright and yet surprisingly playful. Having been almost sacrificed himself, he is confident in questioning God's desire to punish people for sinning. He points out that our lives are not so long anyway and that most of our time is taken up with mundane human activities, so how much can we really sin after all?

You might think that Isaac is being facetious, but he is making a profound point. What can God really expect of us? We're only human, of course we will make mistakes, but most of the time we will just be getting on with living. For Isaac, trying to justify human existence to God is laughable, literally.[42] This is what he learned from the *Akeida*: he was young and innocent and yet he was still nearly sacrificed. We are all God's creations and God can do whatever God wills. Trying to defend our lives to God would be like a character in a novel trying to justify to the author why they should not be killed off in the next chapter.

Amazingly, God accepts this line of argument, for the talmudic story continues with the Jewish people quoting a biblical verse which is interpreted as their thanks to Isaac for defending them when the other patriarchs would not: "For You [Isaac] are our father, because Abraham did not know us, and Israel [Jacob] did not recognize us" (Is. 63:16). The story ends with Isaac saying to them, "Instead of praising me, praise the Holy One." And they do, by completing the verse just quoted: "You, God, are our Father, our Redeemer; from time immemorial is Your Name."

This intriguing talmudic allegory is a direct response to the question of despair. Isaac's perspective shows that life can never be justified existentially, and to this even God has no answer. This is why, despite the experience of the *Akeida*, Isaac could remain committed to God.

Similarly, the tragedy of the Holocaust can never be explained or justified by theology. All we can say is that the *Jewish people survived and Judaism continues*:

42. The Hebrew word for Isaac is *Yitzḥak*, which means "he will laugh." In the Torah, Isaac's naming, birth and personality are all associated with laughter and playfulness, see Gen. 17:17–19, 21:6, and 26:8.

> One writer about the Holocaust records that he met a rabbi who had been through the camps, and who, miraculously, seemed unscarred. He could still laugh. "How," he asked him, "could you see what you saw and still have faith? Did you have no questions?" The rabbi replied: "Of course I had questions. But I said to myself: If you ever ask those questions, they are such good questions that the Almighty will send you a personal invitation to heaven to give you answers. And I preferred to be here on earth with the questions than up in heaven with the answers."[43]

The narratives in the Torah teach us that we can and should challenge God in the name of what is right and just. We might not always win, but we should continue nonetheless.

We Can Be Heroes

Religious protest is integral to Judaism. It plays an essential role in our relationship with God. In essence, God demands that we defend what is right and just through prayer and deed. To train for this, God acts, as it were, like a coach: "Let Me teach you, instruct you the way you should go; let Me counsel you with My own sight" (Ps. 32:8). The injustices of this world should motivate us to make a difference. We are compelled to do this even if it means taking on God, as this hasidic story demonstrates:

> A disciple made the following remark in front of Rebbe Menahem-Mendl of Kotzk: "God, who is perfect, took six days to create a world that is not; how is that possible?" The rebbe scolded him, "Could you do better?" "Yes, I think so," stammered the disciple, who no longer knew what he was saying. "You could have done better?" the Master cried out. "Then what are you waiting for? You don't have a minute to waste, go ahead, start working!"[44]

43. Jonathan Sacks, "The Holocaust in Jewish Theology," in *Tradition in an Untraditional Age: Essays on Modern Jewish Thought* (Vallentine Mitchell, 1990), 153.
44. Elie Wiesel, *Messengers of God: Biblical Portraits and Legends* (Random House, 1976), 35–36.

The preponderance of protest prayers in our tradition gives voice to the frustrations we have with our lives, with our faith, and with the state of the world. Our daily liturgy, and especially the *piyyutim, seliḥot,* and *viddui* prayers, add depth to our conversations with God. Unfortunately, these have become less familiar for many, and so we think that doubts, troubling thoughts, and feelings of rebelliousness have no place in the *siddur* or the synagogue. But the truth is the exact opposite. Generations of passionate and thoughtful Jews have written these ideas and emotions into our prayers, and they can be very helpful if we embrace them.[45]

The tradition of protest demands that we never accept passively the suffering, pain, and unfairness we find, but rather that we do our best to diminish it. This means, like Moses, standing up for our own people, and like Abraham, coming to the aid of the wider world.

Whether helping with *local* projects, such as improving the accessibility of mental health provisions in our own Jewish communities, or supporting *global* initiatives, such as COVAX, which works toward equal access to lifesaving tests, treatments, and vaccines for poorer countries, the fight for what is right and just is an essential part of what Judaism stands for.

This fight is bolstered by speaking out against injustices within society and demanding change, just as Abraham and Moses did. The eleventh blessing in the weekday *Amida,* recited three times daily, reminds us of this on a regular basis: "Blessed are You, Lord, the King who loves righteousness and justice."[46] Indeed, the Talmud[47] says that all the commandments in the Torah can be predicated upon these two ethical principles which were taught to the prophet Isaiah: "Thus said the Lord: Guard justice and do what is right" (Is. 56:1).

Superheroes always have fatal flaws that punctuate their never-ending physical fights, but God's only vulnerability is His commitment to the Jewish people and care for all humanity. *The radical message of the Jewish tradition is that God wants us to exploit this.* God's vulnerability facilitates our strength. For it hands us the keys to this world and energizes us to never give up in the pursuit of doing what is right and just.

---

45. Laytner, *Arguing with God,* 174–76.
46. *The Koren Shalem Siddur,* 120, 218, and 264.
47. Makkot 24a.

Chapter 11

What If You Still Have Difficulties with Belief?

EXPLORING THE QUESTION

Despite being raised within a Jewish home, having had some meaningful religious experiences, and admiring certain rabbis and teachers, there are still many Jews who find it hard to believe in God and the Torah. This is clear from numerous reports and studies.[1] There is no one reason for this. Emotional, intellectual, and social factors all play a role.

Some have had their challenging questions ignored, rejected, disparaged, or just unsatisfactorily answered. Others have found biblical stories far-fetched, or Torah laws morally troubling, and they cannot see how or why God would interact with human beings in this way.

Although Judaism prides itself on the importance of family, a not insignificant number of people were raised in an unhappy Jewish home. They may have suffered from childhood experiences that were emotionally or physically disturbing or, in extreme cases, abusive.

---

1. E.g., "Jewish Americans in 2020: Jewish Identity and Belief," *Pew Research Center* (May 11, 2021), www.pewresearch.org/religion/2021/05/11/jewish-identity-and-belief/; Faranak Margolese, *Off the Derech: How to Respond to the Challenge* (CreateSpace Independent Publishing, 2005); Sergio DellaPergola and L. Daniel Staetsky, *The Jewish Identities of European Jews: What, Why and How* (Institute of Jewish Policy Research, December 2021), 26–32.

Understandably, this may have left them with very negative associations with Jewish life.

Then there is another group who have trouble relating to spirituality. Such experiences leave them cold and unmoved. They look elsewhere for meaning and purpose in life. Others, meanwhile, find it hard to see the value of religion today. The variety of attitudes and lifestyles offered by the modern world speak to them much more than their Judaism.

You may identify with some of the above factors. Many people have struggled with belief, and no two stories are the same. Valuable insights from contemporary psychology, the practice of active listening, and a deeper appreciation of the complexities of human identity have taught us never to underestimate or dismiss the range of factors that influence our feelings and decisions.

Whatever the reasons may be, the result is that believing in God as the Creator of the universe and giver of the Torah has become difficult to accept for many individuals. This book has predominantly focused on intellectual questions, responding to three broad kinds of challenges: the truth and purpose of origin narratives such as Creation, the Flood, and the Exodus; the ethics of the Torah's laws, such as slavery, sacrifice, collective punishment, and chosenness; and the nature of religious belief and arguing with God. However, these questions are frequently entangled with emotional factors. The heart and mind do not function independently. Each reacts to and is influenced by the other. The social and cultural context of the schooling we have received is part and parcel of our overall education and upbringing.

And so, these responses may not be enough for some readers. You may still have nagging doubts that make it difficult to be a committed Jew. This is not always easy to deal with and, over time, can dilute the appreciation of our Jewish heritage. Nevertheless, there is more to say.

It is also important to acknowledge the pressures of expectation and the feelings of guilt which can come from family and community when it comes to religious belief. They might say one of the following:

How can you turn your back on generations of our ancestors?

> Just don't rock the boat.
>
> In the shadow of the Holocaust, we mustn't let go of our traditions; we owe it to the victims.
>
> Please don't disappoint us, you can't just throw all this away.

These types of loaded comments are all too common. No tradition as old as ours could have survived without such anxieties seeping in. Whether expressed aloud or heard internally, they are unsettling and hurtful, even though they may have been said (or implied) with care and conviction. Furthermore, they are all very negative motives for living as a Jew. We should be able to find constructive reasons to build upon, rather than feeding feelings of guilt and the constant desire to meet the expectations of others.

By voicing these worries, parents, teachers, and leaders reveal how much Judaism means to them. However, ultimately, these words and arguments can be damaging. They might help for a while, but to be fully engaged as a human being, it is vital to have positive and stimulating reasons for how to live your life. Having a constructive Jewish outlook is much healthier than continually being warned of the threats of assimilation and extinction.

The issue then is this: If belief in God is difficult, does that have to detract from being excited and inspired by Judaism? Is Jewish life so founded upon faith that without it everything comes tumbling down? Does lack of belief make you a lesser Jew? Is being an unbeliever unforgivable, or are there other paths that can bind us to tradition in upbeat and compelling ways?

RESPONDING TO THE QUESTION

To construct a committed Jewish life that ignores God is problematic. It is, however, quite common. Rather than being ortho*dox*, accepting the principles of Jewish belief, many Jews are what can be termed ortho*prax*, meaning that they follow the practices of Judaism rather than accepting the theology. They deeply appreciate the ethical value of Jewish life, while not being enthusiastic about belief. The social and soulful aspects of prayer are what bring them to synagogue. The joy of family get-togethers is what motivates them to observe Shabbat and the festivals.

These are, of course, very positive and powerful aspects of Jewish practice. Bringing up children in such an environment teaches them many important life lessons, as well as grounding them in the values of a caring family and supportive community. But Judaism has much to say about belief and, in the long run, this is sorely needed to live a meaningful and fulfilling Jewish life.

Whereas chapter 9 presented belief as a quest for God, we will take a different approach here. The aim is not to find alternatives to God, but rather to reframe how we think about belief as a concept and as a lived experience.

It is a commonly held view that belief in God requires a "leap of faith." And so, to answer the question "Do you believe in God?" in the positive means to affirm a truth that cannot be proved. Thinking that religious faith necessitates accepting something that is irrational or beyond reason has led many people to dismiss it. The Hebrew word for "faith" or "belief" is *emuna*. In its various forms, which all contain the same three-letter grammatical root *A-M-N*, it appears thirty-nine times in the Torah. *Emuna,* however, has many more connotations than its English counterparts.

This chapter will elaborate on five of these connotations. They can be categorized as faithfulness, citizenship, loyalty, antiquity, and integrity. Despite all the reservations expressed above, these connotations of *emuna* can transform belief into something easier to accept and much more meaningful for living a religious life today.

Emuna as Faithfulness

If *emuna* were simply belief in God's existence, then we might have expected the word to be used when a biblical character encounters God, to confirm the truth of that experience. But *emuna* never appears in that way.

God first speaks to Abraham in chapter 12 of Genesis, but it is not until chapter 15, which takes place more than a decade later after Abraham has already had several divine encounters, that the word first occurs. God promises Abraham that he will have children whose offspring will be as innumerable as all the stars in the sky. The Torah records Abraham's reaction as, "He believed (*he'emin*) in God, and God reckoned this to his merit" (Gen. 15:6). The connotation here is that Abraham trusted that what God promised him would be fulfilled. His "merit" was that he expressed his faithfulness.[2] We see here that *emuna* means trust in an assured future rather than abstract belief.

Emuna has the same meaning when Moses first meets God, at the Burning Bush. God is trying to persuade him to lead the Israelites out of slavery, but Moses is reluctant, "They will not believe (*ya'aminu*) me" (Ex. 4:1), he says. So God teaches him two signs, his staff turning into a snake and his hand turning leprous. God said: "If they don't believe you (*lo ya'aminu*) by not heeding the first sign, then they will believe you (*he'eminu*) by heeding the second sign" (Ex. 4:8).

The signs are meant to legitimate Moses in the eyes of the Israelites. Moses wants them to trust that he will lead them to freedom. He needs them to be faithful to the cause initiated by God. Indeed, when he does return to Egypt and shows the Israelite elders these signs, he wins their trust: "Then the people believed (*ya'amen*) and listened" (Ex. 4:31). Here *emuna* is the term used for gaining trust from others and committing to a shared endeavor.

Similarly, the response of the Israelites to the splitting of the Reed Sea was to announce, "They believed (*ya'aminu*) in God and Moses His servant" (Ex. 14:31). This does not mean that they now believed that God and Moses existed – after all, they had already known Moses for many months as he initiated the ten plagues sent from God. Rather, it means that with the downfall of the Egyptian army, the Israelites were finally inspired to declare their faithfulness to God and to following Moses. That is why they burst into song: "Then did Moses sing, and all the Israelites with him, this song to God" (Ex. 15:1).

A few weeks later, when the clan of Amalek attacked the Israelites, Moses appointed fighters and then positioned himself on an overlooking hill, raising his hands heavenward to motivate them to prevail.[3] But the battle dragged on and Moses became tired, so he sat down while

---

2. Rashi gives this interpretation of the verse.
3. Mishna Rosh HaShana 3:8.

Aaron and Hur supported his arms: "And his hands remained steadfast (*emuna*) until sunset" (Ex. 17:12). Years later, when God admonished Miriam and Aaron for criticizing Moses, they were told: "My servant Moses is the most faithful (*ne'eman*) in My entire house" (Num. 12:7).

In these examples, *emuna* refers to further features of faithfulness, namely steadfast commitment and enduring reliability.

The philosopher Martin Buber described the profound difference between *emuna* and *pistis,* the Greek word used to describe Christian belief:

> Emunah originated in the actual experiences of Israel, which were to it experiences of faith.... Emunah is the state of "persevering" – also to be called trust.... [Conversely,] Christian Pistis was born...in the souls of individuals, to whom the challenge came to believe that a man crucified in Jerusalem was their saviour...[and] of the acceptance of the claim and of the confession made both in the soul and to the world: "I believe that it is so."[4]

For Buber, the trusting faithfulness of *emuna* experienced by our ancestors is a world away from the propositional faith of *pistis.*[5]

Another nuance of *emuna* is expressed in the Torah's use of the word *Amen*. During Moses's final days, he tells the Israelites to conduct a commitment ceremony on the mountains of Gerizim and Ebal in central Israel, once they have crossed the Jordan River: "And the entire people shall say, '*Amen*.'"[6] This would be the response of the Israelites to the Levites' recitation of twelve blessings and curses, affirming their acceptance of the covenantal relationship with God. We see here that *Amen* does not mean "I believe," but rather "I agree." It is an expression of faithfulness to a jointly agreed upon enterprise.[7] Each time we say

4. Martin Buber, *The Two Types of Faith* (Syracuse University Press, 2003), 170, 172.
5. Building on this, a useful discussion of three forms of faith can be found in Norman Lamm's *Faith and Doubt* (Ktav, 1986), 6–9.
6. In Deuteronomy 27:15–26, this phrase is repeated twelve times. Though in the Torah only the curses are explicitly mentioned, Sota 37b explains that each one followed a parallel blessing.
7. Another example of this in the Torah is the case of the *sota,* the trial by ordeal for a

Amen to a blessing, we confirm our commitment to that enterprise by voicing our faith in it.

In the negative, *emuna* describes a loss of trust. When the Israelites heard the damning report brought by the spies, there was uproar (Num. 14:1–4); God said to Moses, "How long will they not have faith (*lo ya'aminu*) in Me?" (Num. 14:11).[8] Similarly, when Moses struck the rock instead of speaking to it as instructed, God said to him and his brother: "Because you did not trust (*lo he'emantem*) in Me to sanctify Me before the eyes of the Israelites ... therefore you will not bring this assembly to the land" (Num. 20:12). And, when Moses spoke of the future, of times when the Israelites would be unfaithful to God, he says: "For a wayward brood are they, children with no trust (*lo emun*) in them" (Deut. 32:20).

We see that in each occurrence, a lack of *emuna* implies a lack of faithfulness. Only God is unwaveringly faithful:

> And you shall know that the Lord your God, He is God, the faithful (*ne'eman*) God, keeping the covenant. (Deut. 7:9)

> A God of faithfulness (*El Emuna*) ... right and fair is He. (Deut. 32:4)[9]

In the Talmud we find a fascinating description of the moment back at the Burning Bush when Moses himself lacked *emuna*. But faith in God was not the issue. According to Resh Lakish, God reprimanded Moses for not believing in the Israelites, saying to him:

> They are faithful ones, the descendants of faithful ones (*ma'aminim benei ma'aminim*), while in the end it is you who will not have faith (*leha'amin*).[10]

---

woman suspected of adultery to establish her guilt or innocence. She was asked to agree to the terms of the ritual by saying, "*Amen, Amen*" (Num. 5:22).

8. See also Deuteronomy 1:32 and 9:23.
9. See also Psalms 119:90.
10. Shabbat 97a, based on Exodus 4:31 and Genesis 15:6.

The "end" refers to the time Moses hit the rock, just mentioned. Moses had accused the Israelites of being rebellious (Num. 20:10),[11] showing clearly that he had again lost faith in them, just as God predicted. The lesson here is that even great leaders can make the mistake of doubting their flock. They must never lose faith in their followers' ability to renew their commitment to the cause they all share.[12]

Resh Lakish's comment is the clearest expression as to the nature of *emuna*. No one could have believed in the truth of God's existence more than Moses, for "no prophet again arose in Israel like Moses, whom God knew face-to-face" (Deut. 34:10), and yet he is the very one castigated by God for his lack of *emuna*. This makes it abundantly clear that *emuna*, Jewish belief, is focused on trust. It means *faithfulness* more than it means faith.

This is a boon for those who have difficulty with abstract belief. To have *emuna* is primarily to be *trusting*, *committed*, and *faithful* to the Jewish nation and their dedication to God. *Trusting* in the people with whom you share centuries of history, celebrating festivals and life-cycle events with them, and caring for their welfare. *Committed* to your own Jewish community, other communities around the globe, and to Israel, the homeland of the Jewish people. *Faithful* to generations of Jews who despite life's vicissitudes have shared a common purpose, living meaningfully through their culture and traditions, knowing that they could always rely on God.[13]

Consider that even after all his achievements, if Moses still lost the right to enter Israel because of momentarily losing faith in the Israel-ites, then surely it is being faithful to our fellow Jews that is of paramount importance.[14]

---

11. Maimonides argues that Moses's mistake was losing his temper and calling the Israelites "rebels" (*Shemonah Perakim* 4:5).
12. When I was upset at some recent foolishness in the Jewish community and complained to my teacher, Rabbi Sacks, he would say, "Rafi, never give up on the Jewish people, no matter what, they are *ma'aminim benei ma'aminim!*" It is an important lesson that I have never forgotten.
13. See further in Ephraim Urbach, *The Sages: Their Concepts and Beliefs* (Magnus Press, 1979), 31–36.
14. I am reminded of this when listening to the pop song, *If I Ever Lose My Faith in You*,

Emuna as Citizenship

Does this mean that belief in God is unimportant? This cannot be so. Maimonides's well-known "Thirteen Principles of Faith" appear in our prayers and are taught in most Jewish schools. These statements about God's existence, the authority of the Torah, and reward and punishment are widely recognized as the fundamental principles of Jewish belief. If you cannot subscribe to those, even while being faithful to the Jewish people, then have you not abandoned your faith?

Judaism is rooted in religious belief, but the idea of deriving formal principles came relatively late.[15] Maimonides was among the first to attempt this and his list of Thirteen Principles became the most widely accepted. His motivation may have been the urgent need to clearly identify Judaism's tenets in the face of challenges from the powerful forces of Christianity and Islam in his time.[16] Even so, many other rabbinic authorities were hostile to the introduction of this kind of religious dogma.[17]

Leon Roth called this aversion the "'dogma of the dogma-lessness' of Judaism,"[18] but it would be a mistake to underestimate the lasting importance of the Thirteen Principles.[19] A sign of their popularity is their presence in the *siddur* in two different versions. One is the poetic rendition of the principles, known as *Yigdal,* believed to be composed by Rabbi Daniel bar Judah in fourteenth-century Rome. Many communities sing this hymn at the beginning of the daily morning prayers and at the end of the weekly Friday night service.[20] The other is a prose version of unknown authorship which is arranged as a list of succinct declarations, each beginning with the words *Ani*

---

by Sting: "You could say I lost my faith in science and progress. You could say I lost my belief in the holy Church. You could say I lost my sense of direction. You could say all of this and worse. But if I ever lose my faith in you, there'd be nothing left for me to do" (Gordon Sumner, Sony 1993).

15. Marc B. Shapiro, *The Limits of Orthodox Theology: Maimonides' Thirteen Principles Reappraised* (Littman, 2015), 4–5.
16. J. David Bleich, *With Perfect Faith: The Foundations of Jewish Belief* (Ktav, 1983), 15–16.
17. Abraham Twersky, *A Maimonides Reader* (Behrman House, 1972) 401–2; Menachem Kellner, *Must a Jew Believe Anything?* (Littman, 2006), 77–82.
18. Leon Roth, *Judaism, A Portrait* (Faber and Faber, 1960), 125.
19. Shapiro, *The Limits of Orthodox Theology*, 17–27.
20. *The Koren Shalem Siddur*, 24, 370.

ma'amin be'emuna shelema, "I believe with perfect faith." This can be found at the end of the weekday morning service.[21]

Maimonides was not involved in producing either of these versions and never advocated for his principles to be recited in prayer.[22] In fact, when read in their original context, a wholly different understanding of his objective emerges. The principles appear in his *Commentary on the Mishna*, at the very end of a long essay that serves as an introduction to the penultimate chapter of tractate Sanhedrin. This chapter addresses and qualifies the statement that "All Israel have a share in the World to Come."[23]

Maimonides begins his essay with a discussion of the ultimate good that comes to those who adhere to Jewish practice. He bemoans the lack of understanding of the purpose of religious rewards such as the World to Come and the Messianic Era. People fixate on the rewards themselves, rather than on the mindset required for achieving them: "They do not distinguish between the ultimate good itself and the means that lead to this."[24] Deeming it imperative for every Jew to be more sophisticated in their thinking, he now describes in detail some vital distinctions: between external and internal motivations for following Jewish law; between literalness and metaphor in reading traditional texts; and between enjoying physical and spiritual delights in life.

Maimonides continues, "It is appropriate and necessary to mention at this point that the foundations of our faith can be expressed in thirteen principles," and goes on to explain each one in some detail. However, in the crucial paragraph that follows, he stresses the *societal* rather than *philosophical* importance of these principles:

> When a person believes in these fundamental principles and clarifies their faith in them, they are included in the group called

21. Ibid., 202–5.
22. The practice appears nowhere in the *Mishneh Torah*, his comprehensive code of Jewish law. Nevertheless, Rabbi Yaakov Emden (1697–1776) wrote in his *siddur* that a God-fearing person should recite the Thirteen Principles every day.
23. Mishna Sanhedrin 10:1.
24. Maimonides, *Commentary on the Mishna*, Sanhedrin, chapter 10, Introduction. Based on Twersky's translation.

> "Israel" whom we are to love, care for, and treat, as God commanded, with love and fellowship. This is so even if they should commit every possible sin, due to desire or being overcome by their base passions. Then they will be punished for their sins but will still have a share in the World to Come. They are just considered as "sinners in Israel."

Thus, Maimonides views his Thirteen Principles as the common framework for being affiliated with the Jewish community. They express essential Jewish status. He then adds:

> Nevertheless, if a person gives up any one of these principles, they have removed themselves from the Jewish community. They are an apostate, a heretic.... We are commanded to hate them.

At first glance, this appears severe – rejecting the principles excludes you from the Jewish people and brands you a despised heretic. However – and this is important – nowhere does Maimonides ever prescribe a test or examination for believing in these principles. They are not meant to be used as a diagnostic test to check whether a person should be recognized as a Jew. If your birth mother is Jewish then so are you; this is the accepted halakhic view.[25] You are not required to affirm these principles at your bar/bat mitzva or when you join a synagogue. Being born a Jew means that you are "already foresworn and obligated from Mount Sinai."[26]

Maimonides seems to be describing a form of "Jewish citizenship." Being a Jewish citizen means enjoying the support and care of your fellow citizens. The Jewish people are more akin to a nation than a religion – united by a common origin, history, language, culture, country,

---

25. *Shulḥan Arukh, Even Ha'Ezer* 8:5. See also Mishna Kiddushin 3:12, and the analysis of Deuteronomy 7:4 in Yevamot 23a. Of course, conversion is also possible and will be discussed.
26. Yoma 73b; Nedarim 8a; Shevuot 21b. Specifically this means that the commitment made by the Israelites at Mount Sinai binds all future generations. See Exodus 19:8, 24:7, and the renewal of this commitment in Deuteronomy 29:9–14.

and purpose. Our country was lost when Jerusalem was destroyed by the Romans in the year 70, but we remained citizens of the Jewish nation.

A comparison with British citizenship is helpful. Legally, the main determining factor for British status is that if at least one of your parents is British, then automatically you are too. You can also gain citizenship if you marry a British citizen and permanently reside in the United Kingdom; or if you complete a formal naturalization process in which you learn about the country and language, as well as display good conduct and moral character; or if you are granted asylum for political reasons.[27]

Similarly, in Jewish law the determining factor for Jewish status is an automatic one: being born of a Jewish mother. You can also become Jewish through conversion, which is like naturalization, although a much more intense process. Additionally, the Torah discusses the possibility of conversion for those seeking political asylum in the Land of Israel (Deut. 26:16–17).[28]

A person can be stripped of their British citizenship only as a result of seriously prejudicial behavior or actions in conflict with the public interest, such as terrorism, espionage, organized crime, and war crimes.[29] Judaism is different here. As we saw, Maimonides states that even if a Jew commits "every possible sin," they will still remain a Jew. Bad behavior or lack of religious practice does not affect Jewish status.[30]

To be stripped of Jewishness would require a person to formally reject the Thirteen Principles. In practice, this would apply to "one who *says* there is no God."[31] Having doubts and questions is *not* the issue; only if a person publicly announces their rejection of the Thirteen Principles would they become a heretic.[32] This is because making such a

27. https://www.gov.uk/british-citizenship.
28. See the discussion of the "runaway slave" in chapter 5.
29. See https://www.legislation.gov.uk/ukpga/1981/61/section/40.
30. This is based on Sanhedrin 49a, which cites God's words to Joshua, "Israel has sinned" (Josh. 7:11), to infer that even though they have sinned, they are still Israelites.
31. Maimonides, *Mishneh Torah, Hilkhot Teshuva* 3:7. This phraseology follows the language of the Mishna (Sanhedrin 10:1).
32. Menachem Kellner, *Must a Jew Believe Anything?*, 36; Samuel Lebens, *The Principles of Judaism* (Oxford, 2020), 220–21 (note 42).

pronouncement would be a clear negation of the shared purpose and destiny of the Jewish people.[33]

The Thirteen Principles are like a Jewish national anthem; that is why they appear in various forms in the *siddur* at the beginning and end of services. They remind us of our collective purpose, as do "God Save the King" for the British, "The Star-Spangled Banner" for Americans and "O Canada" for Canadians.

As a natural-born British citizen I have never been required to swear my allegiance to the crown, but I am encouraged to sing the national anthem on important public occasions. Similarly, a Jew is never required to affirm the Thirteen Principles because they were never intended to be dogma, but a Jew is encouraged to sing *Yigdal* and recite *Ani Ma'amin* as part of public prayer.

Thus, *emuna* is demonstrated by being trustworthy and faithful to your fellow Jews with whom you share your values and traditions. This, though, is not blind commitment. Attitudes can be criticized, practices can be challenged, belief can be questioned, and trust may require some justification. A Jew may have doubts about religious belief and so they should continue to seek God (as explained in chapter 9), but they will never be denounced for not being fully convinced. To be a Jewish citizen is to throw in your lot with the Jewish people, through thick and thin. As mentioned in chapter 8, this is in line with the first questions asked of a potential convert:

> We say to them, "Why would you want to become Jewish – don't you know that these days the Jews are belittled, disparaged, scorned, scattered, chased from place to place, and suffer affliction?" If they reply, "I know it, and I am not even worthy," then we accept them into the process.[34]

---

33. According to the Talmud (Sanhedrin 99a), this is derived from a biblical verse that shows clear intentionality: "A person who shall act with a high hand… they revile God and shall be cut off from among the people; for they have spurned the word of God" (Num. 15:30–31).
34. Maimonides, *Mishneh Torah, Hilkhot Issurei Bia* 14:1.

Strongly identifying with the Jewish people is the core of Jewish citizenship. Only once this commitment has been ascertained in a potential convert can lessons in religious beliefs and practices begin in earnest: "We then inform them of the fundamentals of the faith, elaborating on God's oneness and the prohibition of idolatry, and inform them of a few simple and a few severe commandments."[35] From the very beginning, it is the willingness to share *Jewish destiny* that counts.

Loyal King Ahab

What if, for some reason, you were to go all out and publicly and deliberately reject these fundamental principles. Would that be it? Would you then have to be branded a heretic and ousted from the Jewish community? Though this was the boundary set by Maimonides, some major twentieth-century rabbinic authorities have shown an extraordinary tolerance in such cases. They felt this was a necessary response to the enormous pressures of emancipation and the advent of modernity, which posed an existential challenge to Jewish life.

Rabbi Abraham Isaac Kook argued that cultural influences of general society had become so enticing that a Jew who rebelled was effectively "under duress" and so could not be judged a real heretic. Rabbi Yeshaya Karelitz (1878–1953), known as the Chazon Ish, found other ways to render heresy inapplicable. Before a person is branded a heretic, Jewish law requires that he or she first must be given a compelling warning. But, he argued, because of declining deference to religious authority this was no longer achievable. Worse still, most Jews would view punishing heretics as unfairly destructive. Instead of preserving religious life, it would only damage it further. Therefore, rather than rejecting nonbelievers, they should be drawn back through "bonds of love."[36]

Similarly, in an effort to maintain the possibility of influencing liberal-minded Jews who had given up on faith, the worldwide recognized authority Rabbi Moshe Feinstein (1895–1986) refused to dismiss them completely. Despite their apparent heresy in rejecting "the principles of

---

35. Ibid., 14:2.
36. These arguments and their sources are explained in Jonathan Sacks, *One People? Tradition, Modernity, and Jewish Unity* (Littman, 2001), 125–27.

the Torah," he argued, they should still be viewed as having full status as Jews. The only context in which he insisted that heresy should not be tolerated was when its aim was to undermine Jewish law or destabilize rabbinic authority.[37]

Thus, if you have difficulties with belief and even come to deny fundamental Jewish principles, the religious community will still not give up on you. Of course, you will be encouraged to increase your commitment, but your Jewishness will never be questioned. Your citizenship among the Jewish people is secure.

Strands of this conciliatory attitude can be traced back to talmudic readings of wayward biblical characters. One example is King Ahab, ruler of Samaria, the northern kingdom of Israel in the ninth century BCE. To say he was a bad king would be an understatement, for "Ahab son of Omri did that which was evil in the sight of God, more than anyone before him" (I Kings 16:30). He took a foreign wife, built an idolatrous temple, provoked God, persecuted the prophet Elijah, caused Israel to sin, and was involved in theft and murder (I Kings 16:31–33; 18:17; 21:19–22, 26). Rabbi Yoḥanan says this king even had written on the gates of the capital, "Ahab has denied the God of Israel."[38] Ahab came to a sticky end and, according to the Mishna, was one of three Jewish kings denied the afterlife.[39]

And yet, despite all this, he reigned for twenty-two years and successfully protected his people all through that period. The Talmud asks why Ahab merited to be king for such an extensive period, and the answer given is remarkable. When Ben Hadad, king of Aram, laid siege to the capital city of Samaria, leading a huge allied army, Ahab had no hope of thwarting this vastly superior force. He sent the message, "Yours am I and all I have" (I Kings 20:4), effectively submitting to become a tax-paying vassal state. But then Ben Hadad asked for more:

---

37. This argument and their sources are explained in Joshua Berman, *Ani Maamin: Biblical Criticism, Historical Truth, and the Thirteen Principles of Faith* (Maggid, 2020), 302–9.
38. Sanhedrin 102b.
39. Mishna Sanhedrin 10:2.

> I will send my servants to you and they will search your house... and it shall be that everything that is precious in your eyes they will seize and take away. (I Kings 20:6)

At this point, Ahab decided to consult the elders and the people about how to respond to this excessive demand. They advised him to refuse, so he sent a courteous but abrupt message back to Ben Hadad: "All that you demanded of your servant at first, I shall do, but this thing I cannot do" (I Kings 20:9).

A prophet of God then assured Ahab of victory against Aram if he were to strike first, which he did with resounding success. But what was so precious in Ahab's eyes that led him to consult the elders and then refuse Ben Hadad? "It must be a Torah scroll," says the Talmud.[40] Rashi explains:

> Ahab said to himself, "Ben Hadad demands this great thing, but the Torah scroll is not only mine; it belongs to the elders of Israel." This is why Ahab consulted them.[41]

In his book on I Kings, Rabbi Alex Israel explains the underlying issue here:

> Ben Hadad seeks not to humiliate Ahab personally, but rather to remove Israel's national symbol. It is this attack on Israel's spiritual roots that Ahab rejects.... As Ahab faces the very survival of his kingdom, he discovers that what matters most to him is his Jewish identity. In a classic gesture that has been exhibited by many wayward Jews who in critical moments of danger... discover their Jewish roots, Ahab demonstrates that at his core is a Jewish sensitivity.... He may not observe the law, but he knew it was the essence of Israel's survival.[42]

---

40. Sanhedrin 102b.
41. Rashi on I Kings 20:6.
42. Alex Israel, *I Kings: Torn in Two* (Maggid, 2013), 276.

We see that the Talmud makes a concerted effort to show that, despite Ahab's denial of God, he was still to be praised for his loyalty to Israel. There is even one opinion that Ahab merited the afterlife after all.[43]

This emphasis on loyalty is adopted for numerous rebellious figures. Maimonides elaborated on this idea; after highlighting the few worthy deeds of Ahab and other problematic biblical characters, he quotes the often-repeated rabbinic principle: "The Holy One, blessed be God, does not withhold the reward of any creature."[44] He concludes that if well-known heretics can be rewarded for the little good they did, then is it not possible for wayward Jews to also be rewarded?[45]

Evidently, finding ways to include Jews rather than exclude them is a major thrust of the rabbinic tradition. Allowing Ahab to rule Israel for more than two decades implies that loyalty to the Jewish people eclipses religious belief. It seems that God will forgo His honor if His people remain faithful to one another.

This shift in focus, from God-centeredness to people-centeredness, is also visible in the first eight chapters of the book of Chronicles. They contain a continuous genealogical list from the very first human to the reigns of David and Solomon, which then become the main subject of the book. The listing is peppered with specific incidents, such as Abraham's name change from Abram (I Chr. 1:27),[46] and Reuben's profaning of his father's couch (I Chr. 5:1).[47] Though these are minor occurrences when compared to the great God-centered events of Creation, Exodus, and the Revelation at Mount Sinai, these three major events are omitted from the beginning of Chronicles altogether. Indeed, God hardly gets a mention here.

Allegiance to God becomes a central issue later on, but in its opening chapters, when Chronicles gives a whistle-stop recounting of biblical history, the emphasis is squarely on the lives of the people and how they

---

43. Sanhedrin 104b.
44. Pesaḥim 118a; Nazir 23b; Bava Kamma 28b; Horayot 10b.
45. "The Epistle on Martyrdom," in *Crisis and Leadership: Epistles of Maimonides*, translation, notes, and discussion by Abraham Halkin and David Hartman (Jewish Publication Society, 1985), 23.
46. Originally described in Genesis 17:5.
47. Originally described in Genesis 35:22 and 49:4.

link from one generation to the next, rather than on God's input. We see again that Jewish faith is framed by the continuity of Jews through time and the age-old tradition they share. Ahab may have rejected God, but he was loyal to his people, and for that he was rewarded. He counts as one of the faithful. This speaks volumes for many Jews today.

Emuna Since Antiquity

For how long can we say with certainty that there has been a Jewish people with a religious tradition? This too is a crucial question for those who have difficulties with belief. If God is in doubt, then maybe much of the Bible comes under question. According to the latest academic research, how far back into antiquity do Jews and Judaism really go? For how long have we kept faith? It is instructive to highlight the oldest and most widely accepted evidence that corroborates the historical existence of named biblical characters and Jewish practices.

Support for the Flood and Exodus narratives appeared in earlier chapters, but no attempt was made to prove the existence of *individual characters*. There is much archaeological data to demonstrate that the narratives of the Torah and subsequent biblical books are in broad agreement with the political, economic, and cultural milieux of their times.[48] There is even mention of our ancestors on ancient cuneiform tablets (the Amarna Letters) and on a hieroglyphic inscription (the Merneptah Stela).[49] But we want to know something more precise: What is the earliest firm evidence we have of specific biblical figures and practices?

Living in London, I have regular access to the British Museum. In Room 6 there are two large stelae which plainly testify to the antiquity of our people. These upright stone slabs, each about two meters high, bear cuneiform inscriptions in Akkadian that relate to the ancient kings of

48. K. A. Kitchen, *On the Reliability of the Old Testament*; Mordechai Cogan, *The Raging Torrent: Historical Inscriptions from Assyria and Babylonia Relating to Ancient Israel* (Carta, 2015); Mitchell, *The Bible in the British Museum*; Sarna, *Understanding Genesis*, and *Exploring Exodus*; *The Koren Tanakh of the Land of Israel: Exodus*.
49. Clyde E. Fant and Mitchell G. Reddish, *Lost Treasures of the Bible: Understanding the Bible through Archaeological Artifacts in World Museums* (Eerdmans, 2008), 37–42, 72–74.

northern Israel. The first is known as the Kurkh Monolith.[50] It gives an account of the reign of the Neo-Assyrian king Shalmaneser III, focusing on his military campaigns. Toward the end, written on the back, there is a description of the battle of Qarqar which occurred in 853 BCE. Shalmaneser III faced a local alliance of eleven kings including one named "*A-ha-ab-bu Sir-ila-a-a.*" There is general agreement that this translates to "Ahab, king of Israel," the very same as in the Bible. This ancient battle, in the northwest of Syria, is well known from numerous inscriptions.

The king appearing just before Ahab on the Kurkh monolith is Adad-idri, who was thought to be Ben Hadad (II) of Aram.[51] As discussed above, Ben Hadad was Ahab's enemy, but after a second defeat they had negotiated a peace treaty (I Kings 20:31–34).[52] The battle of Qarqar is not mentioned in the Bible because it took place well beyond Israel's borders and Shalmaneser was unsuccessful on that occasion, so it had limited impact on local affairs. As is the case with several kings, the Bible admits not describing everything Ahab was involved with: "And the rest of the acts of Ahab and all that he did... are they not written in the Book of the Chronicles of the Kings of Israel?" (I Kings 22:39).[53] Thus, the Kurkh Monolith is possibly the earliest piece of corroborating evidence for a key biblical figure.[54]

The second stela is commonly known as the Black Obelisk.[55] Decorated with reliefs and inscriptions detailing further accomplishments of Shalmaneser, one vivid scene shows a dignitary paying him homage,

---

50. Ancient Kurkh, where the stela was found in 1861, is in the Diyarbakir province of Turkey.
51. Cogan, *The Raging Torrent*, 20.
52. Ahab's motivation may have been to build an alliance to stand against the impending threat of Shalmaneser; see Israel, *I Kings: Torn in Two*, 282.
53. The book referred to in the verse is not extant, though it is mentioned twenty times in the biblical books of Kings and Chronicles.
54. One candidate for corroborating an even earlier biblical character is the Tel Dan inscription found in 1993. Though highly fragmentary, it refers to kings "of the House of David." The inscription "testifies to the existence of a line of kings who as early as the ninth century BCE traced their legitimacy back to David" (Israel Finkelstein and Neil Asher Silberman, *David and Solomon: In Search of the Bible's Sacred Kings and the Roots of the Western Tradition* [Free Press, 2007], 265–66).
55. It was found in ancient Kalhu, south of Mosul in northern Iraq, in 1845.

and underneath it is written, "*Ma-da-tu sa m-ia-u-a mar m-hu-um-ri-i,*" which translates as "tribute of Jehu, son of Omri." This is identified as none other than the biblical Jehu who was appointed king of Israel by the prophet Elisha a decade after Ahab (II Kings 9:1–13). The Bible says that Omri was actually the father of Ahab, not Jehu, but "it was Assyrian scribal practice to refer to certain kingdoms by the names of their founders."[56] Thus, the Black Obelisk is the oldest pictorial evidence we have of a biblical character.

One further stela, known as the Moabite Stone, completes the picture.[57] Unfortunately, on discovery, "it was subsequently smashed by local Beduin, but a paper squeeze had been taken, and from it a copy of the text was published."[58] It describes a war between King Mesha of Moab and King Joram of Israel. Joram was Ahab's son, which places this battle between the events of the two stelae just mentioned, around 840 BCE. Incredibly, this very same battle is described in the book of Kings (II Kings 3:4–27). Thus, the Moabite Stone is the oldest corroborating evidence of an actual biblical event.

These three objects have left no doubt in the minds of archaeologists regarding the existence of the northern kingdom of Israel, as well as specific Israelite kings, as far back as the ninth century BCE.[59] To me, this is staggering. It means that we can confidently trace our people back in time by more than 2,850 years.[60] This is centuries before the empires of Persia and Greece and well before the birth of Christianity and Islam. Our people predate Confucius and Socrates, Alexander the Great and Julius Caesar. Even if you find belief in God difficult, you can be sure that the Bible contains verified ancient stories of our ancestors and their culture which stretch far back into antiquity.

---

56. Cogan, *The Raging Torrent*, 26.
57. It was found in 1868 at the site of ancient Dibon, now Dhiban, Jordan.
58. Mitchell, *The Bible in the British Museum*, 56.
59. Israel Finkelstein, *The Forgotten Kingdom: The Archaeology and History of Northern Israel* (Society of Biblical Literature , 2013).
60. "It is in Ahab's reign that we have the first absolute date, that can be controlled historically, in the entire history of the Hebrew people." Cyrus H. Gordon and Gary A. Rendsburg, *The Bible and the Ancient Near East* (W. W. Norton, 1997), 225.

Whenever I walk through the British Museum, it is filled with people who are fascinated by ancient civilizations. They marvel at the old relics, but they see them as entirely detached from their own modern lives. For them, the past is a foreign country. But not for me. When I look at the artifacts, I see my ancestry – not alien cultures from a bygone age, but ones among which my forebears lived, following their faith and keeping their traditions, just as I do today.

As well as biblical figures, there is archaeological evidence of ancient biblical rituals too. The oldest might be the Ketef Hinnom silver scrolls. They were found at a burial site just outside the Old City of Jerusalem by Israeli archaeologist Gabriel Barkay in 1979. The tiny scrolls were in a tomb dating from the seventh century BCE and appear to have been worn as amulets on a necklace.

When painstakingly unrolled by researchers at the Israel Museum, they found a tiny inscription in ancient Hebrew script. High-resolution photos taken by a team at the University of Southern California in 1994 finally enabled the fragmentary text to be deciphered. Unmistakably, it was the beginning of an ancient Torah blessing: "May God bless you and keep you; may God shine His face on you" (Num. 6:24–26). This was the famous priestly blessing which Aaron gave to the Israelites at the inauguration of the Tabernacle in the wilderness, a year after the Exodus,[61] and which his descendants continue to give today to the people of Israel.

Being rolled up with letters too small to identify easily, the scrolls were clearly not intended to be read. It seems that they acted as a form of spiritual protection for the wearer.[62] It is astonishing that twenty-seven centuries ago this Torah blessing was already so familiar that it was a popular talisman in the kingdom of Judah.

Every week, before Shabbat, I phoned my father to give me this blessing, and on Friday nights my wife and I recite it to our daughters after Kiddush. We are continuing the tradition of a blessing that was known and spoken by our ancestors in antiquity. It is hard to imagine the millions of Jews who have kept this tradition across the generations

61. See Rashi on Leviticus 9:22, based on Sota 38a.
62. Jeremy D. Smoak, "Words Unseen: The Power of Hidden Writing," *Biblical Archaeology Review* 44, no. 1 (January/February 2018).

in such a vast array of cities and countries, spanning the globe. This is another aspect of *emuna*, the tenacity of Jews over the centuries to keep their faith. I do not know the extent of their religious beliefs, but I know that they gathered in communities and observed rituals which my generation and I continue.

Emuna as Integrity

There is one more connotation to be highlighted: the profoundly ethical dimension of *emuna*. At the end of a person's life, says the Talmud, when they stand before the heavenly court, they will be asked a series of questions, the first of which is, "Did you conduct business faithfully (*be'emuna*)?"[63] Before anything else, they are quizzed not on their religious beliefs but on the integrity of their working life. This implies that in Judaism "business integrity is not *a* moral issue, it is *the* moral issue."[64] The Talmud confirms this when concluding its discussion of the core religious reasons for the cessation of Jewish sovereignty almost two millennia ago:

> Jerusalem was only destroyed when there were no people of faith left, as it says, "Search the streets of Jerusalem, see now and know, seek throughout her boulevards, if you can find one… seeking faith (*emuna*) – I will forgive her" (Jer. 5:1). But do we not have a tradition that even in the breakdown of Jerusalem there were always people of faith within her?… Indeed we do, but those were faithful with matters of Torah, while it was those faithful in their business practices that were missing.[65]

According to this opinion, the end came not because of a lack of belief in God, but because people no longer practiced integrity in their business dealings. This indicates that underpinning all the aspects of *emuna*

63. Shabbat 31a. The questions are all derived from phrases in the same biblical verse which begins, "And the faith of your moments" (Is. 33:6).
64. Matis Weinberg, *FrameWorks: Genesis* (Foundation for Jewish Publications, 1999), 175. See chapter 12, "The Business of Faith," which gathers and interprets many rabbinic sources on this topic.
65. Shabbat 119b–120a.

that have been discussed in this chapter are the honesty, fairness, and integrity with which we are meant to treat each other. This is especially true in our daily transactions because they form such a huge part of our lives, where impropriety has measurable consequences. Deceit is the biggest challenge to *emuna,* not religious doubt or the inability to uphold dogma. In the end, "the righteous person shall live by their faithfulness" (Hab. 2:4).[66]

Living *Emuna*

In summation, *emuna* focuses on affiliation rather than affirmation.[67] Belonging more than believing. It binds the Jewish people to each other rather than to a catechism. *Emuna* is a collection of ideas that includes faithfulness, trust, steadfastness, citizenship, loyalty, integrity, and a determination that goes back to antiquity. The rabbis of old never thought to exclude Jews who questioned their beliefs, and in the modern period, many have bent over backwards to find ways to include even those who feel little connection to Jewish principles and practices. We can never abandon each other because we were taught that *El Emuna,* our faithful God, would never abandon us. Even wayward King Ahab, a man whom I am sure really existed, found a place in our faith. Born in antiquity, *emuna* describes the lived experience of our people: not what they professed, but how they carried themselves, and with whom they decided to build a life and pass on their ancient rituals and values. The scope of this shared project is utterly astounding. It carries on, and it carries us, to this day.

---

66. This verse is quoted by the Talmud (Makkot 24a) when it concludes its debate as to which biblical verse *all* of God's commandments are predicated upon.
67. In modern Hebrew, the word *bitaḥon* is also used to refer to faith in God. Though the word itself, in that form, is not to be found in the Torah, its three-letter grammatical root, B-T-Ḥ, does appear several times. However, rather than religious belief they all refer to living in security, free from harm. See Leviticus 25:18, 19, 26:5; Deuteronomy 12:10, 28:52, 33:12, 28. Fittingly, this accords with the other meaning of *bitaḥon* in modern Hebrew: national security. In later biblical books, the root word B-T-Ḥ does occur with reference to God but, like *emuna,* its meaning is much closer to reliance and trust rather than abstract belief. See, for example, Psalms 115:9, 118:9.

Emuna is the glue that has kept the Jewish people together. Even when our predecessors were called upon to give up their lives in defense of Jewish tradition, it is *emuna* that enabled them to overcome their fears and to never give up hope. The moral philosopher Mary Midgley poignantly confirms this:

> A faith is not primarily a factual belief, the acceptance of a few extra propositions like "God exists" or "there will be a revolution." It is rather the sense of having one's place within a whole greater than oneself, one whose larger aims so enclose one's own and give them point that sacrifice for it may be entirely proper.[68]

68. Mary Midgley, *Evolution as a Religion* (Routledge, 2002), 16.

Chapter 12

Why Pray Today?

EXPLORING THE QUESTION

Of all religious practices, nothing comes close to *tefilla*, prayer, because so much of Jewish life revolves around it. The *shul* is the house of prayer, the *siddur* is the book of prayer, and the *luaḥ*, the Jewish calendar, sets the timetable for prayer.

We gather as Jews today in many kinds of settings, on campuses, in community centers, and at residential retreats, but synagogues are still the most ubiquitous and significant, whether measured by absolute number, physical size, or geographic spread. You will find some sort of *shul* in virtually every Jewish community in the world.

Of the countless Jewish books produced, the *siddur* is certainly the most popular. Literally millions exist. Synagogues have stacks of them, almost every Jewish home has one, and new editions are constantly being published with fresh translations and commentaries, made for myriad congregations, denominations, and sects.

Shul newsletters and announcements abound, but they always include the times of prayer services. There is a specific liturgy for daily, Shabbat, and festival worship, as well as for every life-cycle event. Prayer is the primary ritual that punctuates the *luaḥ* of Jewish life.

Judaism today would be unimaginable without the *shul*, the *siddur* and the *luaḥ*, and yet, it seems that the centrality of Jewish prayer is under grave threat. Although there are many pockets of committed

Jews, when we look at world Jewry as a whole, synagogues' pews are vacant most of the time, the vast majority of prayer books see minimal use, and few Jews pray on a regular basis, whether alone or in groups.

What happened? How did a practice that was the heartbeat of Jewish life become so marginalized? Why are so many of us disengaged from prayer? There are four major factors that have contributed to this. For today's Jew, prayer has become unrelatable, uncomfortable, ineffective, and unnecessary.

First, the actual prayers are hard to relate to. Written in ancient Hebrew, employing a poetic style that is rich in archaic imagery, they are filled with copious and ever more elaborate ways of praising God. This does not chime well with modern sensibilities. It is not how we speak today. Consequently the traditional prayers can be difficult to understand and alienating in the extreme. Some people find the use of male pronouns for God in English translations to be off-putting. Additionally, the prayers have a fixed format that is not meant to be tampered with too much.[1] For the twenty-first-century personality, these linguistic, stylistic, and formal barriers tend to stifle a passionate interaction with prayer.

Second, prayer after prayer speaks of the fragility of life, the flaws in the human condition, and our constant need for divine salvation. The raw vulnerability expressed in these texts makes many of us feel uncomfortable. A few selections from the daily morning service easily illustrate this:

> What are we? What are our lives?[2]
>
> Forgive us, our Father, for we have sinned. Pardon us, our King, for we have transgressed.[3]

1. This is called the *matbe'a tefilla,* "the formula of prayer," and refers to the standardized formatting of the prayers, although there was always room for some textual variations within this structure. See Y. Berakhot 6:2 and the Rashba's last comment on Berakhot 11a.
2. *The Koren Shalem Siddur,* 36, from *Ribon Kol haOlamim,* after the daily morning blessings.
3. Ibid., 116, from the sixth blessing of the weekday *Amida.*

> May Your mercies meet us swiftly, for we have been brought very low.[4]

There are many more self-effacing examples in the services for the High Holy Days and public fast days. Conversely, modernity prizes independence, self-worth, and the belief that we are in control of our destiny. We are told to be self-confident, self-sufficient, and to overcome self-doubt. So it is disconcerting to be constantly reminded of our weaknesses and limitations.

Third, prayer does not appear to work. Or at least it does not feel as though it does for many people. It makes promises about God intervening in our lives that do not seem to be fulfilled. Here is a good example from a psalm recited every Shabbat morning:

> I say of the Lord, my Refuge and Stronghold, my God in whom I trust, that He will save you from the fowler's snare and the deadly pestilence.... You need not fear terror by night, nor the arrow that flies by day; not the pestilence that stalks in darkness, nor the plague that ravages at noon. A thousand may fall at your side, ten thousand at your right hand, but it will not come near you. (Ps. 91:2–3, 5–7)[5]

This guarantee of deliverance from harm is not borne out in our real lives. Observance and faith do not seem to save us from danger or make us immune to disease. Depending on God's protection is recommended on nearly every page of the prayer book, but that strikes most people as ineffective.

Fourth, prayer today just seems so unnecessary. So much of what we used to pray for is now within our grasp. When these prayers were written there was only a limited understanding of the science of nature, so we turned to God for help much of the time. This is typified by the

4. Ibid., 156, 234, from the final paragraph of the *Taḥanun* (Supplication) prayer, recited twice daily, except on Shabbat and festivals.
5. Ibid., 418; Psalm 91 is also recited at the end of Shabbat, ibid. 694, 696.

Seyder Tkhines, a popular book of Yiddish prayers for women, compiled in the seventeenth century, which vividly articulates real life concerns:

> When baking: "I come to honor Your holiness and ask You to bestow Your blessing on this dough; send an angel to protect it, so that it may bake well, and rise well, and not burn."[6]
>
> When pregnant: "Take the key to my womb in Your right hand, and unlock me without pain and without suffering, and allow this birth to be free of all harm, without sickness."[7]
>
> For wellness in body and mind: "May my health be good so I may do You justice through truth ... and when I lie in my bed, protect me from bad thoughts, so my body and my heart may lie safely at rest; and do not allow me to be smothered by my covers, so that I may live to honor Your Holy Name."[8]

Today, we know the chemistry of baking bread. Advances in gynecology, polysomnography, and psychology have drastically reduced birthing complications and sleep disorders. Many aspects of mental ill-health have been alleviated too. We no longer need to rely exclusively on God's assistance because we are in possession of so much scientific knowledge.

Also, constantly worrying about the future, which caused humankind to turn to God to ask for help for generations, has now been replaced by something far more effective. *Insurance* is the practical way we reassure and protect ourselves today. Why pray for safe passage when you have car and travel insurance? Why pray for a successful livelihood when you have work insurance? And why pray for well-being when you have health insurance? We handle the fear of our lives going wrong by relying on risk management rather than God.

---

6. *Seyder Tkhines: The Forgotten Book of Common Prayer for Jewish Women*, translated and edited with commentary by Devra Kay (Jewish Publication Society, 2004), 152.
7. Ibid., 163.
8. Ibid., 135.

The displacement of reciting prayers by managing risks is central to modern life. The story began in the coffeehouses of London at the end of the seventeenth century.[9] Fueled by the dark brew, these establishments were open around the clock and became the primary source of news about international trade, which was vital for the business of insurance. A favorite coffeehouse of the sailors and tradesmen from the ships moored on the Thames docks was opened by Edward Lloyd on Tower Street in 1687. Daily news of departures and arrivals, sea hazards, new routes, and conditions abroad was constantly being shared. After acquiring larger premises on Lombard Street, Lloyd formalized the rapid flow of information by establishing a regularly updated "Lloyd's List."[10]

The list was used by merchants' agents and underwriters to negotiate insurance coverage for trade ships and soon expanded to provide news on stock prices and foreign markets. London's insurance industry grew to cover almost any kind of risk, including theft, fire damage, physical harm, ill-health, and even adultery. In 1771, a band of the underwriters who did their business at Lloyd's joined together as a formal group with a self-regulated code of behavior. This ultimately became Lloyd's of London, not only one of the largest and most well-established insurance organizations in the world today, but the sine qua non of insurance itself and a household name the world over.

Modern risk management uses vast swaths of constantly updated information as well as innovative mathematical models to forecast the future accurately. Measuring and weighing up risk has propelled economic growth and technological innovation, and radically improved our quality of life:

> Without a command of probability theory and other instruments of risk management, engineers could never have designed the great bridges that span our widest rivers, homes would still

9. Peter L. Bernstein, *Against the Gods: The Remarkable Story of Risk* (Wiley, 1998), 88–92.
10. Lloyd's List was published daily all the way into the twenty-first century. In 2013 it moved to a digital format and began providing hourly updates. To this day it is a key source of insurance information. See https://lloydslist.maritimeintelligence.informa.com.

> be heated by fireplaces or parlour stoves, electric power utilities would not exist, polio would still be maiming children, no airplanes would fly, and space travel would be just a dream.[11]

As a result of all this, we now make sure to invest in insurance policies rather than saying our prayers. Our age-old reliance on God has been replaced with our modern ability to manage our own future.

In summary, from a modern perspective, our traditional prayers have become more unrelatable, their content makes us uncomfortable, their assurances seem ineffective, and their reliance on God appears to be unnecessary. Once upon a time we needed to pray for the rain to fall, crops to grow, rivers to flow, bread to rise, illness to pass, children to be born, suffering to be minimized, and war to be averted. We wrote numerous prayers to address all our worries and concerns. Talking to God used to be our first thought on waking and our last thought at night. It was the high point of Shabbat and the heart of every festival. But this is no longer. The profound urge to pray has dissipated. For many of us now, prayer is dispassionate, rushed, and brief, if done at all. We turn to innovation, invention, and the latest app to solve our problems rather than to God. So why should we still commit to regular prayer? Why battle to understand these alienating texts? What, for instance, does the daily recitation of the *Shema* achieve for us? Does prayer still hold any importance?

RESPONDING TO THE QUESTION

Most people, including me, have a fluctuating relationship with prayer. It can be deeply meaningful and uplifting, even transformative at times, but all too often it is a routine chore. I have, of course, met my fair share of devoted daily *daveners* and been inspired by passionately spiritual people, but for many of us, daily prayer can be quite challenging.

Interestingly, those who only pray once a week on a Shabbat morning may find it more meaningful and uplifting than those who attend services three times a day. Others find praying in English to be more valuable. Some prefer praying privately, while for others, prayer

11. Bernstein, *Against the Gods*, 2.

is all about gathering as a community and singing together. Every rabbi and Jewish educator I have ever met has developed helpful suggestions and strategies for improving prayer, but this only demonstrates the extent of the problem.

Though the organization and inclusiveness of communal prayer and the specifics of weekday, Shabbat, and festival services are all important topics, we will focus here on the fundamental impetus for the individual to pray in our tradition, and the barriers that can make this difficult.

These will be structured around the four main problems described above: for modern people, prayer has become unrelatable, uncomfortable, ineffective, and unnecessary. Then I will offer a few personal perspectives that drive me to pray every day and help me to connect with the *siddur* and seek to communicate with my Maker. In the end, the pages of the *siddur* relate to all the questions discussed in the past eleven chapters, and so will help to summarize and conclude this book.

From Unrelatable to Personal

The mitzva to pray is highly unusual because it is so unspecific. Maimonides's presentation of the laws of prayer makes it crystal clear that only the *principle* of daily prayer is a biblical commandment:

> The number of prayers is not prescribed by the Torah; the format of prayer is not prescribed by the Torah; nor is any fixed time for prayer prescribed by the Torah.[12]

In fact, the structure, content and schedule of prayer, and even the need to pray communally, are all rabbinically legislated. The basic command is only "for each person to offer supplication and prayer, on a daily basis, according to their ability."[13] Those who were eloquent would expand their prayers, while those less articulate would pray only as they were able. A person could pray whenever they wanted, some doing so several times a day, while others only prayed once.

12. Maimonides, *Mishneh Torah, Hilkhot Tefilla uVirkat Kohanim* 1:1.
13. Ibid., 1:2.

Maimonides says this was the tradition for hundreds of years until the period of Ezra the Scribe in the fifth century BCE.[14] By that time, our ancestors had spent decades in exile, adopted foreign languages, and were no longer able to express themselves adequately, and, therefore, pray in Hebrew. So Ezra and his contemporaries standardized the content of the prayers and established the three daily services, as well as the services on festivals and other holy days.[15]

All this implies that in essence, there is no uniform way to pray in the Jewish tradition, and that the reason for fixing the framework and content of the prayers was to aid a disparate and weakly educated generation. For the sake of communal consistency, we continue to follow this tradition, but reminding ourselves of its underlying flexibility is important when thinking about the unrelatability of prayer, and how it could be more meaningful.

Importantly, there is still much more room for individual freestyling than is generally appreciated. Many people think that praying in English is not religiously "authentic" and prefer to recite the Hebrew, even though they cannot understand most of the words they are saying. Yet the Mishna clearly states that the *Shema,* the *Amida,* and Grace after Meals can all be said in *any* language.[16] The commentaries explain that this is because a person is meant to understand what they are saying when they pray.[17] Indeed, the prayers in *Seyder Tkhines* referred to earlier are emotive examples of personally written pieces in a language that those who used them could understand.

As a teenager I found the poetry and imagery of the prayers offputting. I struggled with Shakespeare at first too. Learning to understand the literary value of texts and delving beyond their surface meaning was part of my education. Now I expect the words of the *siddur* to mean more than they first imply. The writers were reaching to the very limits of language to express their own earnest emotions and their conceptions

14. Ibid., 1:3.
15. Ibid., 1:4–8.
16. Mishna Sota 7:2.
17. See Rashi and *Tosafot* on Sota 32a.

of God. My trying to uncover their implications and latch on to their intentions has been very rewarding.

The *siddur*'s constant and manifold praising of God was also something that left me cold...that is, until I discovered pop music! Then I realized that there truly are an inexhaustible number of ways to talk about loving someone. Though love songs praise romantic love, prayer can be a pathway to appreciating spiritual love:

> Just like a lovesick man, whose mind is never free from his love for a particular woman, thoughts of her filling his heart at all times, when sitting down or rising up, when he is eating or drinking, so even stronger should be the love of God in the hearts of those who love God.[18]

As we grow and experience different kinds of loving relationships – parents, friends, partners, children, etc. – so our ability to love God can also mature. So too, our appreciation of the many different ways of praising God in our prayers takes on more meaning.

Communal prayer was standardized to preserve it through time, but today it seems to have had the unintended consequence of making it less compelling and relatable. Yet the lesson of the essential mitzva of *tefilla* is that each of us has always been free to convey our feelings to God in ways that are individual and intimate. It is this that matters so much more than how much we pray. "Better to say few supplications with real intention than many without."[19]

Discovering the hidden depths of the Hebrew prayers reaps dividends, but there is also plenty of room to experiment with personal language and individual modes of expression. The shortest prayer in the Torah is just five words, "God, please, heal her, please" (Num. 12:13). It was Moses's personal request to God in response to his sister's disease. It should inspire us to find our own words when we ask God to heal our loved ones. What would you say?

---

18. Maimonides, *Mishneh Torah, Hilkhot Teshuva* 10:3.
19. *Shulḥan Arukh, Oraḥ Ḥayim* 1:4.

Opening Up to Your Vulnerability

One of the main purposes of prayer is to admit our vulnerability. This is in direct opposition to the modern glorification of independence and self-sufficiency. It is human nature to want to be in control of your life, but it is hubris to think that you really can. Moses reminded the Israelites of this in his last days:

> Watch yourself, lest you forget the Lord your God.... Lest you eat and be sated and build goodly houses and dwell in them.... And your heart become haughty.... And you will say in your heart: My power and the might of my hand made me this wealth. (Deut. 8:11–12, 14, 17)

Some prayers are meant to make us feel raw and uncomfortable. They are not there to keep us in a state of perpetual fear and anxiety, but to remind us of our weaknesses and limitations. Prayer enables us to bracket out part of each day to remember that we are insecure. We do this even while still recognizing the security modern life has given us:

> Whatever challenges we face, it remains indisputably true that those living in the developed world are the safest, healthiest, and richest humans who ever lived. We are still mortal and there are many things that can kill us. Sometimes we should worry. Sometimes we should be afraid. But always remember how very lucky we are to be alive *now*.[20]

Perhaps we should say "blessed" rather than "lucky" as luck implies feeling fortunate in the face of blind fate, whereas blessing implies a recognition of how we got here. Having emerged from the coronavirus pandemic, we have become so much more aware of the fragility of our lives. Yet in our keen desire to move on from the painful past few years, there is a concern we will quickly forget these feelings. Again, our prayers are there to remind us. The most strident admission of

20. Dan Gardner, *Risk: The Science and Politics of Fear* (Virgin, 2009), 353.

our own limitations is contained in a sentence toward the end of the *Taḥanun* prayer, recited on weekdays:

> We do not know what to do, but our eyes are turned to You. Remember, Lord, Your compassion and loving-kindness, for they are everlasting.[21]

With these words we are admitting that we are unsure of what course of action to take. We do not even know what to pray for. Dwelling on that helplessness for a moment is humbling. It moves us to call upon God's unwavering compassion. This prayer always stops me in my tracks. It forces me to open up to my weaknesses and vulnerability.

The Effectiveness of Prayer

Does prayer have the power to change reality? Do our devout supplications storm the heavenly realms and trigger a shift in our earthly destiny? To declare that they do flies in the face of our everyday experience, for pain and suffering do not suddenly disappear in response to sincere prayer, and yet to admit our prayers do not trigger anything at all implies that our words have no effect, that our devotions are in vain. We need a way out of this conundrum if we are to make sense of prayer.

This can be found by first considering the process of divine reward and punishment. The Torah is unequivocal about the issue. It states repeatedly that God will punish the wicked for their actions while rewarding the righteous for theirs. For instance, in the well-known second paragraph of the *Shema* we are told:

> If you listen to My commands ... to love the Lord your God and to serve Him with all your heart ... then I will give the rain of your land in its season ... and you shall gather in your grain and your wine and your oil ... and you shall eat and be satisfied. (Num. 11:13–15)

21. *The Koren Shalem Siddur*, 234, from II Chronicles 20:12 and Psalms 25:6.

And if we do not, then:

> The Lord's wrath will flare against you and He will hold back the heavens and there will be no rain and the soil will not give its yield and you will perish swiftly from the goodly land that the Lord is about to give you. (Num. 11:16–17)

This is the traditional Jewish view of divine providence, that everyone is directly subject to God's reward and punishment. But does this actually occur in real time? Do the righteous receive rain in season while the wicked swiftly perish? Two common explanations are offered to overcome the obvious disconnect with our everyday experience. One is: "It might not appear that the righteous are rewarded, but who knows who is truly righteous?" And the other: "The wicked may not be punished in this world, but they will be in the World to Come." Both appear unsatisfactory. The first implies that we are all completely oblivious to who is truly good and bad, which is hard to accept, and the second just postpones the issue to a future time. Thus, both serve to diminish the immediacy of the bond between God and humanity.

The approach of Maimonides seems to better accord with reality.[22] He argues that only some people are governed directly by divine providence while everyone else is subject to the general randomness of nature which we regularly encounter. "According to Maimonides, the wicked and the ordinary, constituting much of humanity, are relegated to happenstance.... God's presence and providence, for most people, are mediated via the causal order that He created."[23] Only few merit direct attendance by God, and these are people, says Maimonides, who have striven to improve themselves: "Divine providence is in each case proportional to the person's intellectual development."[24]

How does providence work for these few virtuous people? The response of Maimonides to this question is subject to interpretation.

22. Maimonides, *Guide for the Perplexed* 3:17–18.
23. Moshe Halbertal, *Maimonides: Life and Thought,* trans. Joel Linsider (Princeton, 2014), 338, 340.
24. Maimonides, *Guide for the Perplexed* 3:18.

The conservative reading asserts that these few do enjoy some intimation of divine intervention and are directly rewarded by God. Again, this is problematic as it is at odds with what we see in the world. However, there is a second, more philosophical approach that is more subtle. It was advocated both by Samuel ibn Tibbon, the translator of Maimonides's *Guide for the Perplexed* from Arabic to Hebrew, and his son, Moses ibn Tibbon. Both believed that for the virtuous few, divine providence was built into the natural order itself and that no intervention was required. Instead, *God's wisdom structured the world such that it naturally responded well to these people.*

Samuel ibn Tibbon understood from Maimonides that virtuous people *did* suffer life's hardships just like everyone else, but because they were focused on what really mattered, which is a deeper understanding of God's world and how it operates, they did not *perceive* these as hardships at all. They had succeeded in changing their consciousness. Moses ibn Tibbon read Maimonides slightly differently from his father here. He agreed that these people had a deeper understanding of the world, but rather than changing their consciousness, it made them better able to protect themselves from hardships. Their knowledge enabled them not to succumb to anxiety but rather to rationally evaluate a situation and calculate the risks of one direction over another, so that things turned out better for them overall.[25]

The views of father and son Tibbon are very appealing. Following their approach, when the Torah instructs us to listen to God's commands and observe them, it means that doing so will make us more thoughtful, honest, and reasonable, and will alter our awareness. As a result, we are more likely to be successful (which is Moses ibn Tibbon's view of God's reward), and if we are not, we will not be disheartened, because of our enlightened perspective (which is Samuel ibn Tibbon's view of God's reward). As a result, the rewards and punishments promised in the Torah remain intact as well as still according with our experience of reality. This is also the way to read another key verse in the Torah:

25. Halbertal, *Maimonides: Life and Thought*, 339–40.

> I call to witness for you today the heavens and the earth. Life and death I have set before you, the blessing and the curse, and you shall choose life so that you may live, you and your seed. (Deut. 30:19)

By making a choice about our actions and our outlook we can warrant life or death, a blessing or a curse. Our innately human ability to decide how we live and view our existence, even in the face of extreme hardship, is what will determine our success and failure in this world, and this is what God wants for us.

Now, finally, the effectiveness of prayer can be understood. Taking the time to pray every day is an effective way of regularly reflecting on life and its purpose. *It enables us to live intentionally rather than reactively.* It gives us the space we need to detach from our immediate concerns, take the longer view, and thus alter our perspective. In that sense, prayer really does have the power to change reality, because it allows us to clarify our personal perception of reality.

Earlier, when it was first suggested that prayer does not work, we quoted from Psalm 91, recited every Shabbat, which implies that if you make the Lord your refuge, then God will save you from pestilence, nightly terrors, and war. Rabbi Samson Raphael Hirsch's explanation of this psalm is in line with the interpretation of Maimonides just advocated above. He writes:

> Of course, the catastrophes which shall befall the world of mankind will not remain unknown to you. You will live to behold them all.... You will learn from these calamities that occur in the history of the nations that all evil prepares its own ruin.[26]

Learning the lessons of history will ensure our future. That, says Rabbi Hirsch, is the message of this psalm and why it is worth reciting.

In an essay on prayer, Rabbi Adin Steinsaltz (1937–2020) addresses how we can know if we are deluding ourselves when we pray:

26. Hirsch, *The Psalms: Translation and Commentary,* Book Three, 150. See also Maimonides, *Guide for the Perplexed* 3:51 (toward the end).

> A person may think he is in communion with holiness, in a state of divine love or fear – yet he is experiencing no more than illusions: not an experience coming from a true inner soul connection, but from an almost physiological phenomenon.[27]

He answers by quoting Proverbs: "True speech stands firm always, but a false tongue is for a mere moment" (Prov. 12:19). A prayer recited truthfully will have some permanence. He concludes:

> If after religious rapture passes, nothing remains, the absence of emotion indicates that all along it was no more than the imitation of true feeling. The value of a person's prayer lies not in how much he cried out, how much he swayed, nor even how strong his emotions were, but in what remains of his experience after the prayers are over.[28]

This too reflects Maimonides's approach. The efficacy of prayer is in the lasting impact it has upon *us*. If we are changed in some fruitful way, then our experience was not illusory.

The Necessity of Prayer

It is a mistake to think that advances in knowledge could ever usurp the need for prayer. Human ingenuity was never thought of as a replacement for dependence on God. Problem-solving and risk management were not an alternative to divine protection. The two have always gone hand in hand. This is expressed very dramatically in a particular biblical episode.

Jacob has not laid eyes on his brother for over thirty years.[29] The last time they were together it had not ended well. Esau was incensed that Jacob had tricked Isaac, their aging father, into giving Jacob the blessing that Esau thought was rightfully his (Gen. 27:18–36). When Rebecca, their mother, heard of Esau's plan to kill his brother once their father

27. Adin Steinsaltz, *The Thirteen Petalled Rose*, trans. Yehuda Hanegbi (Basic Books, 2006), 141.
28. Ibid., 142.
29. Rashi on Genesis 28:9.

died, she arranged for Jacob to be sent away to her family in the north (Gen. 27:41–28:5). After a time, she hoped, Esau's anger would subside and Jacob could return. But because of the need to provide for his growing family, Jacob was forced to prolong his absence, and on his eventual return, he heard that his brother was coming to meet him with an army of four hundred men (Gen. 32:7).[30] This worried Jacob greatly – and it is his three-point preparation plan that highlights the relationship between prayer and action. First, he mitigated the risk:

> He divided the people that were with him, and the cattle and camels, into two camps. He figured, "Should Esau come to the one camp and strike it, the remaining camp will escape." (Gen. 32:8–9)

Then he prayed:

> And Jacob said, "God of my father Abraham and God of my father Isaac… I am unworthy of all the kindness that You have steadfastly done for Your servant.… Save me from the hand of my brother…lest he come and strike me, mother and sons." (Gen. 32:10–12)

And finally, he sent ahead a huge stream of gifts to appease and honor his brother:

> He took from what he had in hand a tribute to Esau his brother: two hundred she-goats and twenty he-goats, two hundred ewes and twenty rams; thirty nursing camels with their young, forty cows and ten bulls, twenty she-asses and ten he-asses. (Gen. 32:14–16)

In contemporary terms, he insured against potential loss, appealed to God, and skillfully maximized his resources. In no way did Jacob see his tripartite response as contradictory. It was an integrated approach

30. See Rashi's comment on this verse.

that reflected his outlook; a holistic deliberation on how to survive and succeed in the world.

First, he had to overcome his fear of devastating loss. This human desire to cope with an uncertain future is what led, as outlined earlier, to the industry of risk management and insurance that propels modern civilization. However, though insurance only developed into a sophisticated financial tool in the eighteenth century, it has been employed in more rudimentary ways for over three and a half millennia.

The ancient Babylonian Code of Hammurabi dedicates numerous clauses to a form of merchant ship insurance; Greek and Roman guilds developed cooperatives to care for families whose main breadwinner unexpectedly died; systems of insurance grew in line with the rise of European trade in the Middle Ages; Italian banks in the fifteenth century managed agricultural cooperatives set up by farmers to insure each other against bad weather; and just over a century later a bill was introduced in the English Parliament by Sir Francis Bacon to regulate the growing business of insurance policies.[31]

Yet all these innovations did nothing to hamper the growth of Christianity and Islam, as it was always understood that religious devotion was a response to a different kind of human need. While splitting his camp was a *practical* measure, it could not relieve Jacob's *emotional* distress, and so, he turned to God. Realizing his limitations ("I am unworthy") and articulating his worst fears ("lest he come and strike me, mother and sons") was an emotionally mature way to restore his psychological well-being. Note that the Torah contains no response from God, for none was expected. Jacob's plea exemplified our human need to bare our soul in a time of desperate insecurity.

Having given voice to his vulnerability, Jacob now had the peace of mind needed to solve the problem of how to handle his brother. His open-hearted act of prayer afforded him the composure required to sympathize with Esau's pent-up feelings, and to understand why he was reacting in this way. This, in turn, enabled Jacob to work out the best way to respond to Esau.

31. Bernstein, *Against the Gods*, 92–95.

The pragmatic mode of thought is an *external* response generated for us to function effectively in the world. But it needs to be accompanied by an *internal* response. This idealistic mode of thought focuses on the emotional anxiety involved and the search for deeper meaning that is also part of the struggles we face. Only when we address *both* the pragmatic and idealistic modes of thought, utilizing external and internal responses, can we successfully identify a comprehensive way to move forward.[32]

As innovations in science and technology progress at an ever-increasing pace, we also need to progress psychologically and ethically in order to make sense of where all this is taking us. The impetus to launch ahead into what we can do sidesteps the question of why we are doing it. Hence the need for prayer. In connecting to God, *tefilla* frames our day, gives us space to examine our fears, shows us our place in history, and reminds us of what we hold dear and of our purpose in life.

Why I Pray Every Day

We have seen how prayer need not be unrelatable, how it is meant to make us uncomfortable, and also how it can be highly effective and is supremely necessary in today's world. All this helps me to open my *siddur* each day to pray. But there is one more perspective on prayer to explore, and it is intensely personal.

Jewish prayer has three essential elements: praising, requesting, and thanking.[33] First we recognize that God is the foundation of all existence, acknowledging that our Creator continually maintains the world, and everything and everyone in it. Second, having identified the ultimate source of all that is, we realize our utter dependence and turn to God to ask for all our needs and hopes. Third, having made our requests, we are moved to thank God for all the gifts we receive. This is the structure of the weekday *Amida*:

Rabbi Ḥanina said: The initial blessings are like a servant who formally praises their master; the middle blessings are like one who makes

32. Karen Armstrong connects these modes of thought to the terms *logos* and *mythos* used by the ancient Greeks. See Armstrong's *The Case for God*, 3.
33. Maimonides, *Mishneh Torah, Hilkhot Tefilla uVirkat Kohanim* 1:2.

a request for their needs from their master; and the final blessings are like one who has received reward from their master and leaves gratefully.[34]

Therefore, while praise is the approach and thanks is the taking leave, the essence of *tefilla* is undeniably this: *voicing our needs to God.* When people want to deepen their experience of praying, they are generally encouraged to study the *siddur* and the laws of *tefilla*. This, of course, is worthwhile. But if the essence of prayer is voicing our needs to God, then it seems that a more meaningful way to begin might be for each of us to reflect on what are our own personal needs, and only then turn to the *siddur*.

So, consider the following questions: What do you really want in life? What are your most vital needs each day? If time were short and resources were limited, what do you think you could not live without? Responding to these questions for myself pushed me to consider what truly matters. The process became a worthwhile exercise in self-reflection. After some frank deliberation, I came up with five needs:

a. To make the most of being alive
b. To learn and understand as much as possible
c. To have health, happiness, and wisdom for the ones I love
d. To be helpful and kind
e. To be connected to my people and build a meaningful relationship with God

All these mean the world to me. No doubt they could be expressed in different ways, and some would change a few of the points but, deep down, we all share many mutual concerns. Being awake to life, learning more, caring for those close to us, giving to the world, and being part of a community of faith are desires shared by people across the globe.

Looking through *Shaḥarit,* the daily morning service, are there words and prayers that convey these wants? If *tefilla* is about voicing our needs to God, then this should be the case. And indeed, it is. This can be seen already in the first few pages of the *siddur.* Here are five selections with an explanation as to how they relate to the five needs listed above:

34. Berakhot 34a.

(a) *Modeh ani:* "I thank you, living and eternal King, for giving me back my soul in mercy; great is Your faithfulness."[35] These are the first words we are meant to say on waking up in the morning. Recognizing that life is a gift from God speaks to our wanting to make the most of being alive. Our day begins full of potential, appreciation, and opportunity.

(b) *La'asok bedivrei Torah:* "Blessed are You, Lord our God, King of the Universe, who has made us holy through His commandments, and has commanded us to engage in study of the words of Torah."[36] This blessing can be viewed as the demand to commit to a life of learning in the widest sense. Humans are a learning species.[37] Becoming an educated Jew demands a deep, ongoing study of our Jewish sources as well as the various fields of general culture.[38] We want to learn more every day, about Judaism and about all of civilization. This gives life so much more depth and meaning.

(c) *Yevarekhekha:* "May the Lord bless you and protect you. May the Lord make His face shine on you and be gracious to you. May the Lord turn His face toward you and grant you peace."[39] This, of course, is the priestly blessing that Aaron gave to the Israelites at Mount Sinai, during the inauguration of the first house we built for God (Num. 6:24–26).[40] As previously mentioned, my wife and I bless our daughters every Friday night with these words. But reciting them every morning allows us to express what we want all the time: that our loved ones are safe, healthy, and happy, and are free to live purposeful and successful lives.

---

35. *The Koren Shalem Siddur,* 4.
36. Ibid., 8.
37. As it says in Mishna Avot 2:8, "If you have learned much Torah, take no special credit for yourself, for it was for this you were created." Torah here may be read in an expansive sense; for example, see Proverbs 28:4, 7, 9, and 29:18.
38. This inclusive approach was championed by Maimonides and followed through the generations by a range of scholars, most notably in the last century by Rabbi Joseph B. Soloveitchik. See Isadore Twersky, "What Must a Jew Study – and Why?" in *Visions of Jewish Education,* Seymour Fox, ed. Israel Scheffler and Daniel Marom (Cambridge, 2003), 47–94.
39. *The Koren Shalem Siddur,* 10.
40. See Rashi's comment on Leviticus 9:22.

(d) *Dabkeinu:* "May we attach ourselves to the good instinct and to good deeds.… Grant us, this day and every day, to be graceful, kind and compassionate in Your eyes and in the eyes of all who see us."[41] This is a reminder to be kind and considerate to everyone we encounter throughout the day. To remain calm and caring requires effort, so the prayer asks God to help us to be attached to good sense and to do good.

(e) *Shema Yisrael:* "Listen, Israel: the Lord is our God, the Lord is One. Blessed be the name of His glorious kingdom for ever and all time."[42] Though all three paragraphs of the *Shema* are recited later in the service, it is traditional to say the first line and whisper the second as part of the preliminaries. There are many interpretations of the *Shema*, but an especially valuable one powerfully expresses our daily desire to recommit to God and the Jewish people. It is worth explaining in detail.

The Talmud relates that when Jacob was on his deathbed, he was suspicious of his children. "Perhaps one of you is unworthy?" he said.[43] Jacob had good reason to worry, as his children had caused him considerable anguish in the past. There had been Simeon and Levi's violent revenge (Gen. 34:25–31), the jealousy toward and rejection of Joseph (Gen. 37:1–27), Judah's distancing (Gen. 38:1–5), and the near loss of Benjamin (Gen. 43:1–14). We know of Jacob's worries later in life because of his exchange with the Egyptian pharaoh. Having just reunited with Joseph, we might have expected Jacob to be cheerful, but he is decidedly not:

> Pharaoh said to Jacob, "How many are the days of the years of your life?" And Jacob said to Pharaoh, "The days of the years of my sojournings are a hundred and thirty years. Few and evil have been the days of the years of my life, and they have not attained

41. *The Koren Shalem Siddur*, 30. The translation has been edited to highlight that we are not asking for grace, kindness, and compassion from God in this prayer, but that *God enables us* "to be graceful, to be kind, and to be compassionate, *leḥen, uleḥesed uleraḥamim.*"
42. Ibid., 38.
43. Pesaḥim 56a.

> the days of the years of my fathers in their days of sojourning." (Gen. 47:8–9)

Even to a stranger, he reveals his deep feelings and regrets. Returning to the Talmud's description of Jacob's deathbed, we can now appreciate why he questioned the suitability of his children. He was worried how they would turn out, and he was concerned that he had not lived up to his father and grandfather. But, continues the Talmud, the children responded to their father enthusiastically: "Listen, Israel: The Lord is our God, the Lord is One!" This story cleverly takes the first verse of the *Shema,* which appears in Moses's speeches to the Israelites in the last book of the Torah (Deut. 6:4), and repurposes it as the intimate promise of allegiance said by a group of children to their dying father. Let me explain phrase by phrase:

> *Listen, Israel* – Jacob's name had been changed to Israel (Gen. 32:29), so they were effectively saying, "Listen up, Dad."
>
> *The Lord is our God* – meaning, "The God who you have followed your whole life is our God too."
>
> *The Lord is One* – The Talmud itself expounds on this phrase, "They were saying, 'Just as there is only unity in your heart, so too there is only unity in our hearts.'" In other words, they were saying, "Don't worry, Dad. Just as you are certain about the focus of your life, so too are we; we are unified in following your beliefs."

Jacob was so relieved to hear this, says the Talmud, that he exclaimed, "Blessed be the Name of God's glorious kingdom for ever and all time" – the line we whisper after the first verse of the *Shema.* Every morning when we recite the first verse of the *Shema,* we are reenacting Jacob's deathbed scene. We have become Jacob's children, and our ancestors, living and deceased, are Jacob. We express our loyalty to them and their beliefs when we recite this verse. Like them, we say, we are committed to God and the Jewish people. This reenactment binds generations of

Jews; it reminds us of our mission in the world and is a powerful reason to recite the *Shema* daily. To me, it is compelling.

This whole exercise in self-reflection is helpful in seeing how our personal needs are recognized and expressed in *tefilla*. First thinking about what really matters to us, and only then reaching for the *siddur*, allows us to rediscover what it always was – a collection of heartfelt prayers to God, collected by passionate Jews over the centuries, and put into an ordered structure. *Siddur* literally means "ordering." It should not have been surprising to find our deepest feelings and cares expressed there, for we share them with our ancestors. They too had profound needs, and they poured their hearts and souls into the development of the *siddur*.

This, then, is why I pray every day. To express my most heartfelt desires. To begin my day by focusing on ultimate concerns. To remind myself to be conscious of God and to live with intention and meaning.

Ritualized Theology

To my mind, the central role prayer plays in Judaism is best expressed by Rabbi Dr. Irving Jacobs (1938–2020), who was a scholar of liturgy and a former principal of Jews' College:

> As is well known, the early teachers of Judaism did not perceive prayer to be simply the medium of communication between worshipper and Maker. The rabbis also recognised the importance of prayer as a medium through which they could communicate their concepts and beliefs to their followers. Consequently, Jewish prayer is regarded as ritualised theology. Virtually every liturgical composition and blessing is a statement of one or more of the basic teachings in Judaism.[44]

Theology, the systematic study of the nature of God and religious belief, is not an abstract project for Jews. We analyze our faith not just to know what to do, but to expand and deepen our experience of actually doing it. Discussing God brings us closer to God. Studying the mitzvot enables

44. Irving Jacobs, *The Impact of Midrash* (Oxford, 2006), 1.

us to perform them with renewed understanding and gusto. Challenging an accepted Jewish principle forces us to engage seriously with our traditional texts. Analyzing the principle's underlying theological, sociological, and historical components leads to a deeper appreciation of its aim and essence and can induce a reinterpretation that adds contemporary meaning and significance.

Beyond study, however, Jewish prayer affords us the regular opportunity to articulate Jewish beliefs and ideals in a concrete way. This is what Rabbi Jacobs meant by ritualized theology, the self-conscious expression of religious beliefs. It is faith spoken out loud, and it serves to focus our thoughts and fill our days with purpose.

Every chapter of this book has quoted from our Jewish prayers, emphasizing that we wear our beliefs and values on our sleeves. The prayers cited are reminders of our intense engagement with each of the twelve questions discussed in these pages. The *siddur* is a treasure trove of Jewish thought that has been recited by generations of Jews. In our prayers, we articulate our ideals. We give voice to our national hopes and aspirations. We express who we are as a people.

Epilogue

This has been a book about questions, the ones that are asked about belief by people who are looking earnestly to understand the Torah and develop a deeper connection with their faith. They are questions about the origins of the Jewish people, about the ethics revealed at Mount Sinai, and about the challenge and meaning of our religious beliefs. There are no simple answers, but exploring them engrosses us in an enduring relationship with Jewish tradition.

The process of engaging with these questions has also led to a questioning of contemporary culture and ourselves. The Torah's approach to slavery challenges unacceptable labor practices still in use today. Investigating the flood leads to a deeper appreciation of our responsibilities in the face of climate change. Clarifying the relationship between sacrificing animals and eating them warns us of our obligations to the animal kingdom. Reviewing the arguments Moses and Abraham presented to God highlights the importance of a culture of protest. And so on.

Maimonides believed there to be a rationale for each one of the Torah's narratives, and that we are charged to discover them through inquiry and deduction:

> Know that every story that you will find in the Torah serves a necessary purpose for religious teaching. It either helps to establish a

> correct principle of faith, or to rectify one or other of our actions, with the goal of bringing an end to wrongdoing and injustice in society.... Though the meaning of a Torah text may elude you, there is a good reason for it.[1]

There are moments in the Torah when God explicitly questions humankind. Although these queries are posed to certain characters in specific circumstances, they can be read as existential challenges which reverberate through the generations. Briefly explaining three of these is an apt way to end this book.

God called to Adam after he ate from the forbidden tree: "*Ayeka*, where are you?" (Gen. 3:9). This was a provocative question to Adam about his situation rather than his location.[2] In a wider sense, it can be understood as a question that God asks regularly of us all: Where are you in your thinking? What are you doing with your life? Are you just reacting to what comes before you or are you choosing a path?

God said to Cain after he had killed Abel: "*Ma asita*, what have you done? The voice of your brother's bloods cries out to Me from the land" (Gen. 4:10). The midrash suggests that God used the plural "bloods" rather than the singular "blood" to refer to future generations that would now never come to be.[3] For us, it is a standing challenge about the consequences of our own moral choices: What have you done? Some of your actions have brought pain and sorrow into the world, so what are you going to do about it? As individuals, as a people, and as a world, we face God's questions about our destructiveness. God challenges us to take responsibility.

God said to Moses: "*Ma titzak elai*, why do you cry out to Me? Speak to the Israelites, so that they journey onward" (Ex. 14:15). Caught between the devil and the deep Reed Sea, Moses was unsure what to do and had turned to God for assistance. But God rejected his apprehensiveness and demanded action.[4] Considering our own anxieties, we too

---

1. Maimonides, *Guide for the Perplexed* 3:50.
2. Rashi on Genesis 3:9.
3. Genesis Rabba 22:9.
4. See Rashi on this verse.

are often adept at bemoaning our plight rather than facing up to it. And so, God is still asking us: Why are you worrying so much? Now is the time to move forward, to journey onward. We too must take the plunge.

Where are you? What have you done? Why do you cry to Me? These are three of the profound questions that the Torah poses to each one of us. Just as we question belief by confronting the Torah, so too does the voice of God emanate from its pages and continue to confront us. As much as we question the Torah, so the Torah questions us. It is a demanding book for a demanding people.

Index of Biblical Sources

EXODUS

LEVITICUS

NUMBERS

DEUTERONOMY

The fonts used in this book are from the Arno family

Maggid Books
The best of contemporary Jewish thought from
Koren Publishers Jerusalem Ltd.